T0322974

Negotiating Dissidence

Negotiating Dissidence

The Pioneering Women of
Arab Documentary

Stefanie Van de Peer

EDINBURGH
University Press

For Richie McCaffery

Edinburgh University Press is one of the leading university presses in the UK. We publish academic books and journals in our selected subject areas across the humanities and social sciences, combining cutting-edge scholarship with high editorial and production values to produce academic works of lasting importance. For more information visit our website: edinburghuniversitypress.com

Edinburgh University Press Ltd
The Tun – Holyrood Road
12 (2f) Jackson's Entry
Edinburgh EH8 8PJ

Typeset in Monotype Ehrhardt by
Servis Filmsetting Ltd, Stockport, Cheshire,
and printed and bound in Great Britain by
CPI Group (UK) Ltd, Croydon CR0 4YY

A CIP record for this book is available from the British Library

ISBN 978 0 7486 9606 2 (hardback)
ISBN 978 0 7486 9607 9 (webready PDF)
ISBN 978 1 4744 2338 0 (epub)

Contents

Figures

Acknowledgements

Like all books, this is the result of a long gestation period and many years of thinking and re-thinking. I am indebted to family, friends, colleagues and mentors for inspiring me, for forgiving the little obsessions and uncertainties, and for indulging my single-mindedness.

First, I want to thank colleagues and mentors David Murphy, Michael Marten, David Martin-Jones and Elizabeth Ezra. Their guidance and recommendations were of immense value. I truly treasure their support. I also thank the anonymous reader, who, through pointed questions, provided clarity and confidence. I am indebted to the Arts and Humanities Research Council for funding part of this project, and the Five Colleges Women's Studies Research Centre for providing the time and space to continue to think, discuss and write at a crucial point in my early career.

Second, I am very grateful to the film-makers whose work I discuss in this book – I have been very lucky to interview some of them. Ateyyat El Abnoudy is quick and generous; Selma Baccar is formidable as a film-maker and as a politician; Izza Génini is professional and honest; Jocelyne Saab is entertaining and forthcoming; and Hala Alabdallah Yakoub has been very kind and enthusiastic about the project. I feel privileged to have come across their work. I thank them for making the inspiring films that they did and for allowing me to ask so many questions.

I also thank my many friends and family members who gracefully showed an interest: Clare Clements, Lizelle Bisschoff, Ana Grgic, Jonathan Owen, Allyna Ward, Paige Medlock Johnson, Leen Maes, Öznur Karaça, Laure Van den Broeck, Malikka Bouaissa, Kathleen Scott, Philippa Lovatt, Emilie and Valerie Van de Peer, Marjan Weyn, Dirk Van de Peer, Edmond Weyn, and Mari and Leon. I am immeasurably grateful to Richie McCaffery, my main source of inspiration for always wanting to be and do better.

Introduction

Film-making in the Arab world is often a matter of idealism and activism, especially for women making documentaries. In spite of many practical and ideological difficulties, women have found ways to supply and subtly negotiate dissidence into their films. As a result, all films in this book – whether they are experimental, essayistic or poetic – are political in nature. I trace the histories of women making documentaries in the Mediterranean Arab world, and the inspirational political and cultural statements these pioneers made for their subjects, their spectators and the documentary-making women who followed in their footsteps.

Pioneers are not always necessarily the first: they are the most significant or most influential examples for those who came later. The time frame with which this book is concerned overs an almost a fifty-year period, spanning the early 1970s until the 2010s, and the documentary form has, at several points in this half century in the Arab world (and elsewhere), been contested, problematised and censored. Likewise, the positions of women in the societies under discussion have fluctuated markedly, from relative freedom to increased oppression or vice versa. It is therefore necessary to look at national circumstances as well as transnational developments in women's status and in film-making practices in the Arab world. To make matters even more complex, the term 'Arab' poses problems, in general and in this book, as we look here at countries in the Middle East and North Africa, not all wholly Arab, while one of the film-makers is in fact Jewish.

In this book I discuss seven pioneering women documentary makers: in chronological order I look at Ateyyat El Abnoudy from Egypt, Jocelyne Saab from Lebanon, Tunisian Selma Baccar, Assia Djebar from Algeria, Palestinian Mai Masri, Moroccan Izza Génini and Hala Alabdallah Yakoub from Syria. I call these women 'pioneers' for several reasons, most effectively illustrated perhaps with concrete examples. For instance, while Izza Génini was not the first documentary maker in Morocco historically

(Farida Bourquia was, but Bourquia focused on TV documentaries), she has a consistent style and thematic preoccupation, as she looks at heritage, women, diversity and music in a filmography of more than twenty films. She has moreover made a considerable contribution to the production and distribution of Moroccan documentaries. Sometimes these pioneers start making their own films very late on in their lives, as we see with Hala Alabdallah Yakoub, who only started to make her own films in 2006, after having produced and co-directed countless other films by Omar Amiralay, among others. In other cases they have been the only woman to have made documentaries in their country, such as Assia Djebar in Algeria. Film-making *tout court* in Algeria is a very complex and dangerous undertaking, thus leading to the sometimes exilic and often transnational nature of film-making there. Equally, in Palestine, it is hard to find resident women film-makers as the Palestinian people are so dispersed in exile through-out the world, and finding the means to make films inside the Occupied Territories is extremely difficult. Mai Masri, a Palestinian resident in Lebanon, was the first woman to start to make films about Palestinians in refugee camps throughout the Middle East, initiating trends and tendencies followed by many later political film-makers both inside and outside Palestine. Perhaps the only 'first' documentary-making women in this book are Ateyyat El Abnoudy from Egypt and Jocelyne Saab from Lebanon. El Abnoudy is also called 'the mother of Egyptian documen-tary', as she started in the early 1970s, in a country mostly interested in its cinematic heritage of the golden years of the 1940s and 1950s, with belly-dancing melodramas. Likewise, Jocelyne Saab worked as a journalist of her country's cinema, which was, at the time, growing fast and in parallel to Egyptian cinema (where a lot of Lebanese stars were active), but she committed herself to the less popular and usually controversial form of documentary making when the long Lebanese civil war started. What I aim to do in this book is to show how these documentary-making women developed their dissident film-making practices and ideals, their cultural as well as political dissent, in places where censorship, conservative morals and a lack of investment made it prohibitively difficult to create or distrib-ute documentaries, and how their interests and developments influenced future film-makers' work.

Documentary in the Arab World

I write from the perspective of the awareness that I am an 'outsider' with a desire for a coming together of cultures and peoples through films and solidarity. Watching 'other' films (as opposed to 'foreign' films) shows that there exist whole worlds and peoples that may not be part of one's lived experience, and that it is up to every individual cinephile to use cinema as a means of communication and dialogue, to learn to listen to, to see and understand each other better. Being open to new experiences and seeing things from others' perspectives increases our quality of life, through subjectivity, sympathy and solidarity. This sentiment is similar to Laura Marks' 'friendship' or 'affection' *for* the image, established for an other *through* the image. Marks sees two reactions: an immediate action or, when action cannot be taken, a moment of suspension, where potential 'for new kinds of acts, feelings, or perceptions' vibrates. Both this creative and painful suspension are an inherent part of Arab intellectual culture, where there is a 'keen awareness of the circumstances of their society and its relations with others' (Marks, 2015: 4). I will show in the following chapters that this is not only a contemporary insight in the spectators of film, but also a historical tactic by film-makers and spectators alike to create layers of intersubjective understanding that are 'enfolded', another Marksian term, within perception and meaning. While the director and subject may enfold, it is up to the spectator to unfold and understand in order to really 'see' the intended message beneath all the folds of meaning. The overall framework I use in my approach is therefore philosophically transnational, focusing above all on gazes, looks and the act of 'seeing' complementing the voices in the films. This includes going through psychoanalytic gaze theories of representing subalterns and moving beyond these, to conceptions of the reciprocity of an intersubjective look between spectator, subject and director that results – through the unfolding of histories and stories enfolded by subject-positions – into a feminist solidarity.

These 'other' films, dealing with 'other' subjects, are not Other with a capital letter. Through the affection for and the unfolding of the images, the 'other' on screen approaches the spectator, through which an intersubjective spectatorial identity can be established. Especially once the spectator perceives the Arab subjects as no longer 'Other'. This book looks at Arab film-makers, subjects and transnational spectatorships. The Arab film-makers and subjects are in themselves highly transnational as well. The Arab world, as Viola Shafik says, is not a monolith, but is made up of different communities, peoples, states, and governmental and societal forms (Shafik, [1988] 2005: 1). Laura Marks confirms that we should not 'essentialize ethnicity or religion' (Marks, 2015: 9) in our perception or understanding of the Arabic-speaking world. Likewise, this book engages an imagined community, in Benedict Anderson's term, indicating a shared history, knowledge and culture. This community contains surprising similarities and distinctive differences, and I treat it transnationally: each chapter is devoted to another country along the borders of the southern and eastern Mediterranean, but I also ask the reader to draw parallels and see similarities between countries and influences from older film-makers rubbing off on the younger ones, or the ones that started later. Perhaps then, we need to learn to speak of Arab cinemas in all its plurality.

I have limited the scope of films under discussion to the Arab Mediterranean, as the sea is another space of transnationalism with crossings and connections between Arab nations and European ones, of particular importance at this time of migration and refugees. We look here at a specific type of film-making: all are political documentaries by women from the Mediterranean Arab world, and the result is a diversity as wide as the plurals of cinemas and Arabs implies. Most of the films here deal with socio-political issues pertaining to women, such as poverty, women's rights, and the consequences of war, history and heritage on younger generations, which are universal issues relevant not only for the Arabs on the screen but also to the diverse and varied spectators in front of it. Such a transnational approach demands spectators that are willing to establish intersubjective relationships with the films' directors and subjects, which is why my approach to film is injected with an idealistic and philosophical understanding of sympathy and specifically feminist solidarity.

First, some historical contextualisation showing how the films discussed here grew out of tendencies and inspirations in global film-making, and specifically political film-making is necessary. The first woman film-maker in this book started filming in the early 1970s, a time immediately following the period when two vital manifestoes on film in the Third World and in the Arab world collided. The Third Cinema manifesto by Solanas and Getino had influenced militant cinema in previously colonised areas, while the New Arab Cinema (Chabab Cinema in Arabic) collective announced its aesthetic and thematic plans for Arab cinema after 1967. These two revolutionary film-making practices found their way to former colonies and newly emancipated women making films.

The Third Cinema manifesto based itself in Frantz Fanon's Marxist writings on the independence of Third World countries. Solanas' and Getino's guerrilla film-making practice, including a political message of rebellion against oppression of any kind, reveals a preoccupation with everyday reality. As such, Third Cinema film-making moulded post-colonial film-making practices. The militant guerrilla films they proposed were supposed to be revolutionary reactions against the capitalist system and the bourgeois consumer, in the vein of the violence and militancy Fanon saw as necessary in order for the revolution to be complete and effective. The alternative they envisaged for cinema was a politicised content that turned passive spectators into active contributors and ignited involvement in the struggle against the system. In their view documentary best lent itself to a polemical and political outlook on the post-colonial world. Their manifesto was therefore one that publicised an aesthetic of anger and militancy, whereby the revolution could be successful only if it was political and violent. Solanas and Getino strongly opposed 'fantasies and phantoms' and that which made 'the image of reality more important than reality itself'. They were looking for a cinema of the revolution that was 'at the same time one of destruction and construction: destruction of the image that neo-colonialism has created of itself and of us, and construction of a throbbing, living reality, which recaptures truth in any of its expressions' (Solanas and Getino, 1969: 10). This 'throbbing' reminds one of Marks' 'vibrations' of creative and painful suspension in reaction to affective images.

Solanas and Getino thus preferred documentary: 'documentary, with all the vastness that the concept has today . . . is perhaps the main basis of revolutionary filmmaking. Every image that documents, bears witness to, refutes or deepens the truth of a situation is something more than a film image or purely artistic fact; it becomes something which the system finds indigestible' (Solanas and Getino, 1969: 11). They were more concerned with the masses, themes, information, truth and aggression than with the artistic and visual quality of the film, in spite of the contemporary problematisation of the ontological quality of the reality image. The consensus today is that Third Cinema is very time-specific and its relevance has been contested by Teshome Gabriel in the 1980s and Ella Shohat in the early 2000s. Nevertheless, the context in which the earliest film-makers in this book made their first films is framed by this movement: some are heavily influenced by it, others react against it.

Simultaneously, in the late 1960s, a 'defeat-conscious' Arab attitude, engendered by the defeat against Israel, found its filmic apotheosis in the New Arab Cinema (NAC) Collective, and their manifesto, published at the Damascus film festival in 1968, which subverts the old, submissive cinema of the Arab world, dominated by melodrama, fiction and male directors. There was a significant move towards documentary realism and women's issues. Processing an internal self-reflexivity that reveals the nation's dynamic, women became more outspoken about their own contemporary realities.

This collective was as much a reaction to the stale melodrama that dominated Arab cinemas as to the general malaise in Arab culture. A new generation of young film-makers re-energised and organised a collective new outlook on realist cinema. The emphasis was on the artistic exploration of authenticity of form and content. According to Guy Hennebelle, the search for new forms is founded 'on a series of refusals . . . of the former direction of Egyptian cinema, a refusal of old methods, a refusal of compromises. [They] want to reawaken the public and bring it to share the fight' (Hennebelle, 1976: 5). There was a refusal of three main tendencies: gratuitous aestheticism, mediocrity of form and prostitution of great themes. The 1967 defeat, then, was a wake-up call: a point at which the frustrations of young film-makers who were limited in their artistic freedoms culminated and found an outlet. The power of the collective overcame censorship problems and state involvement. Férid Boughédir (1987) shows in his documentary *Caméra Arabe* that New Arab Cinema thrived on a multiplicity of themes and that this resulted in each director having his or her own genre. The diversity was evident in the themes and content, but automatically also found its outlet in the vision of reality.

The 1968 NAC manifesto held that the authenticity of film and its closeness to the social and political reality of a society is a measure of its value nationally and internationally. It stressed the importance of understanding and assimilating the cinematic experience of the world, and the creative utilisation of this experience to suit reality. The manifesto opposed the star system and the tailoring of scripts to suit a certain director, star and audience. It supported the strengthening of the public sector as representing the basic interests of the vast majority of the Egyptian people. The document pointed out the importance of producing films within the reach and comprehension of the widest audience in a nation that then still suffered with a more than 70 per cent illiteracy rate. It refuted the famous equation in traditional cinematic circles that a good production equals a big budget, and it accused the traditional film-makers of wasting the nation's resources. The manifesto stated that:

> what we need is a cinema that records and studies the movement of society and analyzes its new social and political relations, a cinema that would discover and reveal the meaning of life for the individual in the midst of these relations. (Samak, 1977: 14)

Similarly to Solanas' and Getino's Third Cinema manifesto, these film-makers were working towards what was real and urgent for the people. Cinema was more than ever concerned with contemporary socio-economic and political reality, which was – since 1967 – a different and more self-conscious reality. Reality became the dominant strength of the film industry, reflected in a content that determined the form. Emphasis was placed on a truthful representation of everyday life, which came across in documentaries that – due to this renewed interest in reality – were explored with more enthusiasm. What the NAC had that the Third Cinema did not, was a specific interest in women, as film-makers and as a subject for consideration in films. An organised reaction against the monopolising power of rich (male) individuals established itself in order to explore new challenges within old genres, just as female topics and female film professionals gained the confidence to infiltrate the industry.

While Third Cinema had overlooked the role women could potentially play in this new kind of film-making, New Arab Cinema turned out to be the perfect opportunity for women in the Arab world to reclaim their position behind the cameras, which was lost in the 1950s. Very strong and influential female figures had dominated early Arab cinema (for example, Aziza Amir, Mary Queeny, Haydée Chikly), but they gradually disappeared off the scene as cinema was nationalised and censored. In the 1970s, with the advent of new realism and documentary, women took up the camera once more. Boughédir's documentary *Caméra Arabe* shows Tunisian Néjia Ben Mabrouk assuring us that men cannot represent women quite as effectively as women can. Moreover, as feminist documentarists Diane Waldman and Janet Walker point out, 'relatively cheap, accessible, and lightweight 16-mm film and later video equipment enabled many females to enter media production for the first time and/or to turn their filmmaking skills to issues of particular concern to women' (Waldman and Walker, 1999: 5). As such, documentary is an extraordinarily women-friendly genre.

Economically, documentaries allowed for more freedom of expression as they were less expensive to make and therefore financial support was less influential or even absent. This financial issue points at the political aspect of film and documentary: the funders were largely unwilling to take risks, and therefore did not invest greatly in women as directors. Independent, self-funded projects had the ability to express themselves in a more overtly feminist or political way. Equally, the material needed for documentary film-making was less expensive, smaller and lighter than what is commonly used for narrative cinema. It lent itself more easily to the physical frame of women. Both feminism and documentary are grounded in the need for a material platform for freedom of expression. Both are politically inspired forms of opposition to mainstream presumptions. Politically and socially engaged documentaries illustrate that what tended to be issue-oriented in feminist fiction film has become preoccupied with the specificity of representation in documentary film as a platform for oppressed or silenced voices.

A transnational approach to the region to the south and east of the Mediterranean is imperative in order to give consideration to its rich historical circumstances as well as its hybrid contemporary reality. Being located not at the fringe, but on the hinges of three world cultures, this region has experienced influxes from and migration to roughly all continents. European, Arab and African peoples have crossed borders and settled, intermingling cultures, bodies and economies, while North Africans have settled all over Europe and more widely, and have made films in these diasporic or exilic contexts. In using the concept of transnational cinema, and with a strong subjective belief in the optimism inherent to the term, I follow Naficy and Stam and Shohat's work on this subject. Naficy's accented cinema describes exilic, diasporic and postcolonial film-making. The tension between the homeland and the host land is central to his understanding of the exilic, transnational film-maker. Political idealism, nostalgia and economic motivations lie at the basis of the film-makers' lived experience and their concerns in their films.

As Shohat and Stam show, the world consists of a densely woven web of connectedness, 'the global nature of the colonising process, and the global reach of the contemporary media, virtually oblige the cultural critic to move beyond the restrictive frameworks of monoculture and the individual nation-state' (Shohat and Stam, 2003: 1). Shohat and Stam explain that a nation is constructed on narration and visualisation, which makes cinema the ideal expression of the complexity of that nation. Elsewhere, Shohat has assured us that films of the 1980s and 1990s do not so much reject the 'national as interrogate its repressions and limits, passing nationalist discourse through the grids of class, gender, sexuality, and diasporic identities' (Shohat, 2003: 53).

Shohat's essay 'Post-Third-Worldist Culture' illustrates that Third Cinema has doubly marginalised women, 'both as filmmakers and as political actants' (Guneratne and Dissanayake, 2003: 17). Third Cinema's disregard for women film-makers grew out of its emphasis on the class struggle to the detriment of other forms of oppression. Yet Shohat argues that several women in the 'Third World' have nevertheless made extensive use of the film and documentary medium to express their participation in the struggle for national independence and their double marginalisation within the nation. Shohat shows that while documentary practices by women may not necessarily have been feminist in nature, the new low-cost technologies of video and the worldwide burgeoning movement of independent work by women are two factors that have contributed to the growing number of women taking up the documentary camera. Their work is simultaneously a critique of neo-colonialism and of Eurocentric feminism, which misappropriates the terminology of 'sisterhood' and internationalises displaced priorities. Local variants of women's issues and struggles must be reinscribed within the global feminist context of oppression and resistance: 'any serious discussion of feminist cinema must therefore engage in the complex question of the national' (Shohat, 2003: 54). The heterogeneity of form, genre and of national context is central: the local dynamic of the context in which a socially or politically engaged piece of work is set is crucial for a proper understanding of the argument put forward in the documentary. Likewise, while the term feminism itself remains useful, the heterogeneity of feminisms is acknowledged and confirmed, and the documentaries treated with this awareness.

Women's Status

As mentioned, the films in this book are by women, and tackle issues such as women's rights and children's experiences. The transnational approach to the films is concerned with women, and a main inspiration is feminist film studies. A large part of the reading of the films is based in the theories on the gaze and the voice, the most central points of interest and analysis for feminist film studies. Looking at, 'seeing' and listening to 'other' women in these films builds on Laura Mulvey's seminal work on the gaze in film (to which we shall return later), but goes further to consider reciprocity in an active look rather than a passive gaze. The main, central criticism of her work lies in the neglect of ethnic diversity and transnational cinema. From this psychoanalytical gaze theory and interest in the representation of the subaltern, I move into a philosophy of transnational intersubjectivity and reciprocity with a focus on the tripartite relationships between filmed subject, film-maker and spectator. This tripartite relationship develops into one of trust and solidarity, and even complicity, once spectators start to learn to unfold the enfolded through a collaborative reading of image and sound. It is thus the spectator who is presumed 'active' and who must draw out what is implicit in the political message of the film.

On the topic of gender, feminist post-colonial theorists Gayatri Spivak, Chandra Talpade Mohanty and Ella Shohat have explored the oft-occluded female experience in the history of colonisation and post-colonial life. In her key text 'Can the Subaltern Speak?' (1988), Spivak explores how women from the Third World are marginalised, and thus rendered incapable of truly knowing and speaking for themselves. In works such as 'Under Western Eyes: Feminist Scholarship and Colonial Discourses' (Mohanty, 1984), '"Under Western Eyes" Revisited: Feminist Solidarity through Anticapitalist Struggles' (Mohanty, 2003) and 'Post-Third-Worldist Culture: Gender, Nation and the Cinema'

(Shohat, 2003), Mohanty and Shohat also debate the violent oppression of the post-colonial (and often female) subject. They (in)directly criticise Spivak for underestimating the minority subject's ability to speak. Mohanty states emphatically that 'it is time to move beyond the Marx who found it possible to say: They cannot represent themselves; they must be represented' (1984: 354).

She shows that colonised peoples know themselves and the coloniser all too well, and asserts that claiming the opposite is based on a privileged standpoint rooted in post-modern relativism and Marxist feminism (Mohanty, 2003: 511). From Spivak's point of view, the subaltern is no longer subaltern as soon as she speaks. Mohanty's and Shohat's discourse is more optimistic in allowing space for the possibility that the subaltern, othered woman knows herself and can speak for herself very well. The titles of their respective work moreover suggest a slightly different focus, one that perhaps needs to complement the other instead of contradict it: while Spivak focuses on speaking, Mohanty focuses on eyes, and thus gazes. Both the voice and the gaze are of crucial importance in film and feminist studies. From their discourse it becomes clear that Mohanty and Shohat agree that it is more likely that as outsiders, the 'we' of women in the West have become so used to defining themselves as the non-other, non-subaltern, that they cannot include the othered subaltern in their understanding of the world; that is, they cannot hear or 'see' the other, even if she speaks.

Mulvey looked critically upon the (mainly male) gaze (1975). She used Lacanian psychoanalysis and feminist theory to analyse the gaze and deconstruct the body within the Hollywood fiction film experience. She defined three main looks: the spectator's; the camera's; and the diegetic gazes, that is, those between the characters in the film, all part of a network of gazes. The spectators' gazes were divided between the voyeuristic and the fetishistic gaze. I show here that the spectator is not only capable of those, but also of an active look, one that understands through active sympathy between spectator and subject. Paul Willemen (1994) critically re-read Mulvey and argued that there is a fourth look to take into consideration: the look from the subject in the film to the gazing subject; in other words, the look of the character at the spectator. As Willemen demonstrates, this fourth look has been erased in most mainstream fiction films, in order to ensure the enjoyment of the spectator and his or her ability to remain guilt-free of voyeurism. Willemen reads into the fourth look an unsettling, distancing look turned onto the spectator. Intersubjectively, the spectator is one of the active participants in the communication triangle. The spectator is challenged with the fourth look to engage in a more active way in the cinematic discourse and the interpretation of the narrative, while the fourth look can equally emphasise the acts inherent to spectatorship. The spectator moves to the foreground. This close-up and involved aspect of the look has also suffered neglect due to its incoherent definition.

E. Ann Kaplan interrogates the male and imperial gazes as they relate to spectatorship and representations of women onscreen. She first distinguishes between 'looking' and 'gazing' along the lines of gender and race, noting that 'looking will connote curiosity about the Other, a wanting to know . . . while the gaze involves extreme anxiety – an attempt in a sense not to know, to deny . . . The gaze . . . connotes an active subject versus a passive object' (1997a: xvii–xviii). As opposed to the gaze, the look for Kaplan has the potential of 'bringing to view a hitherto unrepresented portion of society' (1997a: xx), dialogically incorporating both reciprocity and solidarity. This argument focuses mainly on the fact that the cinematic subjectivities of spectators and diegetic characters alike are intimately bound up with cultural and bio-political understandings of race, gender and colonial history. Taking this conceptualisation further, I want to distinguish between 'looking' and 'seeing'. The word 'seeing' implies an ethical reconciliation between two subjects. As opposed to gazing or looking, seeing enables a true intersubjectivity, and implies understanding and acceptance.[1] The activity of seeing is transnationally significant: if one 'sees' the other through the act of looking, one acknowledges the other's subjectivity and therefore establishes a reciprocal relationship based on proximity, allegiance, understanding and solidarity.

Spivak's negative answer to her own question has been widely contested, and we could say that listening and seeing via sympathetic spectatorship renders cinema the ideal medium through which to deal with this problem of female subaltern invisibility and non-communication. However, post-colonial relationships have involved a distinct lack of reciprocity of listening and seeing – speaking and gazing *at* an Other have generally dominated. As a tool to move beyond this one-way traffic embodied by gazing and speaking (rather than listening and seeing), I want to look at cinematic solidarity, in particular in spectatorship, through a critical exploration of seeing and hearing filmic images and sounds.

Mohanty shows how feminist solidarity is able to oppose the violence of colonial praxis. In her view, solidarity is an activist stance: it indicates mutuality, accountability and the recognition of common interests as the basis for relationships among diverse communities. It is not enough therefore to look: 'seeing' and 'hearing' the other in an ethically responsible manner becomes imperative. Diversity and difference are the basis for a reflective solidarity that defies the more common 'them versus us' discourse, and replaces it with the 'you and me can communicate with a third' discourse. This discourse explicitly foregrounds inclusivity and communication. However, Mohanty cautions her readers that this solidarity must encompass an understanding of subjectivity as intersectional; that is, as comprising a variety of identity factors beyond gender or race. Likewise, this multiplicity requires film-maker, subject and spectator to intersubjectively realise their subject-position. Again, then, the tripartite dialogue, which incorporates the image and the sound (the indirect, paralinguistic and covert communication strategies), reveals visually innovative and communicatively challenging films that allow spectators with this strategy to take on new moral positions themselves.

Mohanty emphatically engages with the politics of difference by insisting that Third World women are not one homogeneous mass. She advocates a transnational solidarity between women of colour, white women and women from the areas known as the Third World. She acknowledges the need for a shared frame of reference and a 'search for a common feminist political project, within a framework of solidarity and shared values' (Mohanty, 2003: 502). She further argues that this feminist solidarity must be based on the realisation that women across the globe live with common differences, by which she means that diversity and specificity must not be eroded away by generalisations, but should encourage women everywhere to find a common agenda.

Shohat likewise 'emphasizes the particularities and diversity of local struggles for gender equality, and recuperates gender and sexuality from universalizing narratives of national history' (Murphy, 2006: 14). She focuses on cinema produced by women from a wide variety of countries during the 1980s and 1990s in which women reclaim their bodies from the apparatus of the nation-state. While Shohat accepts the particularities of nationalist struggles and the consequences of these struggles for women, she refuses to subscribe to any notion of globalised sisterhood. Rather, she argues that the 'national' must cross borders and accept its hybridity, while also recognising its particularities.

Shohat's most important point is that the Third Cinema manifestoes were homogeneous and over-generalising, male and overtly heroic in their terminology and rhetoric. Likewise, the neo-colonial state of many Third World nations slipped into a repression of non-conformism, a complete neglect or disregard for diversity that mirrored colonial tendencies. As an alternative, she suggests a post-Third Cinema women's aesthetics that re-writes cinema history and gradually reinstates women into that history. Instead of rejecting one gender and privileging another, it is more constructive to include women and allow female cultural contributions to complement an originally male aesthetics. To see the women's realm as an integral part of cinema allows for diversity and multiplicity rather than a 'grand anti-colonial metanarrative' (Shohat, 2003: 74). This comlementarity is where I see the 'negotiating' in the book's title. While the films are highly political, they are not exclusionary vis-à-vis male subjects or other nationalities. Instead, the film-makers offer platforms to the neglected other subject and serve these platforms up to the spectator as a parallel realm that finally completes the picture of global dissidence.

So we move beyond the psychoanalytic and pessimistic conceptualisation of the subaltern and her voice. Instead, the films here show how negotiating borders in a transnational solidarity with the subjective other (not the Other) becomes possible and indeed crucial. By making both the voice and the look count and through generating understanding and intersubjective allegiances, the director, subject and spectator establish emancipating relationships across classifications and borders.

Subjectivity and Intersubjectivity

Subjects and directors are, as we shall see in the films in the following chapters, often not complete insiders but rather part-insider, part-outsider. They have experience with the issue or situation in the films, sometimes first-hand, and comment on it, but are not always inherent to it: they stand outside, or in front of it. We look, as indicated above, at women who are subaltern but also at women who are extraordinary. The diversity in subject-positions requires from the spectator not only sympathy and solidarity, but also a subjective position, one in which they are flexible with regard to what is in front of them, whether this is a subaltern or an extraordinary woman. Subaltern women subjects here are not those described by Spivak as the ones who cannot speak or know themselves, rather – in spite of being in an oppressed position – they have voices and looks and can use these to their benefit. Extraordinary subjects are those in privileged positions not only in financial or political terms, but also in intellectual and expressive terms. Likewise, the directors straddle these two subject-positions: they have been neglected and oppressed as women, as documentary makers and as Arabs, but did achieve the skills and means to make films. So, the spectators are expected to be flexible and stand in solidarity with these different subject-positions, through intersubjective sympathy. Spectators, directors and subjects form a relationship that acknowledges all are subjects in interactions and enact equality through physicality and permissibility.

As documentary theorist Stella Bruzzi shows, rather than focusing on truth and objectivity, it is much more important to see the productivity of the relationship between real and imaginary (Bruzzi, 2000: 6). She says: 'sometimes it becomes necessary to remind ourselves that reality does exist and that it can be represented without such a representation either invalidating or having to be synonymous with the reality that preceded it' (Bruzzi, 2000: 5). Film-makers and spectators alike comprehend the inherent difficulties with representation in the non-fiction film, but this understanding does not invalidate either the documentary film or the documentary pursuit: a documentary itself is the crucial point at which the factual event, the difficulties of representation and the act of watching a documentary are confronted – if not resolved (Bruzzi, 2000: 7). A negotiating process develops between the reality in front of the camera and the act of film-making. The subject is equally as involved in this as the director and the spectator. The documentary truth is the entirety of the performance unfolding itself in front of the camera. Phenomenology turns to the subjects' *experience* of that reality.

In thinking through subject-positions and agencies in the films under discussion, phenomenology offers an alternative to the post-modern disbelief in the documentary's ability to represent reality. It thinks about art (and cinema) as an event that creates meaning depending on the effect it has on the spectator. These ideas were developed by Maurice Merleau-Ponty, whose work on art provided the inspiration for the anti-semiotic thinking of André Bazin, Amédée Ayfre and Henri Agel. These philosophers believed that art unveils the illogical. In line with Third Cinema, solidarity and feminism, their respect for the individual experience offered more responsibility to the spectator as an active subject, while their reading of films was less analytical and more visceral. In this philosophy, sympathy, solidarity and subjectivity are intricately linked. Documentary as an essentially subjective form of film-making needs to be understood within the preconception of a common human experience of reality.

Phenomenology accepts that others can experience the same receptivity to an event or an object. Its premise is that 'the first truth of the world is the truth of perception', which entails a 'genuine metaphysical decision concerning the ontological status of phenomena . . . such as the experience of signification, of things, of values and of persons' (Ricoeur, 1967: 9). In other words, we have to *decide* to accept a common experience. It follows that it is the experiences or the perceptions of reality that are shared, and the sympathy in intersubjectivity relates to this shared experience. Maurice Merleau-Ponty considered art intuitive, the primary activity, and theory as a secondary activity, victim to reason. Primary activities and art in particular are, in his view 'gateways leading out of the useless labyrinth of logic and to the riches of experience' (Andrew, 1976: 245). In phenomenology, perception is 'a matter of the sense organs . . . and is therefore not a purely intellectual activity' (Grossmann, 1984: 87). Deleuze roots many of his insights into cinema and the experience of cinema in phenomenological thinking when he describes the face as an 'organ-carrying plate of nerves' on which most emotions can be read, 'which has sacrificed most of its global mobility and which gathers or expresses in a free way all kinds of tiny local movements which the rest of the body usually keeps hidden' (Deleuze, 1986: 87). As we will see in the films, the close-up of the (subjective) face often communicates more than (objective) reality can.

Phenomenology attempts to explain reflection and perception without preconceived ideas of their status in reality, studying what presents itself to the senses irrespective of its existential status (Grossmann, 1984: 140). Merleau-Ponty also shows that a belief in the spectator is vital for the artist: 'the spectator submits himself to art in order to listen to the analogies and correspondences of the world which the artist, thanks to his labour and genius, managed to enclose within the structure of his work' (Andrew, 1976: 246). Film is art first and foremost. It requests that we look at reality, a shared external experience of objects; that we look at something in a different way. In order therefore to examine film effectively, one needs to examine it in its totality, consisting of the reality of the subject, the creator's intentions, and the effect on the spectator. Together, these three aspects will reveal 'human truth' (Andrew, 1976: 249) created by the subjective, individual perspective of the analyst.

Intersubjectivity is rooted in the belief that the other can be recognised as a being that is equally as complex as the self. In cinema, the interpretation of the Real and the Truth can be trusted to the critical and the intellectual abilities of the spectators. Intersubjectivity relates to the subjectivity of more than one being in the material world who are aware of each other's and their own existence in the shared phenomenological world. Identification and sympathy are the two main ways in which to relate diverse subjects. The subject's being in the world has meaning only through self-awareness of his or her presence in front of the others. Objects and images look back at us, as they are also entities existing in the world of natural objects (Laine, 2007). The distinction between self and other should not therefore be used to define ourselves according to what the other is not, but attract us to find shared experiences through intersubjective, human sympathy and solidarity.

Spectators are able to experience the other not only as an object of the look, but also as a conscious subject that is able to reduce the spectators to objects in their turn. The spectators become aware that they exist for others just like the others exist for them. The phenomenologists anticipated difficulties with visual art and cinematic perception: Husserl, for example, stated that the other's look, or gaze, is limiting to the self's freedom. The awareness of the other's gaze makes one self-reflexive and aware of oneself in the way one is seen by the other. As Edward Said said: 'we are lookers as well: we do more than stand passively in front of whoever wanted to look at us' (Vogl, 2003: 11). The realisation that the other is looking at us, and that we are looking at the other simultaneously, causes the breakdown of the individual's sovereignty and creates a correspondence between the self and the other. However, if we 'see' each other, an understanding appears, while listening contributes further to this correspondence.

This parallels the cinematic gaze: the camera-eye as one of the intersubjective partners in the event of perception alters the natural performance. This concept of performance is crucial to an understanding of the presence of the camera in the other's reality. The camera as the gaze and as a phenomenon alters reality. Yet even Judith Butler (1990), theorist of performativity, departs from the assertion that existence precedes essence as one is not born a woman, but rather becomes one. Equally, one is not born a subject of a documentary, but one becomes one. Through mutual agreements, director and subject enter into a new reality, which is then also entered into by the spectator. The agreement with the spectator is a phenomenological performance: accepting the extraordinary circumstances of the cinema experience, intersubjectivity can be attained once the represented reality is established as a mutually experienced event. Existence and the intersubjective experience of oneself as object precede the performance. In other words, even if there is a degree of performativity, there is still an sympathetic acceptance of it being grounded in a common experience of reality: a representation neither invalidates nor has to be synonymous with the reality that preceded it.

So, in cinema, at least three parties create an intersubjective experience related to the material world: subject, director and spectator. These positions are interchangeable and fluid. Intersubjectivity is a productive alternative to objectivity. Crucially, what constitutes intersubjectivity is the experience of the other as a subject and as an event: the acceptance that the other experiences the same world perceived by the self. A representation of this intersubjective reality is possible if both participants agree implicitly on perceiving it *as* real. Merleau-Ponty says: 'it [art] neither imitates nor constructs; it expresses that which in some way was waiting to be said' (Brent Madison, 1981: xvi). This demonstrates a strong belief in the possibility of reality and representation, and the representation of reality.

A phenomenological understanding of the material world leads to a dialogue between different subjectivities and shows us that 'documentaries are performative acts whose truth comes into being only at the moment of filming' (Bruzzi, 2000: 10). In documentary history, the focus has too often been one-sided: documentary critics often focus on the daring acumen of the film-makers, the creativity in finding their subject and the revealing content of the documentaries, forgetting to also appreciate the creative cinematic techniques. As Ilona Hongisto shows, 'documentary films engage in a productive dialogue with the world in its becoming' – they help to shape, they co-compose the real. She looks at the soul of documentary, and what documentaries can do. In this, she is especially concerned with artistic and experimental documentaries that do not shape the social sphere, but that 'offer a nuanced take on a perpetually emergent practice' (Hongisto, 2015: 19). In her understanding of the aesthetics of the frame, the world beyond the claims, beyond the voice, creates an 'inexplicable integrity of a reality that unfolds before the camera' (Hongisto, 2015: 13), and as such, the forms within the frame consist of an intensified, focused and intersubjective becoming. She says:

> The demarcating power of the frame, its emphasis on the limit, accords the actual forms in the image with an intensity that exceeds them. More precisely, the frame summons the virtual forces hosted in actual forms and expresses them as sensations that break through the bounds of the frame. (Hongisto, 2015: 17)

This book is also interested in what is inside the frame, and how paying attention to this can create a deeper bond, and unfolding power that connects spectator and subject. But more than this, I am interested in the collaboration between the social sphere and the soul of the documentary, between the voice and the look. This book combines an exploration of reality and its representation with a deeper, more intense focus on the film-maker's creative representation and framing of her subject and the challenge put to the spectator for interpretation. Experimentation with the voice and the look potentially undermine the singular authority of the film-maker and place the authority with subject and spectator, ensuring that the responsibility of the interpretation lies in the shared, intersubjective, negotiated view.

Solidarity, sympathy and intersubjectivity, as well as the political content and form of most of the documentaries here, foreground an aesthetics of negotiation rather than a revolutionary aesthetics. The tone of the directors and the tone of the films engage in a negotiation between directors, subjects and spectators. The directors enable dialogue (both visual and verbal) in a moderate, non-violent way. The political and social situation in which these documentaries are made demands a deeper understanding of national identity and a broader regional identity, as well as attention given to the global situation of women in documentary. As Shohat suggests, but does not make explicit, there is a cinematic way of critiquing not only the (colonial) past, but also the (neo-colonial) present *implicitly*, which goes further than reinscription or compensation. The terminology of solidarity, commonalities and shared experiences suggest a mildness, a moderate tenacity or a stylistic rebellion that might seem slow and patient, but is not necessarily any less effective in its negotiating prowess. Similarly, new modes of resistance co-exist with rebellious and heroic ones. The pioneering women of Arab documentary rewrite, imply and contemplate rather than denounce and attack 'the system' heroically. They do not reject as much as interrogate their situations. Documentary feminists Diane Waldman and Janet Walker suggest that:

> Documentaries initiated by people who take up a camera to film their own lives or by people and filmmakers coming together to tell common stories must be appreciated as at least potentially radical, and these documentaries must be instated in the archives of documentary history. (Waldman and Walker, 1999: 17)

Radical or rebellious documentaries do not need to be violent or heroic, in the same way that they do not need to be made by men. The word 'radical' does not need to connote violence or anger. That would be the first step towards understanding not only the aesthetics of these films, but also the attitude of these film-makers. In order to subvert regional and transnational, direct or indirect censorship, the creativity of the film-maker shows its true political potential in negotiating dissidence. This is paralleled in the film-maker's permissible and sensitive analysis of the political context and the subjects' personal circumstances, a subtlety in expression and voice, and, in particular, the great importance attached to the paralinguistic ways of expression and body language – the returned look, the act of 'seeing' and the resulting complicitness.

The Voice and Gaze in Feminist Cinema

Both voice and gaze have been theorised thoroughly in film studies. Perhaps the gaze has received more attention due to its mystery or meaningfulness. As an audio-visual art form, voice and gaze are central in the communication via screen media. Equally, woman's voice and gaze are at the core of feminist and gender studies. In my analysis I aim to give both gaze and voice equal attention, to show their interaction and complementarity in negotiating dissidence in political documentaries.

Most documentaries in this book use a form of voice-over. The voice is one of the aspects central to my analysis. Chapters include their own more detailed analysis of the voices in the films. Sarah Kozloff, in her study of the voice-over in fiction films, defines it as 'oral statements, conveying any portion of a narrative, spoken by an unseen speaker situated in a space and time other than that simultaneously being presented by the images on the screen' (Kozloff, 1988: 5). In recent documentary studies there is a strong opposition to the authority of the voice-over. More and more, documentary voice-overs explore their 'fluid intermixture of narration with exposition, argumentation, instruction, and poetry' (Kozloff, 1988: 2). The voice in a documentary is not easily defined, and it is not any less or more important than the ongoing 'showing versus telling' debate in documentary theory. We will look at what the film-maker shows, what the subject enfolds or reveals, and what – or how – the spectator is enabled to unfold. Bill Nichols (1991) asserts that film-maker and spectator are always outsiders. Authoritative narration, or the voice-of-god, was prevalent particularly in the early days of documentary theorising. John Grierson commented on the voice that 'while the world is sure of nothing, the voice [in documentary films] is supremely sure of itself' (Kozloff, 1988: 29). This conceit of the voice has long been disputed. Grierson himself used narration liberally, but mostly experimented with poetry and pace, laying the foundations for finding new kinds of voices and modes of narration.

As Stella Bruzzi says, the voice-over should not be burdened with a bad reputation stemming from the elitism of past theoretical discussions. She demonstrates how different uses and experiments with extra-diegetic voice-over narration in documentaries have come to show the potential of not necessarily didactic, undemocratic, authoritarian voices. Self-reflexivity and subjectivity on the part of the director, the subject and even the spectators, aids voice-over in its effectiveness and in the possibilities it offers to be critical and interpretative. Looking at the function of the voice-over in documentaries from a distinctive feminist perspective, it is more constructive to discuss the various ways in which the classic voice-over has been modified and its rules transgressed through the insertion of ironic detachment between image and sound, the reflexive treatment of the narration tradition and the subversion of the archetypal solid male narrator in a documentary.

Bruzzi illustrates this through women subverting the expectations placed on voice-over. A common reaction to voice-over is that narration suppresses the voices of the subjects, yet commentary, intervention and intention can equally carry responsibility if the director realises his or her own subjectivity and if the spectator is willing to interpret that subjectivity in the context of the film. The dialectical co-existence of authorial voice-over and factual representation once again places responsibility on the director and the spectator. The voice-over therefore establishes a complex but necessary relationship between the voice of the director and the interpretation of the spectator. Bruzzi presumes the ability for self-reflexivity and sympathy in the spectator: documentaries represent truth through interpretation not necessarily at the expense of independent thought (Bruzzi, 2000: 56). The voice-over can become a subversive tool: 'the narration becomes a component capable of engendering . . . a dialectical distance, one that both draws the audience into sympathising for the image, and sets them critically back from it' (Bruzzi, 2000: 59). This dialectical distance brings inconsistencies to the surface and thus creates a space in which interpretations by the spectator become possibilities. In this way there is no longer a pressing need for documentaries to stress the 'purity' of reality, because the voice grants metaphoric access to the inner self, thoughts and identity.

A woman's voice is confrontational, moreover, as it directly challenges the conceptualisation of the voice-over as a repressive, ideological and patriarchal tool. A woman narrator subverts the insinuations of patriarchal authority, as female voices are mostly associated with the physical power of utterances; the physicality of women's voices stands out because it is unusual. The very presence of a female voice tampers with the unity and the universality of the male voice-over spectators are used to: it creates a critical distance (Bruzzi, 2000: 64). In the 1970s and 1980s, women's voices gained prominence, and by their presence embodied alienation and intensified politics. The female voice signalled a lack that had until then been masked by the patronising and didactic maleness of the voice: 'the traditional voice-over can be construed as one of the symbolic substitutes for [the] loss of control and omniscience. A female commentary is thus an overt tool for exposing the untenability of documentary's belief in its capacity for imparting truths' (Bruzzi, 2000: 66).

Bill Nichol's (1991) assertion that the director will always remain an outsider incapable of truly knowing the subject is also based on Spivak's texts that discuss whether or not the subaltern can speak. The voice-over cannot be separated from the insistence that the subaltern cannot speak. Moreover, several feminist writers and film-makers have experimented with alternatives to 'speaking for' the subaltern woman: Trinh T. Minh-Ha has explored 'speaking nearby' (Kaplan 1997b: 195–217) and Assia Djebar has experimented with 'speaking around'. Both challenge Spivak's lack of faith in the possibility for the subaltern to speak and thus also the only alternative Spivak sees: that of 'speaking for'. Trinh's speaking nearby

'can come very close to a subject without, however, seizing or claiming
it. A speaking in brief, whose closures are only moments of transition
opening up to other possible moments of transition – these are forms of
indirectness' (Chen, 1992: 87). Similarly, Djebar says: 'it is important not
to presume to speak for – or even worse – about women, at best to stand
at their side and, if at all possible, directly next to them' (Hillauer, 2005:
5). Both seek a position from which to speak. 'Trinh claims that "speaking
nearby" offers a position at once close to but noting the distance of difference. Closeness emerges in the loving way the camera works with the
people' (Kaplan, 1997b: 202). Both Djebar and Trinh insist on the possibility of approaching the other. I argue that sympathising and showing
solidarity are perhaps more effective than approaching or knowing. There
is an alternative to speaking for, speaking nearby and speaking around:
the director can speak *with* her subject and spectator. An agreement
on the performativity of the subject-position and the intersubjective
encounter between director, subject and spectator can enhance trust and
belief. The insider–outsider (director) enables the insider (subject) and
the outsider (spectator) to understand one another. The insiders have
learned to represent themselves, not by finding a voice – because they
always had a voice – but by finding a listener in the spectator. Through
the intersubjective relationship between the subject's and the spectator's
realities, through the mediated opening up of spaces with female self-
reflexive voices, and through the trust between director and subject, the
spectator learns how to listen to the voices. In this intersubjective reality,
the subject-position is made material. Whether the subaltern's message
is communicated effectively depends on the receptiveness of all parties
involved in the director/speaker/listener relationships. It is a matter of
negotiation: who speaks, when, why and about what, and who listens. A
spectator's and director's skills to speak with and listen to the subject help
to enact the permissibility of a film's dissidence through extra-textual
aspects.

Next to the voices speaking and the capacity to listen, the look is
equally important and can, through paralinguistics and body language and
other extra-textual aspects, be even more exhilarating and fascinating to
consider. To truly 'see' and therefore understand the extraordinary subaltern woman, the director and the spectator have tools available to them
through filmic language and form. One of these, which will be discussed in
greater detail in the individual chapters, is the close-up. In addition to the
voice-over, the close-up communicates that which is perhaps unsayable,
not permissible, and counts on the spectator's sensitive understanding
and really 'seeing'. Even if we follow the conviction that the subaltern

cannot represent herself, the medium of film offers extra-textual tools that challenge the limitations of verbal communication in censored areas. The subaltern can look back and communicate beyond what she is saying verbally. The gaze is a much politicised notion in Maghrebi politics, as 'the prohibition against woman seeing and being seen is at the heart of [Arab] patriarchy, an ideological system in which the master's eye alone exists' (Mortimer, 2001: 214). Women challenge the patriarchal system by re-appropriating and frankly returning the gaze: 'the cultural logic of looking is not the monopoly of colonialism even if power relations bequeath to it the appearance of such domination' (Hitchcock, 1997: 70). Colonisers are not the only ones who have the power of the gaze: the colonised can look back, even from beyond borders, gender inequalities and racial prejudice. The gaze is not just in the eye of the beholder, but also in the look of those who are 'seen'.

The primary way for the director to achieve the active look and the interaction between subject and spectator in films is the use of the close-up. It is generally accepted that the close-up of the human face provides the subject with subjectivity. Many critics take for granted the two essentially contradictory aspects attributed to the close-up: defamiliarisation, on the one hand, and a deeper insight into the emotional state of the subject, on the other. The defamiliarising effect of the close-up is theorised in much detail by Epstein and Deleuze,[2] while the deeper understanding of the emotional state of the person in the close-up has been theorised more widely. 'The close-up simultaneously poses as both microcosm and macrocosm, detail and whole' (Doane, 2003: 93). French film theory centring around photogénie (in the 1920s), was theoretically incoherent, but roughly meant to express that which is inarticulable, that which exceeds language. Photogénie is the mystical power of an image taken at a certain instant. It defamiliarises the spectator with the object–body in focus. The close-up is the privileged site for photogénie (Doane, 2003: 89). Doane digs deeper into Epstein's existential confusion. Summarised, according to Epstein, photogénie is that which expresses the inexpressible: it exceeds language, it is a mysterious, indefinable something that is present in the image and that differentiates cinema from all other arts. Explaining that the face expresses more about subjectivity than speech can, Doane attempts to link faciality and photogénie. According to Deleuze, she says, the face is the privileged site of individualisation, the manifestation of social roles or social types, and it is also the primary tool of intersubjectivity, of the relation to or communication with the other (Doane, 2003: 95). Deleuze says that 'the close-up pushes us beyond the realm of individuation, of social role, and of the exchange that underlies intersubjectivity', thus indicating that the spectator is forced into active collaboration with the filmic expression. The close-up alters a spectator's superficial perception and challenges the capacities of the human eye.

Béla Balázs refers to the close-up of the face as an experience by the spectator of the realisation that 'we can see that there is something there that we cannot see'. Through the close-up the optical unconscious becomes aware of several aspects of the world that were there before, but that the person was unaware of because the naked eye does not have the same capacities as the camera. In the 1950s, Béla Balázs claimed that the 'close-up produced revelations of a new emotional and dramatic magnitude in showing the microphysiognomy of the human face' (Balázs, 1952: 55). He talks about identification through changing distance, detail taken out of the whole, the close-up and the changing angle as being a new psychological effect only attributable to the narrative particularities of film. In that way, the 'close-up reveals the hidden mainsprings of a life which we had thought we already knew so well. [As such,] the camera has uncovered that cell-life of the vital issues in which all great events are ultimately conceived' (Balázs, 1952: 55). In addition, the close-up has not only widened our vision of life, it has also deepened it. Close-ups make us look at the world differently. In particular, the face merits a new sort of attention as it reveals the 'most hidden parts in our polyphonous life, and teaches us to see the intricate visual details of life as one reads an orchestral score' (Balázs, 1952: 55). He pays attention to the poetic interpretation of a new way of looking and a new life revealed. The close-up provides us with the drama of life as it opens up the reality of what is happening underneath the surface. According to Balázs, faces express the poetic sensibility of the director in fiction films. Feminist documentaries express the real-life sensibility of the director and the subject, which might be disguised under layers of performance and representation, and offer the spectator a challenge and a way to feel implicated through subjective sympathy and solidarity. Post-Third-Worldist documentaries by women use the close-up on face and body language in very intricate ways. In the films in this book, in their hope of implicating the spectator with close-ups, the film-makers pull in the audience, literally bringing them closer to the subject in solidarity through the image (not the voice alone).

Enfoldment and Unfolding

The close-up and the voice-over are also tools in my approach to Laura Marks' concept of the enfolding and unfolding of knowledge. Marks says that simple representation of complex realities seems impossible, and thus experimental art is the perfect condition for the representation and memorialisation of the civil war (Marks, 2015: 10). Indeed, she says, 'the lost, dead, forgotten and otherwise inaccessible beings and events are still there' (2015: 11), but in life outside of art may have been pushed to the background. As such, artists must 'carry out their own unfoldings, explicating hitherto latent events, knowledges and sensations' (Marks, 2010: 234) in order to reveal that which remains hidden and inaccessible. There are several strategies to do this successfully: 'draw attention, in almost diagrammatic fashion, to what they are prevented from showing [and] revealing the smallest sights and sounds that usually seem unimportant'. Another strategy is to continue to bypass well-known facts, and 'willing certain elements to remain in a state of latency' (Marks, 2010: 237), thus protecting the sensitive and trusting the audience to participate in the activity of unfolding that is suggested by the film-maker.

As Marks understands it, enfolded knowledge is about forgetting (or the withdrawal of knowledge), and unfolding about remembering. It is expressed in experimental documentary through the interweaving of narrative strands. Marks writes that experiments are free acts, not reactive acts, and that they 'gain the power to affect others to the degree that they harness active focus' (2015: 9–10). In this she follows Deleuze as well as Islamic philosophy. The 'fold' is where knowledge gets stored that is sensitive or that historiography generally ignores: the 'small' voices. Marks shows, through the work of Arab philosopher Toufic who looks at history, how memory is imperfect, and forgetting or amnesia are the consequences of difficult and harsh circumstances. In other words, history can be traumatic and may be forgotten. He theorises the 'withdrawal of tradition after a surpassing disaster', explaining that 'after a disaster representation is impossible, leading to material destruction and immaterial withdrawal' (Marks, 2015: 10). This sounds similar to what Adorno struggled with after the Holocaust (Adorno, [1955] 1967: 2). However, Marks emphasises that rather than a withdrawal, there is an enfoldment, and she also suspects that the incapacity to act in fact intensifies the conditions of creativity.

Toufic, Marks says, theorises the neglect of the past as a withdrawal, whereas Marks herself thinks perhaps enfoldment is a more productive term, in that she emphasises that 'the past persists, enfolded, in virtual form, and some of its facets may unfold to some degree in the present' (Marks, 2015: 11). She sees enfoldment in four areas of Arab experimental cinema: in its aniconic or iconoclastic approach to images; in its partiality; in a certain lightness, tenderness and humour; and in the Islamic concept of *taqiyya*, or dissimulation, in which one might say one thing and mean another (I refer here to the facial expressions and body language that may reveal something about what the person under scrutiny may really mean). So enfoldedness, in Marks' conceptualisation, is a way of protecting images from perceptibility. It is a way to keep important things protected by not releasing them into images or other forms of expression, and it illustrates the difficulty or impossibility of bringing history and memory into audio–visual expression.

If we take this a little bit further still, it could also refer to the manner in which film-makers protect the heart of their film – the vulnerable subaltern – from the rest of their narrative and the rest of their interviewees. Intersubjectivity might be the goal between subject, film-maker and spectator, but some information or people might remain too sensitive to really reveal all. Likewise, the voice enfolds the look, explaining and even distracting from the image, while the look helps to unfold the voice. As I describe above, the sensitive information, that due to censorship and taboos in the Arab world's media remains hidden or enfolded, can be revealed and liberated, or unfolded through the act of 'listening' and 'seeing' in the audio–visual art of documentary.

Chronology

The structure of the chapters in this book adheres to a chronology: Ateyyat El Abnoudy was the first to start making films in the early 1970s and Hala Alabdallah Yakoub was the last to join these women in making her own films. Between these early and late starters, we see women variously turning to journalism or high art to frame their documentaries. All have had to contend with taboos and censorship issues, but they each find their own ways of subverting the censor and addressing taboo subjects. The chronological structure of the book thus also reveals a logical development in political and cultural terms, witness to changes on a national and often also international scale.

Ateyyat El Abnoudy from Egypt and Jocelyne Saab from Lebanon started making films in the early 1970s, the period immediately after the manifestoes of Third Cinema and NAC first circulated. In their films it is possible to see an initial scanning of the limits and possibilities of documentary for women, as both film-makers were highly interested in the complex political circumstances in their countries, and specifically the role of women in this era: Ateyyat El Abnoudy looks at poverty and the representation of women in government; while Jocelyne Saab is interested in the complex reality of the sectarian nature of the Lebanese war and her own personal situation as a woman journalist within this. Tunisian Selma Baccar and Algerian Assia Djebar, making their first films at the same time in the mid-1970s, look closely at women's roles in their countries' historical struggles. In their films there is a more substantial existential struggle with womanhood and feminism, and the position of the privileged artist within this conflict between genders in historiography. Palestinian Mai Masri and Moroccan Izza Génini both look at their home countries from the position of an outsider. Génini is a Jewish Moroccan woman who was raised in Paris, while Masri is a Lebanese Palestinian, observing and interacting with the inhabitants of Palestinian refugee camps. They make their films in the aftermath of severe conflicts, but the focus on the homeland does not avoid the history of its politics. On the contrary, both Génini and Masri look back on to history to let it inform their present in diverse ways: Génini in a nostalgic, personal way; and Masri in a hopeful, melancholic, communal manner. Lastly, Hala Alabdallah Yakoub is a latecomer to making her own films, and synthesises many of the tendencies of the pioneers that came before her. She was inspired by and has learned from the politically dissenting work, the experimental experiences of conflict and the melancholic longing for home in the previous women's works. Yet all these different approaches to the negotiation of dissidence have in common a working with the voices and images of women, and with listening and seeing strategies. These directors harbour an emphatic trust in the abilities of the spectators to have a film literacy that goes beyond a simple, passive understanding of contexts and contents. Film-maker, subject and spectator work together in an effort to actively achieve a singular feminist empowerment, with not only sympathy, but also the kind of solidarity that leads to changing differences and subject positions at its centre. A negotiating of dissidence through transnational feminist seeing and listening must result in post-Third-Worldist collective action.

Notes

1. Colloquially, 'I see' often means 'I understand'.
2. Mary Ann Doane's reading of Epstein's struggle with the close-up illustrates its abject nature. The defamiliarising effect of the close-up is captured very well in his discomfort with it. He stresses the hyperbolic nature of the close-up and 'delineates the close-up as a lurking danger, a potential semiotic threat to the unity and coherency of the filmic discourse. The most heavily used close-up, that of the face, fragments the body, decapitating it' (Doane, 2003: 89). The close-up as a fragmented image that does not obviously have any relation to the whole is what poses a potential semiotic threat: 'the world is reduced to

this face, this object' (Ibid.). This defamiliarisation inherent in the close-up ensures the abject nature of the Other on the screen. It depends on the active participation of the spectator into the looking act, whether he or she is going to accept the Other into his or her personal space or not.

CHAPTER 1

Ateyyat El Abnoudy: Poetic Realism in Egyptian Documentaries

Ateyyat El Abnoudy, also called 'the mother of Egyptian documentary', started making films as a student in the early 1970s, and has had a prolific and relatively successful career as a documentarian in the Arab world. Her films have been exhibited at festivals worldwide, on television in Europe and the Arab world, and at special screenings of retrospectives of her work, though not in Egypt itself. Her most successful and internationally recognised film is *Days of Democracy* (1996), and she continued making films until 2006, when she became ill. In this chapter I offer an overview of the consequences of censorship for under-represented documentaries in Egypt and discuss El Abnoudy's exploration of voices and faces in some of her most significant documentary films. Particular attention is paid to her first three short documentaries *Horse of Mud* (1971), *Sad Song of Touha* (1972) and *The Sandwich* (1975), as well as *Permissible Dreams* (1982) and *Responsible Women* (1994). The issue of who speaks or who looks at the Egyptian women and children from the lower classes comes to the forefront. In her later and most famous film, *Days of Democracy* (1996), El Abnoudy becomes more self-conscious and reflexive in capturing women's voices and faces. The Al Jazeera documentary, *Days of Documentary*, about El Abnoudy (and not to be confused with her own *Days of Democracy*) is used as an important resource, as – apart from the occasional newspaper article – almost no material exists regarding her films.

El Abnoudy was born in 1939 and grew up in rural El Simbelaween, Daqahlia Governorate, on the north of the Delta. She grew up in a working-class society and grabbed the Nasserist opportunity to attend the University of Cairo to study law (pers. correspondence, 2009). In Cairo she moved in artistic and journalistic circles, mainly because of her relationship with her first husband, the journalist and poet Abdel-Rahman El Abnoudy (who died in 2015). During her studies she supported herself financially by working in a theatre and as an actress. This interest in law, political journalism and art, combined with her involvement in acting, awakened in her a social awareness of class and wealth, an interest in socialism and Marxism, and a curiosity about theatre and film. This led to her taking up the camera and using her background in law for the social commentaries she made in her films. In what follows, a brief exploration of documentary in Egyptian cinema is followed by in-depth analyses of women's voices and gazes in El Abnoudy's documentaries.

Documentary on the Nile

Egypt was the first country on the African continent and in the Arab world to establish a film industry, which remains popular and successful. The country managed to develop a national film culture in spite of colonial occupation until the 1920s. Moreover, Egypt's political influence in North Africa and the Middle East grew exponentially due to its cultural successes in the 1940s and 1950s. The 'fusion of the new media (cinema, record industry and broadcasting) allowed Cairo to become the cultural centre of the Arab world, dubbed "Hollywood on the Nile"' (Armes and Malkmus, 1991: 11).

Nevertheless, while the 1930s–1950s period was the Golden Age of Egyptian melodrama, many of the films became stilted and formulaic genre films, due not only to the formula's popular success but also to the 1947 Farouk Code. This was the first institutionalised censorship law in Egypt. The Farouk Code was 'rooted in a long Arab tradition of undemocratic legislation repressing the freedom of individuals and shackling artistic and literary expression' (Hafez, 2006: 230). In essence it prohibited realism, as that was associated with subversive leftist trends. The law prohibited, among others, the following representations: images of apparently soiled alleys, of hand and donkey carts, itinerant traders, copper cleaners, poor farmhouses and their furnishings, and women wearing enveloping gowns; the shaking of the social order by revolutions, demonstrations and strikes; the approval of crimes or the proliferation of the spirit of revolt as a means of demanding rights; and everything touching Eastern habits and traditions (Shafik, [1988] 2005b: 132). These very specific censorship rules were a direct consequence of the links the Farouk family had recently created with the Iranian court. In 1947, 'the government issued a series of 61 specific ordinances that hardened the view of tolerable cinematic content' (Cordon, 2002: 59). These sixty-one rules were subdivided into two main categories: one to do with mores and morals, including religion, sexuality and violence; and a second one that included matters of national security and public safety. The monarchy was wholly responsible for these strict censorship rules. After the coup by Gamal Abdel Nasser the film industry was nationalised, and in the 1970s, under Anwar Sadat it was re-privatised.

Although realism permeated Egyptian cinema in the 1970s, truly realist films never reached a broad spectatorship. Like the funding, critical acclaim came mostly from abroad. Realist film-makers had taken the camera out onto the streets, shooting the urban lower middle class, but this urban lower middle class preferred the escapist melodrama from the past. Another inhibition on bringing realist films to the people was the renewed and very strict censorship law of 1976. The censorship laws of the 1940s were relaxed in the 1950s, but the 1976 law 'went back to the 1947 law and, in addition, gave the clergy censoring powers, thus providing fundamentalism with the final say in film censorship' (Hafez, 2006: 230).

This shows that the image of Egypt that the Ministry of the Interior wanted to see reflected on the cinema screens was one that excluded any reference to the reality of the lower classes; it forbade the showing of political ideologies detracting from the ruling one and the demand for social rights (including women's rights). Yet some film-makers managed to continue to test the censor's boundaries. Film-makers of neo-realist films and documentaries adhered to the prescribed national image, unless they were privately funded or supported by foreign money. Even well-known film-makers from that time such as Youssef Chahine and Salah Abu-Sayf, who began to make realist films in this period, used explicitly melodramatic plot lines and the popular dialogue-driven style- while subtly exposing new social evils such as materialism and indifference on the part of the new rich generations. Film-maker and critic Viola Shafik points out that during Nasser's period of Arab socialism no such thing as a social critique could be expressed through the medium of film (Shafik, [1988] 2005b: 138)- and while there was a tendency towards social engagement in a few intellectual films such as Chahine's *Cairo Station* (1958) or Abu-Sayf's *No Tomorrow* from the same year, there was no consistently realist trend to be found within Egyptian cinema.

After the defeat in the Six Day War against Israel in 1967, a general malaise entered the political and public spheres in the Arab world. Both the 1967 defeat and 'the ensuing process of reconsidering the whole basis of the country's social and political life, led to the production of some critical films' (Samak, 1977: 14). Some of these were reluctantly given permission to be screened, others were prohibited, and yet others were screened only after Nasser's death. One of melodrama's harshest critics, Nouri Bouzid, states that pre-1967 Egyptian cinema was ignorant of reality, but the defeat created a schism in time and politics that created a change in Egyptian creative output. As Salah Abu-Sayf, Youssef Chahine, Tewfik Saleh and Shadi Abdel Salam had already shown, there was a growing interest in reality, confronting the trauma of the defeat, questioning and discussing past and future. New film-makers subverted the censorship laws and began to 'refuse prohibitions and unveil sensitive areas such as religion, sex, the authorities, the "father figure" . . . they let the collective memory pour forth' (Bouzid and El Ezabi, 1970: 243), and sought to re-establish the basis of their cultural heritage and identity. Referring to the malaise in the whole of the Middle East and the countries of the Arab League, Bouzid fatalistically calls the defeat the 'alarm bell that aroused the dormant Arab consciousness from its long slumber' of cultural degeneration (Bouzid and El Ezabi, 1970: 242).

The defeat-conscious cinema found its culmination in the 1968 New Cinema Collective, which published a manifesto by the young cineastes wanting to subvert the old, stagnant industry. Before this, the film industry in the Arab world had an unorganised structure. Dependence on censors and public services created a preoccupation with commercialism and financial status. The young film-makers rejected this attitude and instead adopted a new organised collective interpretation of realist cinema.

> The 1968 Cinema Manifesto . . . held that the authenticity of film and its close-ness to the social and political reality of a society is a measure of its value nationally and internationally . . . The document pointed out the importance of producing films within the reach and comprehension of the widest audience in a nation that still suffers from over 70% illiteracy. It refuted the famous equation in traditional Egyptian cinematic circles that a good production equals a big budget, and it accused the traditional filmmakers of wasting the nation's resources. The manifesto said: 'what we need is an Egyptian cinema, a cinema that records and studies the movement of Egyptian society and analyzes its new social and political relations, a cinema that would discover and reveal the meaning of life for the individual in the midst of these relations'. (Samak, 1977: 14)

The emphasis was on auteur cinema, an artistic exploration of authenticity of form and content. Challenging a personal memory to become a collective memory, directors managed to reflect themselves and their contemporary reality in films. The personal thus became political, as illustrated poignantly in Chahine's *El Ard* (*The Land*, 1969).

Many of the young cineastes defined themselves as guerrillas of the image, subverting old values and inspiring new ones. The psychological trauma of the defeat had erased all hope and dreams of the Arab man after the Six Day War. This despair is perhaps best expressed in Chahine's *The Sparrow* (1973). This film had a huge influence on Nouri Bouzid and inspired a whole range of Arab film-makers: Mohammed Lakhdar-Hamina (Algeria), Mahmoud Ben Mahmoud (Tunisia), Souhel Ben Barka (Morocco), and many more (see Boughédir). They all agreed that internal problems needed to be tackled as much as colonialism and independence. These young Arab film-makers injected the film industry with a new energy. Cinema was now more concerned with the political and social power of the content than with form.

This period of extreme change and renewal in Egyptian cinema serves as the context within which Ateyyat El Abnoudy made her first documentaries. She enrolled in the Film Institute in Cairo in 1968. As MacFarquhar (2002) shows, lecturers at the Institute were often drawn from abroad and emphasised film as a social dialogue. Her formative years as a film-maker were heavily influenced by the NAC movement.

El Abnoudy's documentaries are – in her own words – inspired by the 'real' Egypt, and it is her mission to provide her spectators with a 'description of Egypt' (per. correspondence, 2009). Due to government-supported genre-based production, a specific cinematic image of the nation grew in popularity, which caused realist films and documentaries to suffer under strict censorship laws far more than any other films. The distribution of her early films particularly suffered as El Abnoudy explicitly attempted to represent reality as experienced by the lower classes. Stubbornly representing the voice and face of the underprivileged, she confronted spectators with the life of the under classes of Egyptian society. Within the constraints of an oppressive censorship regime she attempted to express her own voice and the voices and looks of Egypt's lower classes. From exploring the possibilities of the documentary genre in the 1970s, she moved on to discover her own voice and subjectivity as a woman documentary maker in the 1980s and 1990s, within a relentlessly changing and frustrating political climate in Egypt.

Nationalisation and privatisation, respectively, made the film industry a popular but also wealthy sector. In the 1970s, as Sadat was in power, the country's capitalist course widened the gap between classes, which resulted in protests against the decline in the quality of life. This was also reflected in films, where the 'synthesizing ideal evident in earlier films is absent: the middle class hero was lost' (Armbrust, 1995: 103). Although production dropped, with the so-called 'New Arab Cinema' or Chabab Cinema film-makers developed a new confidence. The new interest in reality and, importantly, a preoccupation with women's issues went hand in hand with the first full-length feature films that were directed by women in Egypt (Hillauer, 2005: 40). Inas Al Degheidy and Nadia Hamza were successful film-makers in the 1970s who still draw mass audiences to their films today. It was during this period in the 1970s that El Abnoudy made her first documentary.

The historical context in which El Abnoudy's films were made was an era of renewal as well as limitations for film-makers in Egypt. While in the late 1960s an important new impulse injected Arab cinema with fresh energy, Third Cinema thrived in the North African nations in the 1970s. Like Third Cinema, NAC boasted a generation of young film-makers who adopted an organised and collective new outlook on realist cinema. The emphasis was on an artistic exploration of authenticity of form and content. As Nouri Bouzid points out, the individualistic, personal and autobiographical was a vehicle to question the person behind the camera and his or her identity. He identified this as a 'step that must be taken before they may begin to question others' (Bouzid and El Ezabi, 1970: 248). By invoking personal memories and challenging them to become a collective memory, spectators managed to find themselves and their contemporary reality in these films. The power of the collective was necessary to overcome the strong censorship problems and state involvement.

In 1971, El Abnoudy directed *Horse of Mud*, in a style that she likes to call 'poetic realism' (Hillauer, 2005: 15). She was the first woman in Egypt to make a documentary. In her films, the social reality of the lower classes is simply shown – not commented on – in a realist tradition that likes to document the beauty of simplicity rather than to offer opinions or political dissidence. From her first films, El Abnoudy points the camera at the bodies and faces of women. She emphasises hands, facial expressions and body language. The physical presence of these women is crucial for their representation. El Abnoudy also experiments with colours, sound and close-ups. She graduated with this project from the Cairo Higher Film Institute.

The 1980s in Egypt proved to be a conservative era in which New Islamism flourished. Sadat's successor, Hosni Mubarak ruled with a one-party system. He had Egypt re-admitted to the Arab League. At the start of his term in 1981, he re-nationalised all institutions. Consequently, the entertainment industry became part of the public sector once again. The head of state had complete power over the censorship board. New Islamism exercised a great deal of influence on Mubarak's government. They demanded amendments to the family laws (Hillauer, 2005: 37) so that women's precarious rights were abandoned. A stricter religious censorship on cinema 'gradually developed during the 1980s and continued throughout the 1990s' (Shafik, 2006: 296). This determined women's stardom: there was a renewed emphasis on morals and a re-veiling of the female stars. Around the same time, Ateyyat El Abnoudy and Nabeeha

Lotfi formed the Egyptian Women in Film Association in 1990 (Hillauer, 2005: 90). This organisation is one of many aiming to represent women in all aspects of Egyptian society.

Egyptian cinema became one of extreme opposites in the 1980s and 1990s. On the one hand, art films tackled challenging topics attracting no audience at home but gaining international attention and critical acclaim. Commercial melodramas, on the other hand, popular with local mass audiences, did not reach far outside the Arab world. Of course, Youssef Chahine is known to have straddled these two camps in Egyptian cinema as the most important director of the country of all time, addressing his Egyptian audience as well as garnering respect and popularity abroad. Despite all the limitations placed on the film-makers, box-office records showed an increasing number of realist films passed by the censorship board.

Women film-makers who since the 1970s had become interested in representing reality on screen (such as Nabeeha Lotfi, Asma El Bakry and Inas Al Degheidy), did so largely out of practical considerations. As Waldman and Walker illustrated, the material used to create documentaries was more women-friendly. Shafik agrees:

> Prejudices and restrictive morals are the reason why it took women such a long time to reappear in the ranks of film directors. However, this is not the only reason, as it is telling to compare the presence of women in secondary film branches and professions to their feature film directing. Female filmmakers have succeeded in entering in larger numbers the less expensive and more marginal field of the short film and the documentary . . . It must be suspected that the true reason for the shortage of female directors of full-length feature film is that women are not easily admitted to the film industry. They may have difficulties exploiting the so far male-dominated professional networks. Possibly also producers have been reluctant to entrust high budgets to female directors. (Shafik, 2006: 191–2)

One of the most important innovations in NAC with regard to documentaries was 'that they did not comment on the images, a practice that until then [1968] had been considered obligatory in Egyptian documentaries' (Shafik, [1988] 2005b: 51). Perhaps NAC, like any other subversive collective in cinema history, returned to the origins of cinema to explore the possibilities and opportunities within reality and its representation. An organised reaction against the monopolising power of rich individuals explored new challenges within old genres, while female topics and female film professionals started to re-infiltrate the Egyptian cinema industry.[1]

Against all the odds then, women still dominate the documentary genre in Egypt. They 'used documentary, semifictional, and experimental films to counter traditional and commercial cinema with a reflection of real conditions. Despite this political impulse, fed mostly by the disillusionment after the Arab Defeat in the Six Day War, they wanted their "Alternative Cinema" to satisfy artistic and aesthetic demands' (Hillauer, 2005: 15). The idealistic, socially and politically inspired women documentary makers took hold of the camera to rewrite the everyday reality of minorities, un(der)represented on screen. Instead of the 'bearers' of meaning, women became the creators of meaning. As a product of NAC, El Abnoudy took the camera out of the studio and into the poverty of rural and urban Egypt. She insisted on seeing lower-class women on the screen, attempting to give them a voice and a look. With her proclivity for the close-up, she made women's looks emancipatory tools that complimented their voices in an optimistic outlook on the future. She explored creative ways to avoid censorship. Her 'poetic realism' illustrates how in spite of difficult circumstances for a female documentary maker, Egypt is a source of beauty in aspects other than its wealth and cultural history. Her moderate approach to political issues and her intense relationship with her subjects enable the informed spectator to truly engage with Egyptian lower-class women.

As the only consistently independent political documentary maker in Egypt, El Abnoudy stated in *Days of Documentary* that 'the documentary form is one of the most exemplary ways of writing history as it contains that vital combination of sound, image, colour and people's testimonies on the age in which they live'. With her wish to reinscribe women and the poor into Egyptian history, she emphasises that the reality of Egypt must include the subaltern. With her first three short films *Horse of Mud, Sad Song of Touha* and *The Sandwich* in the early 1970s, she established her social involvement with the people. In her loyalty to the subaltern woman in Egypt, she experiments with the voice, and subverts sensibilities with a focus on the beauty of faces and hands that had not been given screen space before. She used the shorts to experiment with her own voice and gaze, and with ways in which to make the voices of her subjects and her own voice interact effectively.

Horse of Mud (1971), *Sad Song of Touha* (1972) and *The Sandwich* (1975)

From a very early age, El Abnoudy was aware of social inequalities between rich and poor, between the metropolis and the countryside, and between men and women (pers. correspondence, 2009). In her films, the binaries are discarded and instead she assumes power and effective dissidence in quietly approaching the truth. The films El Abnoudy made at the

Cairo Film Institute, *Horse of Mud* (1971) and *Sad Song of Touha* (1972), were unusual for the film school as they were documentaries, in grainy black and white, showing the illiterate working classes on the streets and in the mud-brick factories, giving them a platform on which they could voice their grievances. In *Days of Documentary* (2008) she points out that

> It is rare to find a documentary in Egypt. Other documentaries, if they exist at all, focus on general topics, not specific. They do not concentrate on people but keep it general. They are like the news, like reading something off a page, like a comment on what is seen. That does not come from the filmmaker's own mind and not from the people.

She suggests that the voice in film is not usually genuinely attached to the subjects, not personally involved with the topics, and directly or indirectly overshadowed by the state. With these first two films she established her social involvement with the people she films, her reputation as an engaged documentary maker and, most importantly, the style in which she had decided to shoot the people and topics.

The clarity of voice in diegetic or non-diegetic voice-overs is of primary importance to El Abnoudy. In *Days of Documentary* she says that during the shooting of *Horse of Mud* she decided that the microphone should be in the hands of the people on whom the film was focusing. She took the microphone from the sound person and let the people around her decide the direction the film would take by letting them 'truly express themselves in the way that they want'. This set the tone for her own development and involvement in the films as a director and also illustrates the importance she attaches to giving people from the lower ends of society a platform. They may already have a voice and opinions, and El Abnoudy provides them with the technological means and the cinematic platform to utter them on screen. She decided that the multitude of voices present on the site of *Horse of Mud* were interesting and following the instincts of the working people would make the film truthfully Egyptian.

Horse of Mud documents the basic process of mud-brick making in the centre of Cairo, by the city's poorest near the banks of the Nile. The film focuses on the monotony of the task and the beautiful choreography at work. The movement of the workers and their stories are effectively intertwined. El Abnoudy's presentation of street life and working circumstances is not condescending or dismissive. On the contrary, it is an admiring, uplifting view of the lower strata of society. She was criticised and censored for showing the most unappealing side of Egyptian society as, in *Horse of Mud*, *Sad Song of Touha* and *The Sandwich*, she shows everyday life in a mud-brick factory, as a street artist and in the countryside, respectively. Nevertheless, she illustrates the beauty of simplicity and the lyricism in the lives of people that are, like her, connected to their land. She searches her topics and subjects among the people she knows from her childhood in the north of the Delta. In her films, El Abnoudy addresses issues that she, as a lawyer and intellectual, deems necessary and that she, as a daughter of those previously muted, feels personally affected by. The normality, moderation and the relationship she has with the women in her documentaries attempt to resolve problems with representation of the subaltern. Personal bonds between subject and film-maker, as well as the explicit presence of the film-maker, enable self-representation for the subaltern in Egypt.

In *Sad Song of Touha* the self-awareness of the voice that had been appropriated by the subjects in the earlier film changes significantly: made around the same time and in the same context, *Sad Song of Touha* is much more artistic and experimental with the voice-over. The film is a fascinating portrait of Cairo's street performers. It captures the essence of a street culture defined by its social circumstances and its artistic qualities. Once again showing the beauty alongside the bitter realities of the lower strata of society in the big city, El Abnoudy reveals symbolic parallels between their art and their dire situations. Her husband at that time, vernacular poet and Marxist Abdel-Rahman El Abnoudy (Rakha), provides the voice-over by reading out one of his poems. While the visuals show street children practising for their performance during the fair – contortion and exploitation become metaphors for each other – problematising the poverty and the status of these children, the voice-over says:

> The world is a ball, inside the ball are people, who are watching other people. My heart is heavy. My heart! Are you sad or happy? Is the house near or far? Oh, Fate! Is happiness assigned to certain people? And unhappiness to others? People are watching people and the world is a ball. The world is a bouncing ball. Others watched me, laughed, though I wasn't in the mood. As some laughed, others got bored. The world is ugly without people. The world is a ball with people inside. People watched me while I was stretching my hand. They looked and I looked, as if I were drawing a picture and the world is a ball, or are you people as well – looking at these people who are watching people.

The haunting images form a cinematic dream of uncontrollable inequality, while the poem protests the unbalanced nature of society. Long-shots of the fair and close-ups of the children and the bystanders point out contrasts between different strata of society. The act of watching is questioned as well: who is watching whom and for how long. The images painfully reveal the difference between submissive self-conscious smiles, on the one hand, and laughter at the cost of others, on the other hand. The poem parallels the title of the film in its sadness and desperation. While *Horse of Mud* exposed the many voices and faces of the mud-brick factory workers, El Abnoudy has clearly decided to let the poem – with unidentified voice – speak of the atrocities that are actually unspeakable. Images correspond to and illustrate turns of phrases in the poem. Fragments of actions alongside fragments of thoughts express desperation on the part of and sympathy with the performers. The unspeakability of trauma fragments reality and renders it almost indecipherable.

The Sandwich in turn revolves around the rural society of self-sufficient women and children. The film goes even further in the usage of poetic imagery: there is a complete absence of voice, but the imagery – no longer in black and white but in pastel colours – speaks for itself. The film is set in Upper Egypt in a very poor village, where women take care of the food for the children while they herd the goats. The linearity of the images gives the impression that the material is shown in real time. Due to the complete absence of voice, the look of the people becomes crucial: they gaze back at the camera openly and inquiringly. Bringing these images to the attention of the spectator, the film-maker delivers a message that is impossible to ignore: even without words the subjects in the images say 'we are here, you can no longer ignore us'. In close-ups, the spectator is confronted with a face that returns the gaze, and without contextual background it is impossible to ignore the subjectivity of the person's gaze and actions. For a subaltern subject to take centre stage in a close-up is unusual, and this direct confrontation engages the spectator in an immediate sense. As the subject gazes out onto the spectator, she also implicates him or her by demanding a reciprocal look. The spectator can no longer be passive: El Abnoudy forces – through the close-up – both spectator and subject to imagine each other, to see and understand each other, and to develop a sense of sympathy towards each other. A direct bond is created between the subject and the spectator, and the active involvement of the spectator is assured due to the immediacy of the subject's presence.

Horse of Mud and *Sad Song of Touha* created outrage in the press because of the poverty shown and the directness of the criticism, while *The Sandwich* was prohibited by the censor because of the dirt on the faces of the children, the underfed dogs running past the camera and the symbiosis of man and animal. While the films won prizes at foreign film festivals, in Egypt El Abnoudy was accused of placing her camera in the mud of society. For both *Horse of Mud* and *The Sandwich* she was asked to cut scenes out, such as a dirty stray dog and a child with a runny nose. She explained that she appealed to the head of the censorship board, a woman with whom she had a long and difficult conversation. Initially El

Figure 1.1 The symbiotic relationship between a boy and his goat in *The Sandwich*
(1975) © Ateyyat El Abnoudy

Abnoudy argued that as a film-maker she has to show the reality of society.
Eventually she succeeded in convincing this woman to pass the films using
the argument that the films were already so short, it was not worth cutting
anything out (pers. correspondence, 2009).

Giving the microphone to the people, recording the lower social
classes and focusing on the roles of women in society are all factors that
El Abnoudy sees as central to a description of the real Egypt and that
were also vital in the NAC collective. Her affinity with these subjects and
subjectivities comes from her own consciousness of being one of them.
She recognises herself in the mirror of the camera: self sees same (not
Other) in a dialogue between director and subject. The film-maker's own
background in rural, lower-class Egypt parallels that of her subjects. Their
concerns are the same. She is the subaltern subjectivity portraying her own
subaltern identity. The camera as mirror is not a new idea in documentary
studies: Jean Rouch explored this idea that the camera as mirror is a tool
by which director and subject are provoked into collaboration. The acting
out of everyday life in front of the camera confronts subjects with their

own agency. Sympathy and collaboration then are the main tools through which El Abnoudy attains her goals of nuanced intersubjectivity. There is no attempt to 'speak for' in this representation, but the dialogue effectively includes the spectator. Documenting reality from the lower strata of society upwards, El Abnoudy regards herself as the same as her subjects, and brings topics to the foreground in her documentaries that are crucial to her subjects' subjectivities.

El Abnoudy thus distils the essence of documentary making: uncovering details, the director's selectivity and the film's reconstruction. Film reveals the importance of a subject. It is, however, not just the subjectivity of subject and artist that count in documentary making: the subjectivity of the spectator is equally important. He or she is not told by El Abnoudy what to do, but presented with her subtle critique that they are called upon to comprehend. Spectators are enabled to discover their own subjectivity through interaction with the film. She records, and lets the subjects decide on the direction the film will take. In her task as a documentary maker, she presents on screen something for the spectator's consideration. That way our perception of their reality, while not impartial, is presented for interpretation in a visual historiography, the hieroglyphics of film. In *Days of Documentary* she explains:

> During the Pharaonic era, life was described on the walls in hieroglyphics: it is for me a description of the old life in images. Egypt's past is one of greatness, and I want to find a way to record the modern times in as interesting a way as the Pharaonic people did. I want to show how great my country and its people still are, because I love my country and its past.

Reality and truth as they were perceived in the Pharaonic era are recorded in the hieroglyphics and interpreted in modern times. Like her ancestors, El Abnoudy wants to provide posterity with a realistic record of what modern Egypt represents – in opposition to what the state and censorship wish to portray. She shows the real Egypt, not a grand, mythological image of Egypt but the Egypt to which she and her subjects relate. There is an intersubjective relationship at work that relies on a mutual understanding of what Egypt represents: what the reality of the lower-class person in rural and urban Egypt entails. In El Abnoudy's early documentaries, the people do not yet have a discernible individual identity. The film-maker nevertheless provides the spectator with a thorough understanding of their lives and situations. She finds subtle ways to establish a collective identity. The subtlety and moderation with which the film-maker establishes her aestheticism is more effective than explicitly rebellious cinema could be in Egypt. Negotiating the hieroglyphics of the Egyptian present then within the constraints that she experiences as a film-maker, she wants to effectively involve spectators and subjects alike in a permissible manner. Nuances and subtleties drive the narrative forward and implicate spectators in as efficient a way as possible. The sympathy demanded from spectators establishes a bond between both subject and director and spectator. The active involvement of the spectator makes the subjective possibilities of documentary more immediate. Documentaries, therefore, have a stronger message than the hieroglyphics of which she is so fond.

Permissible Dreams (1982) and *Responsible Women* (1994)

El Abnoudy counts on her spectator to sympathise with the women in her documentaries and refuse the appropriating, voyeuristic gaze. She attempts to adequately (re)present the Egyptian lower classes, both rural and urban. She does so most convincingly perhaps in *Permissible Dreams* (1982) and *Responsible Women* (1994). *Permissible Dreams* is about Aziza, a farmer's wife, who has had a dozen children. She works very hard and thrives on her own pragmatic approach to life, but bemoans the fact that her girls are not allowed to go to school. *Responsible Women* also deals with women who work hard to provide for their children, this time in an urban setting. While these films tackle roughly the same subject, the subtle change in the perception of performance exposes the growing involvement of the director in the status of women in Egypt. In *Permissible Dreams* she finds a representative in the rural figure of Aziza and in *Responsible Women* in the multitude of women in Cairo. She also includes herself physically in the documentaries. She avoids the interrogative approach and instead develops an intersubjective rapport with her subjects. The film-maker emphasises their agency. More so than in the first three shorts, in these two documentaries bodies are emphasised in close-ups. The director's personal relationship with and respect for the agency of the women is visualised through the many occasions on which we see hands and faces in close-up. Her own subjectivity as well as the heterogeneous identity of all the women she interviews are crucial for the interactive, intersubjective way of film-making.

Extensive use of the close-up gives the film-maker the opportunity to see facial expressions, the incongruity between what subjects are saying and what they are feeling or hiding, their humour, wit, sarcasm and regrets. Through the close-up the optical unconscious becomes aware of several aspects of the world that were there before, but of which the spectator was unaware because the naked eye does not have the same capacities as the camera. Béla Balázs claimed that the 'close-up produced revelations of a new emotional and dramatic magnitude in showing the "microphysi-ognomy" of the human face'. In that way, the 'close-up reveals the hidden mainsprings of a life which we had thought we already knew so well. [As such,] the camera has uncovered that cell-life of the vital issues in which all great events are ultimately conceived' (Balázs, 1952: 55). Close-ups make us look at the world differently. In particular, the face merits new attention as it reveals the 'most hidden parts in our polyphonous life, and teaches us to see the intricate visual details of life as one reads an orchestral score' (Balázs, 1952: 55). The close-up provides us with the drama of life as it opens up the reality of what is happening underneath the surface. While in fiction, faces express the poetic sensibility of the director, docu-mentaries express the real-life sensibility of the subject, which might be disguised under layers of performance.

The face, that Deleuzian 'organ-carrying plate' (Deleuze, 1986: 87), is the most subjective of all parts of the body, able to express subtleties that language cannot. The extra-textual aspects of facial communication are tools used to their full potential in the facial close-up in documentaries. If North African women have to negotiate their way through the nets of censorship laws, the effectiveness of their documentaries will be flexible and receivable by outsiders only if the language of the face adds to the speech. 'The face is more expressive and honest than words in the isolated close-up of the film: we can see to the bottom of a soul by means of such tiny movements of facial muscles which even the most observant partner would never perceive' (Balázs, 1952: 63). Balázs eloquently calls it the silent soliloquy as he acknowledges that profound emotion can never be expressed in words at all.

In *Days of Documentary* El Abnoudy says that the close-up of a face affords her the opportunity to see the details in the expressions of the people. According to her, a good shot brings into focus the details of the women's lives and bodies on screen, while also focusing on the surround-ing images of the overall context. The close-up is important in order to make the spectator feel close to the subject. The amount of detail pulls the spectator into the documentary, makes him or her feel personally involved and ensures the engagement of the spectator in the topic under discussion.

It is clear from the start of *Permissible Dreams* that there is an intimate trust relationship between Aziza and the film-maker. The film is an in-depth portrait of a rural woman and her views on women's issues in Egypt. Aziza is the one who accompanies the images with a voice-over exploration of her own identity. The presence of the camera challenges her performative self-awareness: she speaks more openly to El Abnoudy than she does to her family. Her frustrations surface precisely because camera and film-maker offer an attentive audience. The camera provokes the subject into asserting her agency through a performative mode. As a speaking subaltern, she is no longer subaltern. It is through static close-ups that the physical, material agency is emphasised. While Aziza insists on her pragmatism and simple happiness through an attitude of permissibility, the camera's presence enables her to also express anger. One of the most important instances in this documentary is the changing tone of Aziza's voice and the intensity of her facial expressions when she mentions the evacuation of Suez during the war with Israel. Footage of this war is particularly rare in Egyptian cinema as it is such a contentious issue. Nevertheless, as Aziza speaks of it, El Abnoudy includes it: while Aziza bitterly reminisces about her anger at the missiles and the fact that she had to leave Suez, the director shows us images of crying children, advancing trucks and ruined buildings in order to illustrate the devastation. It demonstrates a deep agency on the part of the subject. Aziza interrupts her own recollections as she is acutely aware of the camera's presence, she says, 'I never dream of things I cannot afford . . . My dreams are permissible.' Her smile into the camera further reveals her pragmatism and demands the spectators' admiration. A few minutes later, however, her angry face poignantly reveals her frustrations when she says, 'I want to see these Israeli soldiers and wring their necks.' Here, her face reveals a deep-seated frustration and her eyes burn with anger. These two very opposite facial expressions within such a short time span illustrate the immediacy of reactive sympathy and emphasise the spectators' role.

In *Responsible Women*, a film made more than a decade later, the moderate activism of *Permissible Dreams* becomes bitter and cynical. This is evident in the portrayal of urbanised women still suffering the same discrimination that rural women suffered more than ten years before. While modernisation of the state should have established a more equal treatment of the genders in an urban society such as Cairo, the static nature and lack of development of the Egyptian state's involvement in women's issues is further critiqued. The pragmatism and irony present in *Permissible Dreams* are absent from this film, as well as from the women it presents. Some of the women seem desperate in their situation, while El Abnoudy and other intellectuals, who speak their mind in the film, openly show their contempt for the government. It is a far more politically dissident film.

In both films, then, the camera serves as a provocateur. Women are portrayed as emancipated and content for the most part, but different instances of provocation reveal deep-seated frustrations. While Aziza is practical and the film ends on an optimistic note, the women of Cairo in *Responsible Women* are less relaxed about their situation. Both films are

Figure 1.2 Aziza, with her daughter, tells the director that her dreams are limited in
Permissible Dreams (1982) © Ateyyat El Abnoudy

different illustrations of how the personal is always also political. At the same time, the political is personal as its influence on ordinary people is defining. While the film-maker is arguably unable to reach a satisfactory political result, she is able to physically express her rage through body language.

El Abnoudy's films are complex and subjective, but they also illustrate great respect for every individual that comes under the film-maker's scrutiny. The combination of close-ups of people with panning long-shots that provide the spectator with an overview of general life, community and lifestyle never loses track of the focus on people as individuals. At the beginning of *Permissible Dreams*, the camera pans across the rural landscape of the area where Aziza lives. This contextualisation assures in long- and medium-shots that the rest of the film can focus fully on Aziza's face and body. The clearer Aziza's voice becomes, and the better we are introduced to her, the closer the camera approaches her. El Abnoudy points the camera directly at the woman's face in order to establish a very intimate portrait. Aziza introduces herself: we hear only her voice and see only her face.

The documentary is completely focused on Aziza's subjectivity. Close-ups of her face when she is speaking directly to the camera are mixed with images of her working in the fields, baking bread and washing clothes. The camera is not shy of approaching the working woman very closely. As she is bending over the baking trays and the washing tub, the camera-eye deconstructs Aziza. Her bended back, her repetitive movements and the concentration on her face construct an extremely close personal relationship between director, Aziza and spectator. The subtle deconstruction of the female body precisely critiques the disembodiment of the subaltern in other films. Moreover, the camera is no obstruction to normal life, because Aziza forbids it to be intrusive. In this documentary, she regularly gives clear instructions to her children and to visitors not to pay attention to the camera crew and to pretend they are not there. Through this she obviously does precisely that: she deliberately puts all attention and curiosity on the camera and the presence of the crew. They look back and prevent the voyeuristic gaze, instead the spectators' gaze is encouraged to become actively involved in the deconstruction of voyeurism and the construction of a more informed respect of the female body. Aziza asserts her role as the main character. It is she who is in control – and she not only recognises and points out the presence of the camera, she also looks straight into the lens *and* ignores it completely.

In conversation with her husband, Aziza's situation proves to be much more complex. She criticises him and he refuses to acknowledge her voice. She says: 'fine, peace be with you if you do not want to hear my opinion', thus closing the argument but not relinquishing power. The humour in this scene is derived from subtle irony. While she says 'fine' she makes a face at the camera behind her husband's back, indicating her silent rebellion. She might be unable to utter explicit criticism, but displaying her pragmatism in her husband's presence is still possible by turning her back on him and looking straight into the camera, implicitly expressing her inner thoughts. Her facial expressions and body language, which explicitly exclude the man from the composition, reveal her underlying opinion. Because she is in charge of the narrative structure of the film, Aziza can also decide on the persona she displays. Often her face fills the screen as El Abnoudy has zoomed in on her facial expressions, her mouth and her eyes. The facial expressions reveal irony and a deep awareness of the ambiguities of life – it is a female supra-narrative conspiracy. Her light-hearted approach to difficult issues and her knowing look exchanged with the camera, show the moderate nature of her pragmatic attitude and her belief in a feminist complicity with the film-maker and the spectator beyond the camera.

When speaking about *Responsible Women*, El Abnoudy points out that the close-up can become very demanding, as the women who feature in the film often have angry or upset expressions. It is obvious that the women in *Responsible Women* see the camera as one way of venting their grievances. It is an important and versatile receiver of their message. In a situation where no one else can spare the time or space to listen to their woes, El Abnoudy's camera becomes an audience for them, something that acknowledges their identity and existence. In contrast to *Permissible Dreams*, where Aziza mostly smiles, *Responsible Women* is about disappointed widows and single mothers who have nothing to smile about. In the decade between these two films, one senses the permissible radicalisation of the film-maker, both in choice of subject matter and in the approach. El Abnoudy states in *Days of Documentary* that she deliberately chose these women because their expressive faces reveal such hardships. The close-ups of Sanaa (a factory worker), Sabreen (a beautician), Om Ashraf (a garage owner) and Om Fouad (an unemployed elderly woman) reveal anguished faces, sad and angry. A bitter smile and angry eyes accompany sarcastic remarks about the hopelessness of the women's situations.

The discontinuity between what is voiced explicitly and what is implied reveals aspects of the visual power of film providing a versatile spectrum of communication: even if the subaltern subject cannot speak about everything, as spectators we are sensitive to the ambiguities of visual, non-spoken communication. As a consequence of the intersubjective relationship between director, subject and spectator, there is a universal understanding of facial and bodily expressions. A trust in the capacities of the spectator to interpret non-textual and non-spoken arguments is crucial in permissible documentaries negotiating their way through indecipherable censorship laws. The camera serves as a versatile receiver of the lower classes' extra-textual message. This is illustrated powerfully in *Responsible Women* in a sequence where the hopelessness of procedures at the court of personal status law is under discussion. Going there as a divorced woman is futile and expensive. The bitterness about the inability of women to change their situation is first shown as women are intimidated by men at the court's entrance, who also cast threatening looks at the camera. Secondly, the cynicism is reflected in an interview with a female lawyer, Amira Baheyyeddin. The voice-over is the lawyer's, while the images reflect what she is saying: women go to court but their cases are suspended or delayed. She says:

> Courts are known for their long process. When people decide to go to court it is
> because they have no other choice. They have exhausted all possibilities of finding

an amicable solution. It is a long, costly process and women get nothing in the end anyway.

Her frustration about the situation is illustrated in close-ups of her hand dismissively waving aside the court's effectiveness. She closes her eyes, clarifying that the long, slow process at the court is exhausting and ineffective. At the same time, her wry smile says even more than the words she utters. When the lawyer stresses the hopelessness of the situation, we see a sarcastic grin and raised eyebrows expressing bitterness and cynicism about the government's lack of interest in women.

The focus on hands also illustrates industriousness and women's connection to their situations. In *Permissible Dreams*, the focus of the film is on the chronology of providing food – specifically bread – for the family, as in *The Sandwich*. The camera focuses on the hands combining all the ingredients, kneading the dough, placing the dough in the oven, and firing it up, after which the bread is stored or distributed to the children. This is one of the most archetypal motifs of women's documentaries in Africa. The most well-known ones, Safi Faye's *Selbé* and Flora M'mbugu-Schelling's *These Hands*, focus on the linearity of the actions as a context in which women emancipate themselves. Aside from the face, hands are the most expressive tools for communication. Moreover, the hands in El Abnoudy's films are always working, creating and protective. If they are not making or preparing food, they are creating art or they are busy with a means of earning some money to provide for the family.

The importance for El Abnoudy of the facial expressions and the hand gestures in close-up is emphasised in the fact that the majority of her documentaries end on a freeze-frame, a close-up of one of the women in her film while the voice-over goes on. The optimism in spite of the bitterness and the hope in spite of the cynicism are essential tools for the film-maker in her description of Egypt. She usually opts for the freeze-frame of a smiling face while she also gives the interviewee the last word. The film-maker makes an effort to conclude on a positive note: the women she interviews eventually do assert their self-reliance. They may be in an oppressed position out of which there seems no escape, yet this situation has forced them to become fiercely independent. The freeze-frame of a self-assured and confident face at the end of a documentary accusing the government of indifference towards these women emphasises once again their pragmatism and community spirit. One face represents and summarises the message conveyed by a multitude of individual women. The freeze-frame features most prominently in *Responsible Women*. It expresses the subjectivity of the woman on the screen and her anticipation for a hopeful future. It highlights the importance of the facial expression as a coda to the film. In spite of the pessimism that many interviewees express, women do excel in their independence and the film-maker not only represents a positive outlook onto the future, but also sincere pride in these women's versatility. In *Responsible Women*, El Abnoudy ends on a still of Nadia, the last woman who has asserted that she does not need a man in her life. She says:

> I have devoted my life to my children. I want to see them graduate, well educated. What can a man do? So long as I am healthy and I can work and raise them, what need is there for a man? What can he do better than me? He can undertake one job, but I can undertake two.

Nadia is one of the women in the factory, who are asked by El Abnoudy whether they would be willing to ever marry again, and they all assert that their children have priority now. This confirms Womanism and Islamic feminism's preoccupation with motherhood. The body is a reproductive entity through which a new subject with agency is created. This agency is respected by the women El Abnoudy interviews. Motherhood is one of the main themes that run throughout her oeuvre. The body of woman and its function as an independent, nurturing presence is emphasised.

Days of Democracy (1996)

From her 1970s shorts, El Abnoudy re-imagines Egyptian national identity in her documentaries. She goes beyond a stereotypical image of Egypt and proposes, with her documentaries, an image created by the narrative of women occupying the lower strata of society. In *Days of Democracy* her voice as an engaged and politically involved film-maker becomes clearer. Her attitude of negotiation and moderation is still present as she has to function within a repressive cultural environment, but the activism is palpable through irony in voice-over, interviews and extra-textual aspects of film-making. *Days of Democracy* is a politically inspired and outspoken feminist documentary of the women running for the Egyptian parliament in the 1995 elections.

Days of Democracy is El Abnoudy's most widely screened and celebrated film. In it, she interviews women candidates for the 1995 elections in Egypt. The introduction puts the situation in a historical context. In most of her documentaries she introduces the context of the film herself, drawing the bigger picture for uninformed spectators in voice-over. In *Days of Democracy*, however, she chooses to introduce her exposé with white text on a black screen. As in *Days of Documentary*, she mentions the

Pharaonic era as an example to remember in modern Egyptian society and politics. While the film is much more outspoken, revealing the convictions of the film-maker, she deliberately excludes her own voice from this section of the film, as it is so overtly political in nature.

> In the days of the Pharaohs, Egyptian women played a prominent role in political life. The annals of Egyptian kings register the names of six queens who reigned over the Valley of the Nile. The first was queen Meritnet who reigned 5,000 years ago. Egyptian women bore a number of titles and carried many responsibilities in both religious and secular spheres. However, successive waves of invasion, occupation and foreign rule were enough to eradicate the names of Egyptian women from political life and from the echelons of government for nineteen long centuries! Today, at the threshold of the new century, the daughters of Isis are again claiming the role they once played. This film depicts the endeavours of women in Egypt to make a comeback to political life through the parliamentary elections held at the closing years of the twentieth century.

This return to the Pharaonic era shows El Abnoudy's pride about being Egyptian, while it also reveals acute frustrations with the country's contemporary political and social leadership. The large group of women are named and located geographically, covering the whole of Egypt. The interviews uncover similarities in their campaigns, slogans, supporters and intellect. Each woman has her own very distinct voice, but the sheer number of women interviewed gives the impression that all female representatives need and want the same programme to represent them in parliament. In this way, El Abnoudy illustrates the multiplicity of voices to be one united voice speaking out against the inequality in Egyptian politics. The independence of all interviews reflects a struggle with objectivity in the main body of the film. Instead of giving the subject the power to lead the camera, as she did in the three shorts in the 1970s, here the movement of director and subject are deliberate and purposeful. The subject as a political woman takes the lead in representing her constituency and her political programme, and the director takes a secondary but present role. She refrains from building up a constructed argument and lets the women speak for themselves. El Abnoudy wants the spectators to learn and draw their own conclusions. While she is much more explicitly and physically present in this documentary than in earlier ones, she leaves her own convictions outside of the film and lets the spectator decide.

Each of the women is introduced with either a voice-over from the film-maker or a spoken introduction by the women themselves in voice-off. Each chapter reveals the same enfolded structure: outside–inside–outside. After the voice-over, usually filmed outside among rallying men and women, the candidates are subsequently interviewed inside their homes with no one around but the film-maker. Next, they move outside again, to witness the rallying chants and to see the women among their supporters, enfolded as sensitive and vulnerable information in between the folds of political and public discourse. The personal interviews are thus filmed in isolation from the supporters. Remarkably, these intimate interviews are the only times the women openly and enthusiastically mention the specific women's issues they would like to see on the agenda of parliament. This is arguably due to the premise of the documentary and the questions they are asked by the director. When they are outside, however, addressing their supporters in rallies, they hardly ever mention women's issues, presumably because their audience is predominantly male. Yet the spectator is tasked with the trust of unfolding this information, and 'seeing' its relevance for politics in contemporary Egypt.

On several occasions, when she does not get a spontaneous answer to something she is interested in, the film-maker interrupts what someone is saying and insists on a question or answer she needs. It adds to the subjectivity and to the personal involvement the film-maker is trying to achieve. Her agenda is clear: she is critical of the lack of women in parliament and wants to find out the women's ideas on this matter. Whereas before, the director tried to stay in the background and let the subjects lead the narrative, in *Days of Democracy* the film-maker's voice is urgently present, unfolding women's issues hidden in social discourse that is similar although the interviewees are very diverse. This results in multiple voices reflected onto the screen in the multitude of faces and stories. It is an attempt at a liberating subjective, subtle, moderate and moderating presentation of the rural and urban lower-class women of Egypt. The film-maker's agency is more overtly present through her involvement in the structuring of the argument and particularly when she enters the frame in a reportage-style quest. Interrupting interviews to find parallels between her own and the interviewees' ideas or between the different interviewees' agendas, indicates a preoccupation on El Abnoudy's part with specific women's issues. Nevertheless, instead of spoon-feeding the spectator an overt message, the repetition of phrases and structures provides implications rather than messages. They present spectators with detailed accounts of injustices and leave him or her to decide for themselves on their reaction and response. She places the spectator in the shoes of the subjects inside and outside of the film. She invites reactions, opinions and questions instead of trying to provide 'true' representations and answers.

After numerous interviews of a similar nature, *Days of Democracy* gains momentum and becomes more subjective, showing more immediate solidarity as the film-maker enters the frame when searching for Nafisa.

El Abnoudy made this film with the intention of confronting the spectator with the near-impossibility of a woman being elected to parliament
in Egypt. In the last chapter of the film this is literally illustrated when it
is a real struggle to find Nafisa, one of the candidates. This motif builds
tension and provides a climax. In the introduction to *Days of Democracy*,
she demonstrates that it has not always been like this. In the film her goal
is to link the past to the present. The introduction tells the life story of Dr
Doreyya Shafiq, who came to be known as a rebellious woman fighting for
women's issues as she founded a women's magazine, *Bint al Nil* (*Daughter
of the Nile*) in 1945, a socialist union in 1948 and a political party in 1953,
all concerned with suffrage and women's rights. She is most famous for
storming parliament in 1951. She declared that women are half the nation
and should be represented as such (Hassan, 2001). El Abnoudy is driven
by that same argument in *Days of Democracy*: in the final part of the film
she is asked by male bystanders why she wants to speak to Nafisa. She
explains: 'We're making a film about women running for parliament.' The
men question her further: 'Only the women?' To which the film-maker
defensively responds: 'When they're represented by 50% we won't make
films about them.' This links her directly to the cause Dr Doreyya Shafiq
was fighting for and gives the film its feminist vigour. Both El Abnoudy
and Dr Shafiq are aiming to represent 50 per cent of the population, the
'other' half, the women, and give them a platform. A female documentary
maker gives a platform to female political candidates who are representing
half of the population. The subaltern is thus given a truly political voice.

After asking questions and following the political candidate with the
portable camera, the director finally makes herself visible on camera as
well. The repetitiveness in structure and content has enfolded the crux
of their feminist agendas. The last chapter of the film, however, pulls
the spectator back into the action rather than the discourse, as the film-
maker herself becomes physically involved in the search for Nafisa, a
rural woman from Edfu, who is an independent candidate for parliament.
Tension is built up in an almost fictional way. There is no voice-over.
Instead, El Abnoudy enters the frame, asking people in the street whether
they know of any women running for elections in Edfu. At this point not
only El Abnoudy fills the screen, the sound person and the sound equipment also enter the frame. The film turns into a reportage-like quest for
the documentary ideals of the film-maker and the political ideals of the
candidate. El Abnoudy and Nafisa become heroines in an adrenaline-
driven story. When Nafisa is found, the tension has been built up by our
curiosity for this woman who was difficult to track down and for whom
the film-makers travelled so far. The narrative techniques of building up

tension and the meta-narrative techniques of making the documentary more subjective add to the involvement the spectator feels as he or she is pulled into the quest. The repetitiveness of the first part of the film and the sudden surge in adrenaline balance each other out effectively: the representation of the many voices at first seems droning, almost stubbornly proving a point, which towards the end is hit home by the interaction between the director and Nafisa. Nafisa's strong personality and clear passion for her programme is a counterpoint to, as well as a continuation of, the rest of the film.

The multiplicity of voices we hear in the documentaries by El Abnoudy results in an unusual type of narrative structure. The amount of detail we are presented with and the almost ethnographic understanding of women from the lower strata of society, result in what at first sight seems to be a lack of linearity, a lack of logical structure to the film. The film-maker presents her spectator with an incredible amount of intricate details and personal stories that at times threaten to overshadow the overall message. Her artistic treatment of reality conveys a surfeit of information in the form of a mosaic: from up close it is difficult to see the bigger picture, but from a distance the patterns of the film, the dialectics can be seen at work. The same is true of the close-up. El Abnoudy favours the faces of the women she interviews, which often results in a forceful presence of the subaltern in the spectators' look. Spectators are made to 'see', to understand, the subtleties of the dissident voices unfolding on screen.

The vast amount of information spectators are presented with when watching El Abnoudy's documentaries is translated aesthetically in the form of a focused point of view and a return of the appropriating gaze. In *Days of Democracy*, again, the film-maker makes extensive use of the close-up. It presents her with the opportunity to focus on the faces of the women interviewees so that we see the incongruity between what they are saying and what they are feeling or hiding, their humour and wit, their sarcasm and their regrets. In documentaries, the close-up is a natural shot if the director is conducting an in-depth interview with the woman or man on screen. Nevertheless, in El Abnoudy's films, where the focus is so clearly on women and the troubles or issues they are facing in their turbulent lives, in a country where not everything can be expressed freely, the facial expression can reveal and explain much more implicitly than words do explicitly. She is not looking for narrative identification through the close-up, but for recognition and alignment and allegiance: a universal solidarity through a subjective individual focus on the face that comes with the voice. The subconscious or deliberately hidden context of the conversation can be deduced from, for example, smiles, meaningful glances and eye movement. In *Days of Documentary*, El Abnoudy says that the close-up of a face lends her the opportunity to see the details in the expressions of the people. A good shot, according to her, is bringing into focus the details of the women's lives and bodies on the screen, while also focusing on the surrounding interview and on the images of the overall context. In her poetic style, she reveals many layers of detailed description, testimonies and images of the everyday lower-class Egyptian. The close-up is important in order to make the audience feel close to the subject. The amount of detail therefore pulls the spectator into the documentary, makes him or her feel personally involved and ensures an engagement of the spectator in the topic under discussion enabled to unfold sensitive information as the political becomes personal and vice versa.

El Abnoudy then focuses on the people she knows and with whom she identifies. This not only makes her documentaries subjective, with many different kinds of agency and personalities involved. It also makes her films complex subjective points of view, while they reveal great respect for every individual that comes under the film-maker's scrutiny. Through the combination of close-ups of people with panning long-shots that provide the spectator with an overview of general life, community and lifestyle, she never loses track of the focus on people as individuals with agency. The importance for El Abnoudy of the facial expressions in close-up is emphasised by a still image, a close-up of Nafisa while the voice-over goes on.

In *Days of Democracy*, Nafisa sums up her and other women's reasons for running for parliament: it is important to think of the past and of women's rights and to find inspiration there. She is an uneducated but clever woman showcasing her knowledge of the past and her hopes for the future: 1979 was the year of democracy she says, because it was the year in which a legislative amendment earmarked at least thirty seats for women in parliament. Nafisa thus shows her pragmatism and emancipated spirit in wanting to be one of the women in parliament, representing Egyptian women from her area. She emphasises that she wants to speak out. The optimism is palpable in her enthusiasm and in her spontaneous reactions to the director and the camera. El Abnoudy draws attention to this as the frame closes itself around a still of Nafisa's face.

Conclusion

This chapter has illustrated the subtlety with which Ateyyat El Abnoudy tries to subvert the post-colonial state's fabricated national identity by questioning the rigid gender divisions inherent in the state's popular consumer culture. While her critics reproach her for putting the camera in the mud of Egypt, El Abnoudy's films are now occasionally screened in Egypt and at international documentary festivals. Even though the rural–urban divide creates different types of documentaries and views, the people in El Abnoudy's documentaries are offered a platform, a spectator and a listener. While the Egyptian female subaltern may be occupying the margins of society, being handed the microphone and being followed by a camera that explicitly asks to hear her voice and see her face encourages the lower-class working woman to defy under-representation and express herself from the periphery. In her three earliest short documentaries, El Abnoudy experiments with style and voice, offering the microphone to the people in her film or leaving voice out completely, relying on facial expressions and the poetry of life. In her most popular film, *Days of Democracy*, this results in a political choir of voices projected onto the screen parallel to the women's faces. Her documentary oeuvre is an attempt at a subjective, subtle, moderate representation of the rural and urban lower-class women of Egypt. Within the limits of her society, she tackles complex issues in a permissible manner. With these voices and looks, she places the spectator in the shoes of the subjects inside and outside of the film, ensuring that spectators can build up allegiance with the subjects through an unfolding action towards a listening and seeing/understanding fellow global citizen.

Note

1. *Layla* (1927), a film produced by Aziza Amir, is widely regarded as the first 'truly' Egyptian film, and dealt overtly with women's issues.

CHAPTER 2

Jocelyne Saab: Artistic–Journalistic Documentaries in Lebanese Times of War

Jocelyne Saab is the unacknowledged pioneering woman of Lebanese documentary. Lebanese cinema is defined by the country's civil war (1975–90) and so is Saab's film-making career: she started making films at the beginning of the war. While film-making in Lebanon before the war was dominated, as was the whole region, by Egyptian popular cinema, the war really turned Lebanese film-makers' attention to their own society. Before the war, Lebanese cinema was growing rapidly and had the ambition to outdo Egyptian cinema with genre films such as the Bedouin film, the spy and police film, and the fedayeen film, but since the 1980s the war film has confidently dominated Lebanese cinema (Livingston, 2008: 41). In fact, Lina Khatib writes, the civil war ensured that most film-makers, if they continued to make films during the war, turned to documentary film-making and fictional war films after the war. The cause was threefold. First, due to a re-awakened social and political awareness, film-makers became interested in their own contemporary realities. Moreover, the Lebanese civil war coincided with the worldwide liberation movements, the cinematic interest in Third Cinema and the pan-Arab focus on political realism in cinema, thus raising the awareness in film-makers that the camera could be used as a tool in the struggle and as a means of handling the past, the present and the future of the Lebanese people. Secondly, the war caused a brain drain: producers and directors interested in Egyptian cinema fled the country. There was a sense of 'exhaustion' (Livingston, 2008: 41) with the political and sectarian tension in all of Lebanese society, and the civil war was the catalyst which really made them want to pursue their careers elsewhere. Thirdly, a drain on resources followed the destruction of infrastructure, with those who stayed turning to documentary partly out of necessity: a lack of resources and infrastructure led to film-makers re-focusing their activities on the considerably cheaper and practically more independent documentaries. Others turned to making film for video and television, or worked in distribution, exhibition and advertising.

Saab, a newsreader and reporter, turned to film-making in her own city of Beirut when the war started in 1975. She was born in 1948 in Beirut, and was educated in francophone schools. She obtained a postgraduate degree in Economic Sciences from the Sorbonne in Paris. She has made more than twenty films, both fiction and documentary, short and feature-length. Her first feature-length documentary *Le Liban dans la tourmente* (*Lebanon in Torment*, 1975) followed closely in the footsteps of Maroun Baghdadi, Lebanon's most famous documentary maker. His first film, *Beirut Ya Beirut*, also from 1975, was a remarkable prediction of what would happen with the civil war, while it was also a precursor of the many Lebanese films that later came to deal with the predicament of children during the war. Saab had started her career in television, hosting a pop music programme on national Lebanese radio. She became a news anchor and a reporter on television and a journalist for European television, and the civil war really brought her to the front line, in the field, as a war reporter. The physical risks she took to report on the war in Lebanon made her the first woman in the Arab world to bear witness to the horrors of war around the globe, but with an intense focus on Beirut. She has covered war in the Middle East and Iran, as well as the Polisario war in the Maghreb. Her independent films have received numerous international prizes, as they are accessible to both an insider and an outsider audience: her own transnational status has made her documentaries hybrid works, influenced by a European gaze and interest, as well as an insiders' gaze and knowledge.

Her many documentaries, mostly made in the 1970s and the 1980s, are both journalistic and artistic in nature. *Lebanon in Torment* (1975), *Children of War* (1976), *Beyrouth jamais plus* (*Beirut Never Again*, 1976), *Lettres de Beyrouth* (*Letters from Beirut*, 1979) and *Beyrouth, ma ville* (*Beirut, My City*, 1985) combine reportage and experimental elements. These documentaries engage the representation of the absence as well as the presence of memory in a war zone. She also addresses her own and her fellow Beirutis' longing for tolerance and freedom in the post-colonial context in the Middle East at large. In her lament, which is also a celebration of the history of Beirut, Saab observes the city and its architecture, people, streets and parks. At the same time, the voice in the film engages with literary and poetic sources from the city, commenting indirectly on the images. It is particularly in the manner in which she structures her films that the spectator becomes aware of the artistic merit of the films, and the power of this extraordinary woman's voice. Montage is a central technique with which Saab sets herself and her films apart.

Apart from her documentary work, Saab has also worked on and directed several high-profile and popular fiction films. Her move from documentary into fiction is explained through the lack of reality: 'I make images. First, they were war images, and then I started to invent them, because when everything was destroyed in front of my eyes, I couldn't collect the real anymore. I had to reinvent everything. This is how I moved into fiction' (Saab, 2009, in Mostafa, 2015: 38). In 1981, she was assistant director on Volker Schlöndorff's film about the Lebanese civil war, *Circle of Deceit*. In 1985, her first feature film *Une vie suspendue* (*Suspended Life*),[1] the first film shot entirely in Beirut during the civil war, was selected for the Cannes Film Festival. In 1991, she directed her best-known film *Il était une fois, Beyrouth* (*Once Upon a Time in Beirut*), which is dedicated to the anniversary of a century of cinema and the founding of the Lebanese cinemathèque. It is an experimental film that edits together scenes of Beirut taken from global cinema, where the city has been appropriated by foreign spies and businessmen. It is a riposte to the 'many western films featuring Beirut as a spy haven [in the 1960s] which led the government to protest and insist that all foreign film scripts were vetted for approval before shooting could begin' (Livingston, 2008: 39). In a framework story of two young girls and an elderly cinephile visiting these foreign representations of Beirut and searching for a connection with their contemporary reality, the film critiques the appropriation of the city as the Paris of the Orient. Perhaps Saab's most widely screened and accessible work is *Dunia: Kiss me Not on the Eyes* (2005), a film made in Cairo under difficult censorial circumstances, as it engages with the physical expression of a woman's desires through belly dance, and an intense discussion of female genital mutilation, a custom forbidden but still very prevalent in Egypt. *Dunia* stands out among her films, as it does not refer at all to Beirut or Lebanon – whereas the city is one of the main threads that runs through the rest of Saab's work. Her latest feature, *What's Going On* (2010) returns to Beirut, and is again a complex, experimental film looking at contemporary life in the city, and its failure to resurrect itself, still, after two decades of post-war reconstructions. All her work, then, as Mostafa confirms, deals with a focus on the question of identity-formation and coming-of-age experiences of urban women. She is interested in city life and how it impacts on women's sense of self (Livingston, 2008: 36).

Saab is a transnational artist, commuting between Beirut, Paris and Cairo and claiming all three as her home. Her films are funded and screened internationally at some of the world's most significant film festivals, and she has won several international prizes such as the Arab Critics' Prize of the Year (1975), the Catholic Jury Prize at Oberhausen (1976), the Golden Spike at the Valladolid International Film Festival and the First Documentary Prize at Oberhausen (1982). *Dunia* won over ten international awards. Saab's work has received a retrospective at the Lincoln Center in New York in 2010 and the Paris National Film Archive, the Cinématheque Française in 2013. However, while the exhibition and success of her work is transnational, Saab regrets not being appreciated in Lebanon itself. She would like her films to be seen as part of Lebanon's heritage of wartime film-making. Nevertheless, most of the content of her work maintains its intense focus on Beirut.

In 2007, the film-maker turned her attention to photography. She presented her first collection at the Dubai Art Fair and Art-Paris Abu-Dhabi. She also exhibited a multimedia art installation entitled 'Strange Games and Bridges' at the Singapore National Museum. This installation consisted of photography, experimental video and a 'floating garden' suspended in the air on a structure that reminds of a bridge, designed by Laurence Rasse, a garden landscaper. In 2008, she presented a controversial photo exhibition in Beirut titled 'Sense Icons and Sensitivity', which dealt with Occidentalism, as a response to Orientalism, and specifically with the image, representation and reception in the Middle East of white Western women's bodies.

All her work, across forms and genres, indicates a consistent preoccupation with, on the one hand, the city of Beirut and, on the other, a cross-cultural East–West communication, or the lack of it. Her work defies simple categorisation, but is consistent in its reflection on Lebanon's and the Middle East's violent past and present, and the 'Orient's' dissatisfaction with orientalist representation. Within that space, as we shall see, Saab is especially interested in the situation of women and children.

In what follows, I focus on Saab's first three documentaries that are most explicitly about Lebanon: *Lebanon in Torment* (1975), *Beirut Never Again* (1976) and *Letters from Beirut* (1979). These were made during the first five years of the Lebanese civil war and already reveal an interest in the mix of documentary as reportage and as art, which became more obvious in her later work. Jocelyn Saab is more directly outspoken than Ateyyat El Abnoudy: her voice is at the centre of the documentaries and is powerful in its agency and in its sarcasm. The look here is used in an illustrative manner: the indexical relationship between the voice-over and the image remains strong and challenges the spectator. At the same time she also expresses a stinging nostalgia for the past beauty of Beirut, and uses the past and present to illustrate her outspoken political opinions. This reflects Saab's journalistic interests, which are complemented by her interest in artistic and experimental strengths. The experimental nature of her later work, specifically *Once Upon a Time, Beirut* (1995), has been discussed in more detail by Mark Westmoreland, in his writing on Lebanese experimental cinema. He explores the experimental nature of the editing in the film, which projects the shallowness of the representation of Beirut in films from around the world, as well as the beauty of pre-war Lebanon. Through the juxtaposition of these two positions vis-à-vis Beirut, Saab unfolds both a nostalgic image of the city she loves and a critique of what it has come to represent on screen.

In his analysis of experimental film and video in Lebanon, Westmoreland states that film- and video-making in Lebanon is the result of an aesthetic ambivalence with mimetic modes of mediation, which points out the limitations of a post-colonial discourse and the politics of representation (Westmoreland, 2009: 41). The experimental documentaries that fall under his exploration of film and video, he says, problematise documentary methods for procuring knowledge and producing meaning. Instead, non-linearity, a Deleuzian 'becoming', and the intersubjectivity of subject, director and spectator in the films politicise representation, something Westmoreland refers to as a post-orientalist aesthetics. Non-linear, non-causal structures in the film, the subversion of historical representation and the expression of the impossibility of providing a unified national narrative, represent the failure of the nation. Lebanese cinema delineates a country perhaps, but not a nation (Livingston, 2008: 37). Saab, Westmoreland states, critiques both the West and the Middle East for their inability to deal constructively with Beirut as a stage for war and sectarian conflict. In an interview, Saab told me that she is always searching for a Beirut that no one knows or remembers. In this statement, a sense of nostalgia becomes apparent, but what is also always apparent is an anti-orientalist, philosophical and poetic preoccupation with a city in turmoil. This becomes apparent in her films' non-linear structure, poetic voice and the trust she places in her audience when it comes to understanding the experimental representation of the city. In what follows, I explore how the marriage of reportage and experimental cinema in Saab's early work attempts to draw in the spectator in order to establish an intersubjectivity that can lead to solidarity.

Lebanon in Torment (1975)

The title of her first film, *Le Liban dans la tourmente* (*Lebanon in Torment*, 1975), clearly communicates that Saab is worried, and upset, about the escalating violence and the start of what will become known as the Lebanese civil war. Being 'in torment' carries the meaning of a passive, innocent suffering, one that is perhaps undeserved. 'Torment' also implies a protracted period of pain and torture, and, above all, ignorance. It is clear from the film that Saab wants to illustrate this torment, and also try to explain it, although she accepts that explaining the situation in Lebanon might be too difficult, and perhaps even unwanted. She says

> Beside me there were few filmmakers who wanted to show what was going on in the country. But nobody used to go and see these apart from those who were affected, the lower classes. In the end I was criticized by the bourgeoisie, my own people, because I said, 'look at yourselves, let us look at ourselves'. So they hated me. And the lowest class, they said, 'what's she doing, this woman, that's not her place. How dare she change things and talk about us.' Everybody was disturbed by what I was doing – and the more I worked the more alone I felt. (Hillauer, 2005: 174)

The war has often been described as a war of others, fought on Lebanese soil. This tendency to displace responsibility, Lina Khatib has emphasised, served as an excuse for a willing, self-imposed amnesia in Lebanese social and political life. Leaders as well as common Lebanese people stubbornly decided that the war, while it was being fought on their territory, had nothing to do with them. Instead, the popular myth states that Israel, Palestine and Syria fought over and on Lebanon. What Saab does with this film, and what cinema does in Lebanon since this film, is confront the Lebanese people with their own role and responsibility. Outside forces were indeed deeply involved in this civil war, but by no means was there a complete lack of interest from Lebanese people. *Lebanon in Torment* emphasises and lays out Lebanon's stake(s) in the war.

This first film is also her most journalistic one. Animated maps show which area of the country is under consideration, she is seen interviewing people with her microphone, and newspapers illustrate what interviewees talk about. The film attempts to explain the extremely complex social and political situation on the eve of the civil war. It shows Saab's preoccupation with national memory loss and the (mis)representation of Beirut and its peoples.

The film starts with a male voice-over describing how beautiful Lebanon is, with its stunning countryside, delicious food, modern cities and fun-loving, youthful demographic. As this voice-over describes Lebanon as a pleasant tourist attraction, we see ex-minister Khalil El Khoury, relaxing with friends, filmed in a luxurious setting, with smiling young people bedecked with jewellery and wearing fashionable clothes. His discourse on the 'Lebanon of tomorrow', where, as he says, the establishment will have to take into consideration the social underclasses, is contrasted to his actions: revelling in the luxurious surroundings, fashionable women and abundance of food on the tables.

These images of wealth and beauty are contrasted to the next shot, where a gun is cocked loudly, bullets are divided among the actors, buildings are riddled with bullet holes, and the soundscape is also dominated by gunshots, cannon fire and buildings collapsing. Cut to Saab herself, giving an impromptu speech on the Corniche in Beirut, explaining to tourists that Lebanon is a small but beautiful country. This is an ironic performance and she is interrupted by peacekeepers. The voice-over switches to a radio voice, wishing the tourists an enjoyable evening in the clubs and music halls of Beirut. Next, television images of tourists swimming in the sea and sunbathing, followed by a tennis player explaining that the country is ready to explode like a grenade, and he is armed, like everyone else. This montage of images illustrates Saab's sarcastic attitude towards the rich and famous, the tourists and those painting an image of Lebanon that persists: that of the playground of the rich, and Beirut being a cosmopolitan, attractive city. She bursts this bubble by juxtaposing these images with what comes next.

A child explains to the camera that he has 'come to learn to shoot a gun'. This interview is filmed at a paramilitary training camp, where everyone is armed. Saab asks everyone she meets, men, women and children, 'why have you decided to bear arms', and the answers vary only in the political party the individual opposes. Everyone who is armed mentions that it is out of self-defence. Most often, this is against the far right political group of the Phalangists. In succession, we identify Pierre Gemayel (leader of the Phalangists), Abou Sleiman (president of the Maronite League, extreme right Christians), Mussa Sadr (Shiite leader and preacher), Raymond Edde (politician of the moderate right), Ghassan Fawas (communist), Farouk Moukadem (militia leader); in short, every possible sectarian leader and commentator is given a voice, identified on screen with his political leanings to illustrate the scope of the complexity of the political, religious and ethnic situation in Lebanon. While Saab does not manage to interview every one of these leaders directly, she does manage to film them as they give interviews for television or on other public platforms. The diversity of leadership and ideals is impressive, but what is most surprising and interesting is the degree to which all agree with one another as to the reason why they are arming their respective groups: self-defence. Some are 'morally obliged' to defend themselves, others are 'forced' to do so. And while they may be successful at finding a voice and a platform to communicate their messages, the messages themselves remain unclear and confusing, precisely because the discourse of each is so similar to all the others, yet they are identified as being from opposing religious sects. The question indirectly posed by Saab here then is: if everyone says the same thing, and the discourses repeat one another, does anyone really know what is going on in 1975?

Moreover, Saab shows on animated maps throughout the film that she travels the length and breadth of the country to meet these leaders. She travels from Beirut to Bekaa, to Tyre, from the cosmopolitan centre of the country to the agricultural south and the northeast, where poverty holds the unemployed and disenfranchised in its grip. In other words, she places the politicians and religious leaders in their home territories, and indicates that Lebanon is more than just its centre, Beirut. Like so many tourist marketing videos, something the government invested in heavily before the war, she shows the diversity of landscapes in Lebanon, but instead of emphasising their attractions and beauty, Saab highlights their implication in the conflict that is slowly but surely escalating around the common people of these regions.

Not only does she explore the diverse landscapes, ethnicities and politics of Lebanon, she also hands the microphone to those the voice-over calls 'the proletariat': the workers and farmers, just like Ateyyat El Abnoudy did in her early work from the 1970s. First, we get extended interviews with Palestinian refugees, who saw Lebanon as their last resort after having been expelled from or forced to flee their own land. They express their shock after seeing the country they have fled to also spiral out of control. This 'being out of control' is repeated several times by their political leaders as well, and used as an excuse to arm their followers. If Lebanon was the Palestinians' last resort, they say, they have become equally oppressed by Gemayel's Phalangists, thus feeling the need to arm themselves. Secondly, there is an interview that takes place at a tobacco farm, where the workers are shown to be working in desperate conditions, but the factory bosses plainly state that they pay their workers under the going rate, and women earn only half of what the men earn. This sparks Saab's interest, and so she turns her attention to the women workers on this farm, interviewing them about their working conditions: child labour, exploitation and underpayment, and especially bad working hours: 'we don't stop working, from 3am to 6pm'. Thirdly, Saab looks more closely at how children and young people deal with the turmoil in Lebanon. The voice-over states that while the old find work in agriculture, the young often take 'the route of the exodus' from the rural to the urban environment, precisely because they lack work and secure rights. Illustrated with newspaper cuttings, emphasis is put on the injustice done to innocent children and aimless youth, easily impressed and moulded by charismatic leaders. The result is a young demographic constantly on the move, ending up unemployed and poor in the slums surrounding Beirut, contributing considerably to the politicisation of religion and sectarian conflict.

The film's return from the countryside to Beirut and its focus on the slums once again gives the impression that the intended audience for this film is perhaps not those who know the area. With detailed maps, spectators are given a step-by-step guide to the demographic and sectarian make-up of the many suburbs surrounding Beirut: from Bourg Hammoud, En Nabaa, Tell Zaatar, Aïn Roummani, Chuyah, Bourg El Branjeh to Sabra and Chatillah. These are shown in animation: from Beirut on a map of Lebanon alone, we see the suburbs appear in clockwise order and in different colours, in a simplified visualisation and clarification of what is in reality an extremely disorderly cluster of slums. German war film scholar Eileen Rositzka describes the use of animated maps in war films: 'cinematic maps give us multiple (or "split") viewpoints on a certain terrain – the sense that we are able to grasp a place at first sight and yet the place itself holds several secrets and dangers' (Rositzka, 2016). The animated geographical illustrations make it possible to show a perspective on the issues, an overview for unfamiliar audiences and what cannot otherwise be shown.

Perhaps the most interesting section of interviews in this film is the one dedicated to artists. Saab interviews journalists and artists with whom she identifies much more strongly than either the political leaders or the disenfranchised farmers and factory workers. Etel Adnan, for example, is a personal friend of the film-maker and a poet of the left, and Samir Frangié is a leftist journalist. It is in conversations with these people that Saab really takes an active part in the dialogue. We hear her questions and we see her getting much closer to these figures than to anyone else in the film. She emphasises their opinions through the setting of the interviews and the extended time she spends with them. Precisely because of her own status as a journalist and an artist, she identifies very closely with them. In fact, the spectator comes to suspect that they are friends. She returns to Frangié three times in the course of the film, as if he is not only a representative of the leftist journalists with whom he is associated, but also as if he is a voice of reason serving as a counterbalance to all the militant and religious discourse we hear from the other interviewees. Frangié became a famous and influential journalist and later also a politician. His political stance was directly opposed to that of the many militias during the civil war, and he was one of the initiators of movements that promoted dialogue during the war and national reconciliation after the war. He was never elected to parliament, but he did inaugurate a foundation called 'Lettre de Beyrouth' in 2003, an organisation that retains its political faith in development, democracy, civil society, transparency, women's rights, equality, freedom and trade unionism.

While Etel Adnan is only interviewed once, and the interview is rather short, the setting within which this interview is conducted stands apart from all the other interviews. Adnan is a close friend, as we shall see, and she returned to all three films discussed in this chapter. She is both a commentator on events and the poet who provides illustrative voice-over texts. In fact, Adnan's poetry is used in, and even written especially for, Saab's documentaries *Beirut Never Again* (1976) and *Letters from Beirut* (1979). In *Lebanon in Torment*, Adnan does not yet serve as a poet, but rather as a commentator. She is interviewed in her car, and from the informal atmosphere it becomes clear that they are intimate friends, or at least allies in their outlook on and approach to the role of the artist in the war. Saab told me about this presence in the film:

> When I made *Le Liban dans la tourmente*, Etel was a must. I interviewed her. Etel, painter and poet, is inherently related to Lebanon of that time (before and during the war). She is a key figure in the country. (Interview with author, 2010b)

Adnan herself said about the film:

> This is an extraordinary achievement. It catches the Lebanese environment which led to this war in a way no previous document, whether written or filmed, has ever done. Through her political courage, moral integrity, and profound intelligence, Jocelyne instinctively grasped the essence of this conflict. No document about this war matches in importance Jocelyne's cinematic achievement in the three films she has dedicated to Lebanon. This is not only a rare work of fundamental importance for the history of our country, but also a study whose implications stretch beyond Lebanon, and should be taught on university courses devoted to sociology and contemporary world politics. (Brenez and Hadouchi, 2005)

Indeed, Adnan is a widely celebrated poet, novelist and painter, who lived in the United States and became a central figure in Arab–American cultural life. She now lives and works as a painter in Paris. Saab worked for Adnan in the period when both returned to Beirut just before the war, which is how they knew one another. Saab appreciates Adnan's philosophical and poetic style, obvious from this interview, but also from the contributions to Saab's other films. Adnan is admired and loved by Saab and this personal bond comes forward through the intimacy in their conversations. Frangié, in contrast, is interviewed in a more formal setting, at a table in a garden, but his body language clearly illustrates that they are colleagues or friends: he leans back and smiles when Saab speaks, and leans forward when he explains something. He rolls and smokes his cigarettes, and generally partakes in a lively dialogue between two intellectuals.

As a piece of journalism/reportage, the film lays out the complex situation between the different factions, ethnicities and religious sects in Lebanon, as if explaining for an audience who might not know about these. As such, it seems to address a foreign audience, although the situation was so complex that it may have been intended to clarify the situation to a home-grown audience. As an experimental documentary, however, it unfolds slowly and intricately, like an unusually complex pattern that is decidedly non-linear and does not seek to create logic out of the complex situation. All the interviews and sound bites do not make up a logically unfolding narrative. While the visuals give the impression at times that the intended audience is one that is not knowledgeable about the different sects and political parties, the diversity of voices is not presented in a way that explains things through a structure that is immediately comprehensible to outsiders. It could be argued that the situation is in fact so complex that Saab is indeed explaining things to an audience that is supposed to know. The way she explains it is pertinent to an Arab audience. Saab herself refers to this explicitly, in an interview, when she says that she refuses to structure her work logically. She says she speaks in the language of her fellow Arabs, and that this at times upsets them. The unusual structure is non-Western (in fact, it is anti-Western) with a view to eliciting solidarity from a local, regional audience, rather than an international one. As such, the film created an outrage, mainly because of montage and structure. Saab said:

> The Islamic world . . . is disturbed by the representation of things. Painting and film only imitate European painting and film. I broke with this way of seeing in my films, by going back to Arab narrative traditions: not like in the Occident with the beginning, the middle, the end. No, you have boxes, like Russian matrioshka dolls, one going into the other. If you show things in this way, people suddenly identify with it. It disturbs them because the art is not foreign anymore, it is theirs. I feel I can communicate with people this way. (Hillauer, 2005: 175–6)

The way she describes her editing process is reminiscent of Laura Marks' theorisation of enfoldment in Arab experimental film. To illustrate this, I will first describe and then schematise the enfolding structure of Saab's first film. (1) In the opening sequence that focuses on the ex-minister and his colleagues and friends relaxing in an opulent setting, we see their jewellery, their shoes, clothes and their fashionable living conditions. The set-up seems to be informal, but it is obvious that the ex-minister is speaking not just to Saab's camera but also to others. It has the feeling if not the look of a press conference. (2) This is followed by a large number of open-air and set-up interviews with religious as well as political leaders. These are all very formal talking-head interviews: most of them are at official occasions, where the press has clearly been invited to meet and interview the speakers; others are set-up especially for Saab and her crew, for example, the one with Pierre Gemayel, the leader of the Phalangists, who takes her into a conference room, where he takes a seat at one end of the table and requests that Saab sits at the other end. (3) Interviews with journalists and artists follow. These interviews are much more informal and feel more like conversations, where Saab is a contributor to the discussion and where there are people that agree on ideas and ideals. (4) After that, we get to the vulnerable, central issues: the fate and troubles of the workers. She talks to tobacco farmers, fishermen and factory workers, both men and women, old and young, on their farms, in their factories and in their homes. These interviews are much more impassioned and urgent. Here the voice-over sympathises directly with the plight of these people (who are left anonymous, in contrast to the names and functions of the leaders and journalists she interviews) and both directly and indirectly lays the blame for the complex and unfair situation with the leaders: there is no support from the so-called leaders, no acknowledgement of the workers' conditions, which, as the voice-over states, has led to these people either escaping to the city and ending up homeless, which leads them to the urban militia camps, or, if they stay in the countryside, they become militarised there, also in (rural) militia camps. (5) Next, we see continued interviews with religious and political leaders, now emphasising their involvement in the militia camps and detailing their role as trainers and ideological orators. The first interviews here are in the countryside, both in the south in Tyre and in the north in Baalbek, followed by interviews with militias in the urban centres and suburbs of Beirut.

The structure and the content of the interviews are reminiscent of some interviews in El Abnoudy's *Days of Democracy*. In Lebanon, the militia leaders are all surrounded by their followers, as the women politicians were in Egypt. As a consequence, these interviews seem to be conducted in disorderly fashion, in loud voices, with people talking over one another in their attempt to clarify their political or religious stance, and to convince the interviewer of their cause. (6) We return then to another interview or two with journalists, again around a small table and with drinks and cigarettes being shared and Saab taking part in the conversation. (7) The film ends with another ironic look at the rich and famous, with a shot inside the house of a minister, surrounded by women and men in fashionable clothes, the camera lingering on their jewellery and shoes. The difference this time is that while the man is talking politics, and we hear the same discourse we have now heard several times in the film, clichés and slogans, the camera focuses on the facial expressions and body language of a woman in the room, who is clearly well educated and has opinions on what the man is saying. The man is sitting at the other end of the room to where the camera is, the woman is sitting closer to the camera, and Saab focuses on her precisely because her facial expressions and body language say much more than she could in public. It is obvious from her facial expressions that she is critical of what is being said: she moves uncomfortably in her chair, wipes her hair out of her face and raises her eyebrows. While she does not look into the camera, the camera clearly focuses on her because it is more interesting and perhaps more real than the performance by the man at the other end of the room. The camera then pans around the room and points out among the crowd a few other men and women looking uncomfortable.

A schematised overview of the sequence of things in the film could perhaps help to clarify the enfolded structure:

1. the rich and famous (focus on jewels, shoes, filmed in opulent houses);
2. politicians and religious leaders of different sects (talking-heads);
3. journalists and artists (informal interviews);
4. interviews with workers, i.e., tobacco farmers, fishermen, factory workers;
5. politicians and militias (chaotic interviews);
6. journalists (informal discussions);
7. the rich and famous (focus on jewellery, shoes, opulence).

The sensitive information at the centre of the film needs to be protected. This is the fold. Gradually, in the film, we see an opening up of the conversation, an unfolding of a situation that has, at its centre (4), the vulnerable information: the words of the farmers, factory workers and fishermen, which reveals the 'truth', as opposed to the clichéd discourse. What is in this fold, the sensitive statements, are, however, surrounded with interviews that steal the attention away from the 'proletariat', and steep the conversation in political discourse, loud voices, clichés and rehearsed platitudes. The real conversation is hidden in the fold of the enfolding structure, and over-run by the louder, more dominant voices. In Saab's understanding, the smallest of the Russian matryoshka dolls, the central one, is dedicated to the farmers. One needs to dig deeper to reveal their meaning and their value. The spectator is entrusted with the action of unfolding the enfolded information.

In *Lebanon in Torment* we also witness folds within those sections of the interviews that focus on the dominant voices. The audience is here also invited to help to unfold the essence. As leaders are interviewed, the camera lingers on those listening and witnessing. As the voice of the male speaker seems central, it becomes background noise, and in the folds of his discourse, the repetition, the clichés, we witness dissenting looks and body language, or we hear the voices of his subjects repeating these clichés. This reveals (unfolds) the irony in the manner in which Saab's camera observes the leaders. Background faces and voices are foregrounded in rural and urban militia camps, and in the leaders' wealthy surroundings, we witness dissenting opinions in the facial expressions and body language of the women and a few men in the room.

Lina Khatib emphasises that art in Lebanon is in fact the *only* place where the reality of the war is acknowledged and attempts are made to get it represented. In Lebanon, Marks writes elsewhere, 'filmmakers cannot approach history directly' – history is enfolded – and instead must delicately hint at experiences and evaluations rather than confront them directly (Marks, 2010: 243). This delicacy in film and art, Marks posits, results in experiments in form and style, and renews art. As such, art is an unfolding power. In other words, the trauma of the civil war in Lebanon may be conducive to the creation of art, and art is perhaps the only way to deal with the trauma of war: the spectator is requested to help to unfold the art at the centre of an otherwise journalistic body of work. Saab, I have shown, does this through the montage, in structuring her films in such a way as to enfold delicate matters and peoples into discourse, while trusting the spectator to assist her in the unfolding act. Unlike Marks though, I would say that this is an inherently political act not a pre-political given.

Reality enfolds, and art unfolds. Representation is replaced by performativity. Indeed, Lebanon after the war was obsessed with reconstruction. There was no time for reconciliation. A blanket amnesty and a refusal to deal with the implications of the war and the consequences for the country enfolded the war's central causes and concerns. A rhetoric of looking forward diminished the importance of closure, and thus many scholars claim the war stopped, it did not end, evident in the fact that Lebanon has been and is still under constant threat of escalating violence – see, for example, the devastating summer of 2006, and its precarious situation as Syria's neighbour in the current conflict.

While experimentation in Marks' eyes is pre-political, she does agree that it creates a foundation and a source of strength for political acts. The enfoldment in itself is a political act. This is especially true in the case of Jocelyne Saab, who Marks sees as an early proponent of experimental cinema in Lebanon (although she places the film-maker in a French context). But Marks looks at Saab's later work. Here, I deal with Saab's first documentaries, in the 1970s, when she worked as a journalist for Lebanese and European television. Saab's films are a mix of experimental and journalistic styles, and create a political act by encompassing art and journalism. The unfolding and encompassing of art within journalism is at this point an inherently political act.

While war may be seen as disruptive of the narrative potential of life, and the trauma of war in Lebanon has led to a degree of national amnesia, cinema has, in large part because of Saab's early work, managed to focus on the civil war and confronted the country's audiences with their past and present realities. Saab addresses her fellow Lebanese as her intended audience in an unfolding manner, and she has found a way of speaking to them directly in their own language through montage and structure, as she explains through her matryoshka dolls. Hers was the pioneering work inspiring Lebanese post-war film-makers to confront the war and the people's fragmented memories. Khatib shows that post-war cinema in Lebanon was the only locus where the memory of war was confronted. I claim here that it is through Saab's work that there is a heritage of confronting the war at all. She has stated her desire to be seen as someone who played a vital role in archiving Lebanese cinema and visualising Beirut as a part of Lebanese visual heritage:

> I am waiting for someone in Lebanon to regard my films as heritage, just like I gathered the heritage of others (in *Once Upon a Time, Beirut*). [In 2005] someone showed my films in Lebanon . . . for political awareness as part of the 30th anniversary of the end of the Civil War. If I had not done that, your generation would not have seen them. (Khatib, 2008: 42)

With this statement she confirms the political intentions behind, and content of, her films, while she also acknowledges the importance of dealing with and confronting reality in spite of the nationwide tendency to forget the past. Only cinema is a possible 'substitute for systematic collective amnesia': Lebanese experimental cinema is an 'archive in progress . . . mixing true and false, probable and improbable, through which [the filmmaker] inoculates the body of a diseased reality with an antidote of invention, the denial, the return, the subversion' (Cohen Hadria, 2005: 35). While Saab may not abide by official Lebanese ideology and state rhetoric of moving forward and forgetting the past, she has given Lebanese cinema its lively and healthy incentive to engage with the past without fail. In my view, Saab's early work initiated and spurred on Lebanese cinema's success and its renaissance.

Beirut Never Again (1976)

Exactly like *Lebanon in Torment*, *Beirut Never Again* starts with the idea that Lebanon is the ideal tourist destination. Or rather, that it was a popular tourist destination: 'one in two travellers have been here but the city does not exist anymore'. It is now, instead, a ghost city, and its inhabitants live from one day to another. This film really illustrates Saab's preoccupation with children at war. Her focus on children in this film foreshadows another of her short films, *Children at War*, also from 1976. In both films, this preoccupation with children works as a reflection on how memory works in Lebanon, and on how the war destroys memories. CIA statistics show that almost 50 per cent of the Lebanese population is younger than twenty-five and 40 per cent between twenty-five and fifty.[2] This is in large part due to the war, and to the baby boom and relative economic prosperity of the city after the war. In 1976, when these two short films were made, the war had been raging for a year, and the director reflects on her own childhood and youth. In effect, she is still only in her twenties herself, and identifies with the young people she films and interviews. This is already visible in *Lebanon in Torment*, where young Lebanese hippies, teenage militia soldiers and Palestinian children are interviewed alongside the older generation of leaders and politicians.

In *Beirut Never Again*, the director follows the deterioration of the walls in Beirut for six months. Every morning, between six and ten o'clock, when the militiamen from all sides are resting after nights of fighting, she 'goes into town' and observes the developments of the war as they are imprinted on the walls of her city. She reflects: 'the older the war gets, the younger the soldiers become'. This is significant and illustrative of what she worries about with regard to Lebanon's memory: she worries that too many people are dying, buildings are destroyed, and with these people and buildings the history of the country and the memories of the older generations are lost. She says: 'these children have no memories, no fears. The war makes a playground for them that they have never had before'. Ziad Doueiri seems to directly refer to this statement and confirm it in his famous film *West Beirut* (1998). The longer the war goes on, the more people die, and as the militias mostly consist of adults, adults are also the first to die. Because children and young people are the only ones left, as street kids, looting and stealing, or as child soldiers, single-mindedly trying to finish a war they did not start and do not understand, Saab sees not only orphans and troubled kids, but also a devastating consequence for Lebanon's future. She fears a future without a past, where it is not only ignorance of the complexity of the warring sects and factions that ensues or a willing amnesia in a post-traumatic, post-war reality, but also a forgetting of the past due to a sheer lack of memories.

She most ostensibly turns to children in her short film *Children of War* (1976). The film takes place few days after a massacre – with 1,500 dead – in the Karantina slum near Beirut. This is where the director discovered children who survived. She approached them by offering pencils to draw with. They let her film their games and violent warrior-like acts: they re-enact the horror that they witnessed, and the re-enactment of the trauma in fact shows how the children deal with their own war, how the war in Lebanon is experienced differently by different generations and social classes. As I will explore in more detail in a later chapter, children serve as symbols for interrupted memory and amnesia, but also, paradoxically, for collective memory. Children represent the adult and his or her memories of youth and childhood. It seems to be the case then that children often lose their agency in film. Karen Lury (2010) implies this as well when she theorises the child as Other, as an interruption, and as passive. Children in fiction films are often representative of a rupture of everyday modern temporality. War films, Lury further explains, articulate the relationship between witness, memory and history through the presence and character of the child. She indicates that very often the child comes to stand for the adult's traumatised, interrupted memory. The child is presumed to not have the authority on the facts of war, yet their representation of it is visceral, of and on the body, demonstrating how the interweaving of history, memory and witness can be powerfully affective. Lury writes about Western feature fiction films, and I want to posit here the idea that in war documentaries from Lebanon (and Palestine), children are not left without agency. Saab focuses on them in image and voice-over, and describes them as 'the kings and queens of today'. They are also interviewed, and give powerful statements, and in that way become the means through which the film-maker manages to appeal to a large audience: these children are clever, they have insights into the present that many adults do not because their minds may be clouded with memories of sectarian strife and the complexity of the pre-war situation. Children are not innocent bystanders to this war: they are intelligent commentators.

Children's innocence and naivety is a European construct. Numerous articles have been written about the role of children in humanitarian and political social justice documentaries, with the big-eyed, wide-eyed, sad-eyed children, where the goal is to elicit a contribution from the spectator (Pullen, 2008; Smith, 2009; Martins, 2011). Their portrayal as victims worthy of compassion, in need of protection – in other words a sentimentalised and diminutive representation – is not what Saab subscribes to.

She purposefully moves away from that. These Beiruti children are not naive, and they are no longer innocent. Instead, they have lived through a war and they have, out of necessity, had to make it their own. The older the war gets, the younger the soldiers get. In the film Saab says: 'they understood quickly that they are the sole masters of their decisions', making explicit their agency and self-awareness as soldiers and Beirutis.

However, while some of these children who are interviewed by Saab clearly know what they are talking about and in some instances display more clarity than any of the political and religious leaders could in *Lebanon in Torment*, there are some sad-eyed, wide-eyed children. As they fight, they construct a new memory, one that mythologises the past. They may not remember the causes of the war, they perhaps never knew or understood the causes in the first place. Instead, what they say, they appear to be repeating from something they have heard elsewhere. They remember whom they fight and who they have killed. They know it has to do with religion, but they have forgotten what they are fighting for. Many of them, interviewed by Saab, sound bitter and disillusioned as soldiers would, but they do not know an identifiable reason for their own fighting. One interviewed boy says: 'I am disgusted with everything, we always lived together, I do not understand why we cannot do that again. The country is destroyed. It will never be like before. All together, we destroyed it. I have lost friends and family, and I revenged them. I have killed people.' Their short-term memory serves them as soldiers, for being able to continue their fights, and therefore makes it difficult to really end the war.

In *Beirut Never Again*, more than any of her other films, the indexical relationship between voice and image is immediate and direct. Saab parallels what she says with what she sees and explains: 'these children', 'that girl', using indexical language to identify the children she speaks about. She explains to the spectator what 'this child' is doing as she worries about them and their futures: 'what is going to become of this child if he is already mixing his life with that of rats and waste'. There is a sense of judgement in this statement. Perhaps not for the child him- or herself, but certainly for the society in which the child lives. Mostly though, there is a sense of worry for their future. The children have replaced the elders on the battlegrounds and have become the sole masters of their fate. Saab says that bitter poetry has replaced the carelessness of the past, so she does hear a certain poetry in what the children say, she does grant them agency, and respects their insights and analyses of the situation. While order has broken down, as she films broken glass, she says there are little suns reflected in the fragments of glass, referring to the fact that the city and its buildings are destroyed and leave behind nothing but detritus, but the children are not to be seen as detritus. They are not broken, they are the little suns, and represent hope for the future of Lebanon.

For the voice-over in *Beirut Never Again*, Saab returns to Etel Adnan, as a poet-commentator on the war. Adnan co-wrote, with Saab, the voice-over for the film. Their collaboration has not been explored before, not in the extensive work done on Adnan's writings, nor in (the very few) studies on Saab's work, yet it is easy to see how the two women found one another in their poetic, counter-hegemonic treatment of the war in Lebanon. Etel Adnan was born in 1925 and studied philosophy at the Sorbonne in Paris. In 1955, she moved to the United States and worked at the universities of Harvard and Berkeley. In 1972, she returned to Beirut as a journalist, and became a cultural editor for both *Al Safa* and *L'Orient le Jour* (the newspaper Saab is seen to be reading in *Letter from Beirut*). She stayed in Lebanon until 1977, and wrote her most famous work in that year: *Sitt Marie Rose*, a novel that has become a classic of war literature. Adnan has said that 'poetry is the purpose of life'. She sees poetry as 'a counter-profession, as an expression of personal and mental freedom, as perpetual rebellion' (Majaj and Amireh, 2002: 14). She appears in *Lebanon in Torment* and wrote the texts for both *Beirut Never Again* and *Letter from Beirut*.

Like Saab, Adnan likes an enfolded style, with a composite of diverse styles and forms. Her literary experimentation is a political critique of life (Majaj and Amireh, 2002: 18). Also like Saab, Adnan makes the city of Beirut the protagonist of her many works especially *Sitt Marie Rose*. In it a handful of characters describe their experiences of the civil war. There is a 'resistance to narration' in her novel, and as well as a decentrist style and form, the novel displays a decentrist attitude to characters and content. In a post-modern reading, the novel 'exists largely as a form recording its own impossibility' (Foster, 1995: 60), and moves from first-person narration in the first half to a fragmented series of monologues in the second half. The novel tells the story of Sitt Marie Rose, a Syrian charity worker in Beirut, who is killed by sectarian violence. The repeated sequence of monologues in the second half of the novel illustrates, says Foster, the decentrist attitude of the author, where seven separate monologues repeat, in diverse ways, the story of Sitt Marie Rose's death. As such, the novel undermines the assumption that anyone can speak for or represent an Other, or 'the people' at large (Foster, 1995: 63). This illustrates the breakdown not just of literary representation, but also of political representation in a country where different sects and political parties fail to adequately represent their followers. At the end of the novel Egyptian Nasser's conceptualisation of the Arab world as a series of concentric circles is expanded to include the whole world. Adnan shows the conflict in Lebanon to have repercussions for the whole world, while it 'represents the simultaneous breakdown of and desire for an ideological framework where national identity can be conceptualised as a pure and homogeneous interior space' (Foster, 1995: 65).

It is clear then that the enfoldedness, the matryoshka dolls, the concentric circles and fragmentation of the narrative aim to represent the same thing: the impossibility of representation. The experimental nature of Adnan's novel and Saab's films illustrate the two women's like-minded view on the world during the war in Lebanon. But the failure of representation does not prevent them from trying. As Adnan has said in an interview, she believes that women have different options for representing violence and war. She says: 'women pay particular observation to details . . . they translate tragedy into everyday life events. [We] see tragedy in its details and in its suffering in terms of practicalities . . . As women we have a particular sensitivity toward tragedies and disasters, and this is why more women have written anti-war novels than men, especially in Lebanon' (Saba, 1998: 4).

In the early 1970s, when these films were made, Etel Adnan led the cultural department of *Al Safa*, a French-language Beiruti newspaper. Saab was a music journalist at that time, and worked for Adnan. She told me:

> Etel taught us a lot. We admired her. We admired her thinking. She was a philosopher about the world. She was a poet and we were left very free in what we did and wrote. (Interview, 2010b)

One of the instigating factors for Saab to ask Adnan to write the voice-over for *Beirut Never Again* was Adnan's poem 'Jebu', from the collection *The Arab Apocalypse*.[3] Saab found it very prescient and told me it impressed her a lot. During the making of the film, she felt the need to break away from the conventional voice for documentary. She wanted to break with the reportage style she had used in *Lebanon in Torment*. Because normality had disappeared, she saw no more referent to reality:

> I felt I had to liberate myself from the traditional channels and become a totally independent creator. When I look back now, there was in me such strength of conviction about the need to shoot and keep the memory of places and do it my way. The city was being raped, crushed, set to disappear. The way I shot Beirut day after day disintegrated before my eyes. It is very personal. It is the garden of my childhood that disappeared in front of my eyes. (Interview, 2010b)

But she wanted to focus on life, not death. And that, she says, is where she found the poetry that emerges from life: a surreal poetry: 'I do not allow the spectator to trivialise the war.' Using someone else's words and voice is part of that strategy, as she says the war is both personal and political, both collective and intimate. For the editing, therefore, Saab and her editor Philippe Gosselet took their footage to an isolated place, in a convent, where the heat wave in France in the summer of 1976 did not bother them, and where they could distance themselves from the outside world. She calls the editing, creating the enfolded form, an editing of four hands, as in a piano duet. When they had finished the editing, they agreed the film looked like a love poem for Beirut, which reminded Saab of the poem, 'Jebu' and so she decided to call on Adnan, who was in Paris at the time, to watch the film once and write the voice-over for it. Adnan took two days and Saab adapted the text to the film in what she calls 'a natural way'. Adnan's commentary suits the image, as it is reflexive and incorporates history and future – reflected also in the children. Both Adnan and Saab, therefore, move away deliberately from the morbid side of a city under siege that is exploited in news reportage and other documentaries. The poetry and reflexivity, the distance and the children, then, are all tools to emphasise the life in a place of death, and to reflect on 'a philosophy of life', as Saab sees it.

Another voice in *Beirut Never Again*, is that of a singer. Saab illustrates the underbelly of the past Lebanon that she pointed out at the start of the film, with images of poker rooms and bordellos. As she says that Beirut was not only the prime tourist destination in the Middle East, but also the capital of sin, she plays the music of Sabah, a diva-singer of the 1950s, and her medley of *Lebanese Legends*. Again, there is an irony in the juxtaposition of nostalgic legends of times past with the images of the capital of sin. She takes this irony further when she laments the demise of the cafes and shopping centres, destroyed by cruelty, a 'paradise we will never have again', while the soundtrack moves from *Lebanese Legends* to an experimental soundscape that reminds of a train screeching to a halt on its tracks. This unpleasant sound of metal on metal stands in stark contrast to the sung legends as well as to the image on screen, leaving the indexical relationship between sound and image behind at this stage. Instead, Saab is satirising the image of a Beirut that political leaders would like people to maintain: that of an exotic place that is familiar enough to visit, but where one is still free to smoke the water pipes, watch belly dancers and visit bordellos.

The sudden return to the armed children, who are wiling away time until their next battle, is confronting and dark: they are in their early teens, but carry automatic rifles and speak of the atrocities they have committed. The manner in which these images are not only juxtaposed but also enfolded again reminds of the preoccupation with protecting and revealing knowledge. Moving from the descriptions of Beirut as the ideal tourist destination, with entertainment and hedonism at its centre, to children as victims of the war that was started by adults, to children as thieves and looters, to the poetry of the past and children's hopes and futures reflected in shards of glass, to the singer Sabah and her 1950s *Lebanese Legends*, to Beirut as the capital of sin, and lastly back to child soldiers – the film enfolds the children's future at its centre into so many layers of complex reflections of Beirut's past, present and future that it is clear, upon reflection, that it is almost lost between them. But the last scene of the film, with the child soldiers, is so shocking that the audience is aware of these children's centrality to the director's concerns. Unfolding this central concern for the future is something an audience must do for the sake of the children, and it is something the experimental nature of the documentary allows for: the lack of a linear narrative and the experiments with sounds, indexicality and juxtapositions are what pulls in the spectator and enables and encourages them to embody an intersubjective relationship with the children, and watch in solidarity. The experimental nature of this documentary, then, does not alienate but approaches its audience successfully, through its preoccupation with children and the affective nature of children's embodied experiences in war.

Letter from Beirut (1979)

The fragmentary nature of history, memory and storytelling is further explored in Saab's 1979 documentary *Letter from Beirut*. The epistolary structure of the film emphasises the fragmentary nature of life in Beirut not only in the content of the film, but also again in the way the film is structured. She writes to a friend – this is the voice-over, again co-written with Etel Adnan. Saab puts herself centrally in the frame as the letter writer. She describes her experiences of being in her beloved city after a few years' absence, and seeing it so destroyed. She finds it hard to re-adjust to life in a war zone, and admits it would be easier not to remember. If she could forget about the past, she writes, she would not worry so much about the future. But she remains traumatised and, having come back to her city, the repressed memories return. The letter takes on a confessional mode and she admits that everyone is a prisoner of their own thoughts.

As Hamid Naficy writes in *Accented Cinema*, epistolarity is often a consequence of the reflective nature of the exile. It reveals the split subjectivity of the character speaking (reading or writing the letter) in voice-over, and the non-linear structure of the thought process and the way in which

Figure 2.1 Jocelyne Saab writing a letter to a friend about seeing Beirut again after years of absence, from *Letter from Beirut* (1979) © Jocelyne Saab

the traumatised exile deals with memories (Naficy, 2001: 103). There is also an archaeological aspect to letter-writing, but in reverse: 'instead of digging deeper for information, it is added, layer by layer'. While the layers here are different to those that an exchange of letters could illustrate, they are present. Saab decides to ride buses in Beirut, and interviews people who board the bus. She changes route at least ten times, and as such adds layer after layer of interview, confession, testimony of witnesses of the war, of the deterioration of the city, and of the fighting between militias and sects. Naficy says that 'each letter compels spectators to revise their earlier hypothesis about the writer' (2001: 114), and in *Letter from Beirut* Saab compels the spectator to revise their opinions about Beirut and Lebanon with each bus she boards and each interview she films. The film is fragmented not only through the letter-writing and the bus-hopping, but also through the military checkpoints Saab has to stop at as she travels through the city and the country. Every checkpoint has its own sectarian ideology, but all want the same thing: control over who passes in and out of their territory. A repetitive structure, as Naficy writes, 'results from the inability to close the gap of exile' (2001: 114), and it is in this film then that

Saab's distance from Beirut is made more explicit than in the two previous ones. The gap in this film is twofold: there is a gap of exile, but there is also one as a result of the trauma of the civil war. There is a distance between Saab and her home town, and there is a distance between the time she left Beirut and the time she writes about. The constant return, both in space and in time, to the Beirut she knew, this constant search for the past space, emphasises the vast changes the city has had to undergo since 1975. This 'regime of erasure and desire' (2001: 114) aims to redress historical wrongs, but ultimately fails to do so. Each sequence is a fragment, or maybe a paragraph, in her letter, without there being a larger picture of the situation presented to the receiver of the letter or the spectator of the film. She says: 'we live between chaos and sadness, second by second, in an involuntary nomadism'. No one feels at home anymore.

In epistolary films, Naficy writes, the voice is of central importance. There is an orality and an acousticity of the voice that is foregrounded in these films (2001: 120). Accented epistolaries, moreover, emphasise the co-existence of orality and literacy, of the colonial and the post-colonial. There is a unique relationship between voice, interiority and identity, where the voice-over reads out the letter (being written or being read), where the writing is inherently self-reflexive, and where the identity of the speaker, the owner of the voice, can switch between writer and reader without the audience being aware of the identity switch (Naficy, 2001: 121). Taking this further, the way letters are read out over images in films foregrounds the non-synchronicity of these films, and as such these letter-films or film-letters are actually counter-hegemonic. Silence, voice, non-synchronicity and doubt about who is speaking – the writer or the reader, the speaker or the listener – potentially create ontological doubt regarding the owner of the voice.

The voice-over writing/reading the letter coincides with the act of writing the letter only at the very beginning of the film, where Saab is seen on the terrace of a café by the Mediterranean. She is writing/reading about the 'psychosis of violence' and her struggle to come to terms with how Beirut looks. The letter is very self-reflexive, signifying the writer's torn subjectivity about having been abroad and being removed from the developments in Beirut. While she is seen writing, she is being photographed with an ancient static camera on a tripod, by an old man struggling to make the machine work. The self-reflexive voice-over discussing the shock of being back in her home town, the trauma of being in a war zone, and the memories of Beirut before the war and at the start of the war are framed by letter-writing and vintage photography. Both these tools, the pen and paper, on the one hand, and the camera, on the other, are indications that there is a certain nostalgia at work. Saab confronts reality at the start of the film by returning to older times, referring to a Beirut before the war, the Beirut she knows from childhood, a home that was not yet destroyed. This emphasises her exilic identity, and it also problematises memory. The action of letter-writing soon stops, and is replaced by filming on buses and travelling through Lebanon by car, in an old Beetle.

Again Saab's interest in poetry appears: she co-wrote the voice-over with Etel Adnan, apparent in such poetic reminiscences and reflections as when she says that the race course is the barometer of war: if there is too much tension, there is no race and the track will be deserted. If there is no tension, they will run. But even when they run, the horses run faster than history, which represents the collective attempt to forget: Lebanon's collective amnesia. She emphasises that the horses are pure-bred Arabian horses, which makes the pleasure of the game more intense and their ability to run faster more symbolic.

Riding the buses in Beirut, she also films apparently spontaneous conversations between passengers. It becomes obvious though that these conversations are not as spontaneous as they appear at first sight. Saab emphasises the snapshot aesthetic of her film on the bus: she seats students together who have political debates, older men who sing nostalgic songs, women who talk about their families and their children, as well as social workers who ask one another about their charity work. As in *Beirut jamais plus*, the film-maker's contributions become indexical and commanding: she says 'listen to this woman', 'listen to this man'. This seems to foreground the people's voices in compensation for the earlier dominating voice-over of the letter-writer/reader. The film-maker in this part of the film no longer wants to do the interviewing. At the centre of this documentary is a part where she is moving away from the reportage-style film-making. It is a tactic on the part of the film-maker to extinguish her own voice and foreground that of the passengers. Nevertheless, in spite of the frustration she films, her voice-over returns in epistolary mode once in a while, and she says 'but I am happy to be here, to see familiar things, and the city I love', returning to the letter and to her own voice.

Saab's own memories in the letter-writing, the memories and testimonies of the bus passengers, and her reflections on who and what she witnesses while riding and filming on the buses, is followed with a return to reportage journalism in the latter half of the documentary. Here, she travels around Lebanon in her Beetle in order to interview UN soldiers. On the road, she films a family who are loading everything they own into a car, as she reflects in her typically poetic tone: 'These refugees live from second to second. This is a new form of nomadism, typical for our century.' She says: 'In March 1968, there was an exodus of nomads, and in May 1968 they all returned.' This is accompanied with sepia images of the Palestinian refugees, and is followed with images of the car full of Lebanese refugees, thus emphasising the parallels between Palestine and Lebanon in their struggle with the Israelis, and the perpetual nomads, or refugees, of the Middle East. She asks rhetorically: 'Can we say there are non-refugees here? No one is at home anymore.'

As she drives south, closer and closer to the Israeli border where most of the UN soldiers are stationed, she claims that 'this is a no man's land, for the sake of Israeli politics. They erase every trace of what they have destroyed, and the Palestinians launch a style of mimicry,' critiquing this adaptive style of copying. On the road the Syrian Army, Fatah, the Lebanese Army Forces, Palestine Liberation Organisation (PLO), Popular Front for the Liberation of Palestine (FPLP), and the UN all check her identity and her car. Once past these checkpoints, she points out that everything is close together here: that she travels through ten countries in five hours, pointing out the camps of the international UN soldiers. Drawing parallels with the nomads and the bus passengers, as well as her own epistolary and voice-over reflections, she points out that even the UN soldiers experience homesickness: 'being international is hard', the voice-over reflects, and she interviews soldiers who miss their families, who do not enjoy being in Lebanon. She finishes with the French soldiers, who have returned, not for the sake of the Tricolore this time, but for a much more complex issue which they do not entirely understand. As all these soldiers are replaced by colleagues when they go on leave, she says that they are just replacements of the status quo, and nothing is ever resolved. This is reiterated when in the last five minutes of the film, she focuses on Arafat and his emphasis on return to the homeland. She celebrates the power of his discourse and the celebrations of those who live and die for their homeland, but indirectly reveals the endlessness of the battle: out of Arafat's long speech she highlights the parallels he draws between their fight and that of Godfrey of Bouillon, who also fought for the Holy Land long before the Israeli state was established. The repetition of the word revolution is juxtaposed with the boredom experienced every day by the UN soldiers, the sectarian militias and the Palestinian fedayeen waiting to go to battle. Time consists of patience when you are Palestinian, she says, and meanwhile life goes on just 50 km north of here.

'Nothing is better than an evening in Beirut, but what do we talk about? The War.' Again, there is a hint of nostalgia for the old Beirut of her youth, and the realisation that this is now impossible. A discussion with friends shows her that there is a constant uncertainty: the situation is not really a war but also not peace. And the voice-over returns with 'this situation grabs me by the throat'. On her trip back to Beirut she admits: 'if we continue calling this war an event, it is precisely because memory does not function anymore. Disaster follows disaster like the waves of the sea,' thus referring to the collective amnesia and the fragmentary nature of memory. She laments: 'if the young generations are separated and there is no dialogue, the country will have no past and no future'. She visits the painter Aref el Rayess, whose artwork combines the beauty of Beirut's landscapes with the machinery of modernity and war. This leads her to visit a Ferris wheel, which is empty but somehow still working, turning without passengers. This might signify a return to the buses going around the city, full of people with no memories but plenty of stories to tell. She says: 'Beirut turns, as it always has, but it is empty, and with her, time is blind and history is banal. But this is my country, in fire and blood.' The free association at the end of the film, between the painter and the Ferris wheel, as a reiteration of the busses and their passengers, shows Saab's willingness to commit memory to poetry and experiment with the voice and the look of the film-maker. She is speaking about and looking at Beirut through the eyes of an exile, who embodies the lived experience of the Lebanese as well as the distance of the foreigner. The complexity of her identity (Lebanese and transnational), of form (art and journalism), of style (unfolding the enfolded) and subject matter (children and ancient cultures) reflect and parallel the complex developments of war and sectarian conflict in Beirut.

Conclusion

Jocelyne Saab's early documentaries about Lebanon and Beirut are experimental in nature. With a strong voice and an attentive ear, listening to the poetry of the Beirutis, she shapes an image of a complex country. While she was influenced by European journalistic tactics, and reportage-style documentaries are at the centre of her output during this time, she also speaks directly to her fellow Lebanese and Arabs. Through the non-synchronicity of voice and image, the fragmentary nature of the content of the film, of the journeys she undertakes and of the structure of the films, she emphasises interrupted memory and the difficulty of reconciling past and present. The enfolded and unfolding structure of *Lebanon in Torment*, *Beirut Never Again* and *Letter from Beirut*, a preoccupation with children and young people in all three films, and a dominating self-reflexivity as a journalist, an artist and letter-writer, all indicate an ultimate preoccupation with the future. If Lebanese cinema is the only space in Lebanon where the past is remembered and where reconciliation is starting to be considered, then Jocelyne Saab was a frontrunner of this tendency, as the mainstay of Lebanese cinema at large. Saab's earliest experimental documentaries not only deal with the past through reflections and discussions, they also deal with an enfolded historiography as they are unfolding their matryoshka doll structure, and reveal a preoccupation with the future of Lebanon's children and young people, mainly through self-awareness as a reporter, a young person and a returnee. It is not only a home-grown audience, then, with which she manages to communicate. A larger, transnational audience is able to identify with her and with the subjects in her film, as solidarity is elicited from a self-reflexive, compassionate and knowledgeable oeuvre.

Notes

1. Not to be confused with Palestinian Mai Masri's documentary *Suspended Dreams* (1992).
2. As a comparison: in the United Kingdom just under 30 per cent of the population is under twenty-five and 40 per cent is between twenty-five and fifty.
3. The third edition of this book, published by Post-Apollo Press in 2007, has a foreword written by Jalal Toufic, the philosopher whose work is used by Laura U. Marks when she theorises withdrawal and enfoldment.

CHAPTER 3

Selma Baccar: Non-fiction in Tunisia, the Land of Fictions

Tunisian Selma Baccar challenges the form of documentary film. The country has a solid reputation in film with its Golden Age in the late 1980s and 1990s, but due to censorship and restrictive and divisive official life, Tunisian film-makers usually remain in fictional territory. This chapter focuses on Baccar's first and most important feature-length film *Fatma 75*: a feminist essay film about women's roles in Tunisia throughout history. She has since also made *Habiba M'Sika*, a biopic of a Jewish singer who was immensely popular in the 1930s in Tunis, and *Khochkhach*, part biography, part fictional retelling of the life and times of Baccar's aunts. Between the main women film-makers in the country such as Moufida Tlatli, Nejia Ben Mabrouk and Raja Amari, Baccar was the first, and she remains the only one, experimenting with aspects of the non-fiction form. In her films she deals with extraordinary women whose voices are dominant and self-assured, as their looks and intersubjective relationship with the film-maker and spectator establish a feminist complicity and solidarity.

Tunisia, known as the land of fictions, has struggled with serious censorship issues. Post-colonial cinema in Tunisia is known throughout the world for popular films like Férid Boughédir's *Halfaouine*, Nouri Bouzid's *Bezness*, and Moufida Tlatli's *Les Silences du Palais* from the so-called Golden Age in the 1990s. It has become known as a cinema that deals with women's sensuality and the magic and beauty of the old Tunis: palaces and labyrinthine medinas feature prominently as settings that determine the plot lines. In many historians' eyes, such as Hedi Khelil and Férid Boughédir, Tunisian cinema is a cinema of the mythical feminine. Khelil calls Tunisian cinema 'le cinéma au féminin'. Nevertheless, there is a much more problematic gendered spatiality going on in Tunisian cinema than most commentators care to illustrate. The identity politics in Golden Age films foreground women as the bearers of the nation's troubles, while Tunisia's liberal and democratic status in the Arab world denies even the existence of any troubles. Boughédir acknowledges that 'the image of the family is at the heart of Tunisian cinema: the family is often the micro-cosm that represents the nation, and the generations that live together are therefore the representation of the schism between tradition and moder-nity' (Gabous, 1998: 174). He analyses women's themes running through-out Tunisian film history and discovers several strands that contribute to the strength of the female figure in the family and the nation: the absent father, the orphaned hero, domineering mothers, the hysterical woman, unequal couples and the Oedipus complex. In the broader political context of the Arab world, in which the Arab man has been oppressed by colonialism and defeated in the many wars in the Middle East, this is what Nouri Bouzid called the defeat-conscious male in cinema. Both Bouzid and Boughédir emphasise that these themes run through men's films in post-independence cinema, as even after independence it took until 1975 before a woman, Selma Baccar, made a feature-length film.

The year after Tunisian independence in 1957, the modernising state set up a film production company, the Société Anonyme Tunisienne de Production et d'Expansion Cinématographique (SATPEC). The first president, Habib Bourguiba, was eager to monitor production and dis-tribution of Tunisian films. SATPEC controlled imports and prevented Hollywood films from entering the country for wider distribution, but since SATPEC was not that productive – on average two films per year were produced – it was an unsuccessful attempt to promote indigenous film-making. However, the government department supervising culture and information was led by Tahar Cheriaa, who promoted indigenous film-making with unprecedented vigour. Cheriaa produced the first local films and was the founder of the Journées Cinématographiques de Carthage, Tunisia's biennial film festival, in 1966. SATPEC seemed doomed from the outset, and while it did encourage young film-makers and the indigenous film industry, it never effectively supported them. In the late 1980s, it eventually gave in to independent producers and interna-tional co-productions (Armes, 2005: 48).

While in most government-supported Tunisian films there was a tendency to move away from social realism into pure fiction and magic (Armes, 2006: 65), the growing amateur movement moved in the opposite direction. Amateur cinema was an important contributor to the develop-ment of the Tunisian film industry and its Golden Age. Due to deficient and inactive state management of film funds, young film enthusiasts set up their own amateur clubs. The Fédération Tunisienne des Cinéastes Amateurs (FTCA) was set up in 1962. There was no greater plan for the federation than to bring together amateurs in order to enable them to make films. The government was suspicious of the independent and heterogeneous composition of these clubs. Political repression in the 1960s and 1970s was shaped primarily by the government's mistrust of trade unions or independent organisations. The amateurs reacted against the system, fashioning militant films and mobilising a cultural and intellectual environment for artists (Khelil, 2007: 26). They called their cinema 'the cinema of national disenchantment', critical of the inherent contradictions and disappointments of post-colonial Tunisian society. This was also true of the film-makers who had enjoyed an academic education in France or Belgium. Upon their return they were confronted with censorship and internal blockages. The result was a body of films that truly engaged with the reality of the present and opposed it to the hagiography of the past.

The most prolific cine clubs were in Kairouan, Hammam-Lif, Tunis and Sousse. Most films were collaborative ventures, resulting in a well-scripted, clear discourse of the reality of Tunisia. The films dealt with social preoccupations and local phenomena. Most names attached to these films, however, were male. The first effort by a woman resulted in a silent, black-and-white short titled *L'Éveil*, made by Selma Baccar in 1967 at the club of Hammam-Lif. Her club was most active towards the end of the 1960s and the beginning of the 1970s, and was preoccupied with fiction films in which biting criticisms of the government, the state of the nation and women's status was expressed. This criticism increased as the government repression of the clubs grew, and inspired more outspoken and political commentary. In the 1970s, as political dissent and the social preoccupations of the film-makers increased, and as film-makers that had learned their craft in Europe returned with ideals about critical realism, the documentary scene grew, slowly but steadily, within the amateur clubs.

The general trend in Tunisia, then, has been that not a great many films were made due to strict government control and funding problems. However, the films that were made were often of outstanding quality and tended to do very well at international festivals. As to the reason why only a small number of documentaries were being made in Tunisia, there are many theories. Hédi Khelil offers two explanations. He notes that in the Arab world, documentary making has political implications and consists of unavoidable subject choices. According to him, it is the link between the collectivity of the criticism and the individual that is explored by the documentarist (Khelil, 2007: 80). Its long absence from the Arab world, he says, is due to the fact that no individuals have dedicated themselves completely to documentaries. Documentary film-making, if it exists, is mainly seen as a prelude to a more sustainable and profitable career in fiction. He claims that Tunisia, as a land of fictions and myths, is not comfortable with documentary presentation. Hillauer agrees that documentaries have a bad reputation, as Tunisians are not accustomed to discussing their problems in public (Hillauer, 2005: 363). Boughédir adds to this that in Tunisia there is a ruling 'tendency to synthesize influences . . . transforming them in a nice, happy, moderated way. It's a culture that smooths off the sharp edges' (Barlet, 1998). But Khelil notes that as documentary gained importance in Europe and Latin America, North Africa followed. He acknowledges that the division critics and practitioners tend to make between documentary and fiction are artificial and superficial. Tahar Chikhaoui agrees that:

> partly as a result of their freedom from many of the social and political concerns which were so vital to their elders, the newcomers have shown 'more confidence in the camera and in reality, from which stems the place accorded to the suggestive force of the image, liberated from the process of narration, and the growing interest in the documentary'. (Armes, 2006: 156)

This chapter will focus on *Fatma 75*, an essay film of feminist inspiration that plays with reality: both as it is represented officially and as it is actually perceived by women in Tunisia. Baccar films extraordinary women talking with ordinary women, setting up sympathies along emancipatory lines. In 'the land of fictions', where woman is a symbol of the family and the nation, she negotiates her dissidence in rebellious terms, both explicitly, with words from the essay framework, and implicitly, with facial expressions and body language.

Fatma 75, a Feminist Manifesto

Selma Baccar (b. 1945) was the first woman in Tunisia to make her own films. Part of a group inspired by the bohemian atmosphere of the southern suburb of Tunis, Hammam-Lif, she became interested in cinema at a very young age. She studied psychology in Switzerland and film studies in Paris. These influences remained vital throughout her life as a filmmaker and producer, as her approach to directing a film is very hands-on, probing into the psychological lives of her characters. Her inspiration lies in a hybrid of Tunisian stories and French philosophy. After she made *L'Éveil* (*The Awakening*, 1966) collaboratively at Hammam-Lif's cine club, she worked as assistant director on several films with Moufida Tlatli, Nouri Bouzid and Férid Boughédir. Bouzid said that 'she is less competent in secondary roles, she is better in the more important roles, the roles in which she has to make decisions' (Gabous, 1998: 166). He encouraged her to pursue projects on her own terms, and she became the first female film producer in Tunisia. Tlatli became the editor of Baccar's first feature film.

Her first feature-length film *Fatma 75* was made in 1975 and came out in 1978.[1] It was an openly feminist film, made during the UN International Year for Women. With *Fatma 75* she wanted to show that it was not only President Bourguiba who had changed history for women. The historical context of women's ongoing activism needed to be addressed as well. The film was banned for thirty years, and never shown in commercial cinemas. Her next two films did not suffer directly from censorship, but did flirt with (at times very) controversial subject matter. In 1995 she made *Habiba M'Sika* or *La Danse du Feu*, a very popular film about a Jewish singer and dancer from the 1920s and 1930s, M'Sika from La Marsa. The film sets out not to mythologise, but instead rationalises the tempestuous life of Habiba M'Sika. Baccar's latest project is 2006 film *Khochkhach* or *Fleur d'Oubli*. Once again, the film focuses on an independent woman, Zakia, whose fate is to break out of the expectations a conservative society has of women. The different manners in which she fails or succeeds are portrayed in a sensitive way, as the unusual decisions Zakia makes towards the end of the film challenge expectations. Baccar wants to break away from stereotypes aiming to balance a simplistic perspective on women. She sets out to make films that are accessible to a larger audience and aims to inspire new insights and dialogue between the genders in Tunisia. Since 2011, she has been an active member of the Assemblée Constituante as a representative of the socialist party Al Massar. She stands up for women's rights and freedom of the media, thus letting her voice be heard outside the cinema, where she has too often been censored.

The main theme recurring in all Selma Baccar's projects is the fight for women's status and their freedom of speech. Freedom of speech is a contested concept in Tunisian politics. While President Ben Ali upheld the image of democracy for a long time, Tunisia was a dictatorship while he was in power. The discourse employed by Ben Ali was obscure, and the freedoms of women in his 'liberal' Tunisia were equally dubious: discourse was one thing, reality another.

Baccar has always been preoccupied with these two sides of Tunisia: since Bourguiba's Code of Personal Status was initiated in 1956, legally women had equal rights to men, but the Ministry of Women, Family and Children's Affairs, run by Mrs Bebia Bouchnak Chihi, a fervent campaigner, remained powerless when other official institutions and police officers practiced a different policy. Baccar told me this is a constant theme in her work. From *L'Éveil* onwards she has had an interest in representing women, and their (lack of) options and choices. She said that the freedoms that she has experienced in her life as an artist, and as a student abroad, taught her a lot about emancipation and women's rights (she was in Paris in 1968). Being so fervently preoccupied with women, especially in a Tunisian reality, she knows the policies of the government very well and acknowledges the efforts made by Bourguiba. Nevertheless, she also criticises the hypocrisy of the state. The Tunisian reputation for liberal policies clashes with reality, and she is genuinely worried, for example, about more and more young women wearing the hijab.

From *L'Éveil* onwards, her films have dealt with this choice faced by Tunisian women. The confidence of a legal discourse on emancipation is shattered when faced with discrimination in schools, at work or in everyday life. That is why in *L'Éveil* we see an intelligent female student who graduates and wants to pursue further studies.[2] Her father protests against this option: she ends up compromising her ideals by settling for a job as a secretary. It is, again, a senior man who limits her future prospects: her boss sees her as a sexual object and she is forced to leave. When she makes the decision to live independently in her own flat, and offer private language lessons to students, the men in the street disapprove and sabotage her plans once more. The ending is deliberately ambiguous. Baccar refuses to solve her problems. Instead, the film's ending shows her sitting on the beach looking at the sea, contemplating her options. It ends with a lengthy close-up of her face, eyes expressing anger, determination and resilience. The subtleties in the facial expressions of the protagonist bring across the struggle between her own emancipation and the repression she experiences from the men in her life.

Fatma 75 continued along this path, but the film is more openly feminist. It is an essay film with an explicitly didactic feel to it. In the late 1950s, Bourguiba contributed significantly to the rights of women in Tunisia, and his inspirational personality and speeches changed conservative attitudes. However, with *Fatma 75* Baccar wanted to illustrate that it was not only Bourguiba who changed history. While he certainly expressed these sentiments at the right time and in the right place, the whole context of women's activism needed to be re-evaluated. The structure of *Fatma 75* incorporates three different eras: 1930–8 and the first appearance of the Union of Tunisian Women; the national struggle and women's roles during the fight for independence between 1939 and 1952; and the intricacies of the personal status laws as they were introduced in 1956 and 1957. The three epochs are brought together in the fictional story of Fatma, a female student at university, discussing the historical relevance of women's movements throughout the twentieth century in an essay she is writing for her degree. It delineates Baccar's preoccupation with an internal conflict when it comes to the discourse on women as opposed to the reality of women's lives.

Habiba M'Sika is set in the 1920s and 1930s. Habiba was a popular Tunisian singer and dancer, of Jewish background, with a loyal fan base of adoring men. The biopic paints the historical circumstances of colonialism and fascism, in order to portray the historical relevance of this strong independent woman's story. Poetic, romantic and tragic, the story incorporates the choices Habiba is unable to make due to an increasingly suffocating political atmosphere. Her struggle to remain independent and successful culminates in a tragic dance spectacle, which she experiences as an expression of her anger. Once again the film-maker chose to discuss the difficulties for a woman to decide her own destiny. Eventually the struggle between her own internal fight and those that society places on her leads to her tragic ending. The strength of the passion that eventually burns her, remains very strongly present throughout the final stages of the film: her choice to express her anger – however controversial – was one that Habiba made on her own terms, through her power as a performer.

In *Khochkhach* this choice that women ultimately need to have is the culmination of a lifetime of struggle and bitterness. The main character, Zakia, is a sensual woman who becomes sexually frustrated because her homosexual husband does not desire her. She suffocates in her wish to be loved and becomes more and more determined to teach her daughter to be free to make her own choices. Her addiction to poppy tea (khochkhach),[3] however, turns her into a selfish creature. Paradoxically, when she is imprisoned in a mental asylum, she becomes truly free. In this irony lies the power of the film: Zakia is finally free and able to make her own decisions within the confines of an asylum. Her choice to stay when she is declared healthy is determining for her self-confidence. In the asylum she may be confined physically, but she feels free mentally. It is thus the ultimate belief in the power of women's choices that Baccar emphasises with the ending of the film, even if it is completely opposed to societal expectations.

Women's freedom of choice is a thread running throughout all Baccar's films. Férid Boughédir's conviction that 'Tunisian cinema has a feminist thematics' rings true with Baccar's thematic choices (Gabous, 1998: 147). Nevertheless, she disagrees with Boughédir. She insists that she is not a feminist, and that her inspiration, while influenced by the circumstances of the Tunisian woman, comes from her own experience as a woman in a family of female storytellers. She is interested in the psychology of women within the structure of family and community. The women that inspire her are members of her family: mother, aunts and grandmothers. She creates the women in her films from composites of the women that used to be in her life as a child. Along the lines of what Nejia Ben Mabrouk, another female film-maker from Tunisia, said in Boughédir's *Caméra Arabe*, Baccar feels men do not possess the power and the insight into the complex psyche of women and therefore it takes women film-makers to correct male film directors' visions on women. According to Baccar, a woman director adds an extra dimension to the psychology in the representation of women on the screen. Moreover, when Boughédir labels the themes of Tunisian films as feminist, Baccar believes that he does not completely grasp what the term entails. She rejects the label. She told me in an interview that, although she grew up during the 1960s and respects the necessity of the movement in Europe and America during that time, as a North African woman she prefers to distance herself from it. She refuses to use a word that refers to white privilege, and says that she simply does what she does because it is her passion, not because she follows an agenda. Still, if we take on Mohanty's understanding of feminism, as a worldwide attitude towards women's issues rooted in solidarity and sympathy, Baccar's films *are* deeply feminist. She deals only with women's issues and emancipation, in a highly politicised manner. She represents the different stages in a woman's life, growing with her cinematic output. In a political move, she moreover consistently ends her films on an optimistic note. The main inspiration for this political–philosophical move comes from Albert Camus' essay 'The Myth of Sisyphus', and in her adaptations of the myth, women's stories take place in extraordinary circumstances in a Tunisia that desperately needs hope for the future.

In 'The Myth of Sisyphus', Camus adapted the ancient myth of the man defying the gods and being punished for it. It inspired Camus' concept of the absurd. Sisyphus is the absurd hero facing eternal punishment from the gods who have condemned him to a hopeless struggle. As Sisyphus has defied death and disrespected the gods, his punishment consists of pushing a rock up to the top of a mountain, only to have it roll back down every time he reaches the top. The gods believed that for a human being, there is no more dreadful punishment than futile and hopeless labour. Camus is most interested in Sisyphus at the moment of his change of consciousness when he is up at the top of the mountain and sees the rock roll back down. He says that this myth is tragic only because the hero is conscious of his fate at that moment on the top. But he knows himself to be the master of his fate. If the rock is Sisyphus' life, then the effort to roll it uphill is enough to make him happy. Camus concludes that one must imagine Sisyphus happy (Camus, [1942] 1955: 123). Camus is convinced of the absurdity of life. There is no meaning, except if we escape that meaninglessness into a faith (a quest for God who decides on fate) or in suicide. Camus wants to explore a third possibility next to faith and suicide: living with the absurd and maintaining a constant awareness of it. Facing the absurd allows us to live life to its fullest. Only when a person can see and accept their life for what it is, can they ever truly achieve happiness and fulfilment. Camus finds that Sisyphus' punishment represents life: he must struggle endlessly, but as long as he accepts the meaninglessness of the struggle he can find happiness in the fulfilment of the task. Baccar told me:

> The women in my films are all in a similar situation [to Sisyphus]: they find themselves in circumstances that are absurd, and while they struggle in daily life, they also decide to get on with it and not despair. This optimism is necessary in any absurd situation. According to me it is what makes life bearable and worthwhile. (Interview, 2010a)

However, her characters do not find happiness in the absurd situation of life for women in Tunisia. They do not derive peace from it as Camus' Sisyphus did. This is particularly the case precisely because they are conscious of it. In *L'Éveil*, the protagonist stays determined to rebel against her situation. In *Fatma 75*, there is also no solution or acceptance of the absurdity of the situation of women in Tunisia. All interviewees and historical figures fight for freedom and rights, and Fatma does not accept women's fate, she rejects it fiercely. Habiba M'Sika does not manage to find happiness; she is so restless and such a rebel that she cannot find peace. While financial freedom seems attainable, in the end she literally burns up. Only in *Khochkhach* does the heroine find peace and happiness in her situation. Maybe this latest film by Baccar is the one in which Camus' Sisyphus seems to be reflected most effectively. This may illustrate Baccar's struggle to express her own feminist voice. Camus' essay inspired her outlook on life in absurd Tunisia and the attitudes of the women in her films, but she also remains frustrated and has to keep fighting difficult political battles. In fact, her films show a critical re-reading of Camus, and reject an acceptance of absurdity. In that she is also a feminist. In most of her films she actually shows that if the effort to rebel against the system is futile, one must live life reacting against it. Even though the feminist fight might not necessarily provide solutions immediately, it remains a worthy struggle that in itself gives women's lives meaning. This is also how the look works in *Fatma 75*. The absurdities of women's situations in Tunisia are pointed out in facial expressions and body language directly aimed at the spectator in an attempt to connect over the male idiocy, and as such establish a dissenting look to the film that adds to the explicitly dissident voices of the women.

Baccar's films are about women that are extraordinary. Like Baccar herself, they are different to the average woman in Tunisia because of their status as intellectuals, performers, outsiders of society. Fatma is a privileged literature student in the 1970s who, through her name, gives shape to every Tunisian woman. Baccar told me that she called the heroine Fatma as that was the name every Arab woman received from the colonial administration. The title of the film and the name of her heroine count perhaps as a reappropriation of this identity and an assertion that Fatma is not every woman, but an *everywoman* in Tunisia. Habiba is a successful and adored performer in the roaring twenties. Zakia is a sexually frustrated but very wealthy woman. Because of their intellectual and financial status, they are able to say and do things out of the ordinary. Baccar's outspoken criticism of the hypocrisy of her country's government with regard to women and the family laws is condoned only because of her reputation as an artist and as an outsider. Moreover, she learns that fiction is more effective and permissible than documentaries or essay films for putting her message across. Arguably due to her reputation as a rebel, fiction provides a means of escaping the strict government censorship when it comes to politics. Even though the stories in her films are based entirely in reality, history and everyday life, the effectiveness of the stories is measured by their relation to fiction.

In a land of fictions, reality is incompatible with the official discourse of a fictional democratic narrative. Intersecting and blurring the boundaries between reality and fiction is the strength of *Fatma 75*'s response to this situation. *Fatma 75* is a hybrid film, located somewhere between fiction and non-fiction, difficult to classify. I have argued elsewhere that the film is a docu-fiction or docudrama, but would say it is more productive to speak of an essay film, as Laura Rascaroli (2008) describes the form. As the framework of the narrative in the film is indeed a university essay, argued in a particular structure by Baccar's reflexive and subjective 'enunciator' Fatma, dealing with a particular committed and political vision of the world through an active, single voice, it is literally and structurally a film about an essay and an essay film. The political vision opens up a particular discourse on a problem with thought-provoking reflection that results in a conversation, an interpellation and a dialogue with the active spectator, through direct address and the convergence of film-maker and subject. Docudrama, as Rhodes and Springer explain, combines the recording and the representation of the 'real'. As another hybrid form of film-making, docudrama represents 'an attempt to present factual material through the organising aesthetics of fiction and narrative, and inevitably it uses certain forms of narrative patterning and visual composition that facilitate audience identification with the "characters" – even when these characters are well-known historical figures' (Rhodes and Springer, 2006: 6). While these characteristics are also present in the film, it seems more effective to consider it an essay film. The distinction between documentary and fiction is simply unproductive when discussing documentary in general and the film-makers from Tunisia specifically, as storytelling techniques inherent to the country and the region take centre stage in documentary. In an analysis of *Fatma 75* we need to take care not to let the dominance of voice and narrative blind us: it is equally important, though less obvious, to look much closer at the visual subtleties and contradictions, where the interpellation of the active spectator lies, 'each spectator is called upon to engage in a dialogical relationship with the enunciator, to become active, intellectually and emotionally, and interact with the text' (Rascaroli, 2008: 36). While the dramatic storytellers are presenting as well as representing a version of reality, it is in the visual approach to this reality that the key to understanding the essay film's position towards the spectator lies.

Fatma's Dramatic Storytellers

There are two storytellers in *Fatma 75*: the subject and the film-maker. Although we are dealing with material rooted in reality, in the essay film the subject and the film-maker converge in the voice-over. Selma Baccar's status as the pioneer of Tunisian women film-makers has become so important precisely because of her opinionated and direct approach to politics. The discourse in *Fatma 75* deals with a specific problem: the oppression of women through the ages in Tunisia, and shapes 'a supple form of cinewriting' (Rascaroli, 2008: 31). The essay film offers opportunities to be didactic and give her audience an unambiguous message through the dominance of voice/word, 'which [it] cannot do without a poetic, intelligent, written text by a voice-over' (Rascaroli, 2008: 29). Baccar attaches enormous importance to the voice of a film in script and dialogue. She told me that even if the story is based on real-life events, it is the director's specific task to bend real life in order to deliver a story that is interesting, didactic and entertaining. So where and how does the third party in the common tripartite dialogue feature in this essay film? First, this chapter describes the voices in the film, to move on to how this dominant voice is complimented with elaborate looks, where the spectator is implicated most effectively in the discourse on the 'in-depth, personal and thought-provoking reflection' (Rascaroli, 2008: 35).

At the start of *Fatma 75* the spectator is introduced to a number of historically significant women. The film starts with a quote from Tahar Haddad and his interpretation of Islamic rules on the treatment of women: 'We love woman as victim, but hate her as a free and conscious person, because we can enjoy her body but not her mind.' Haddad was an early male feminist from the 1930s, who wrote *Notre femme, la legislation islamique et la société*, defending ideas such as universal education and women's participation in society. This grounds the film firmly within a discourse that rebels against dogmatic interpretations of the Koran and places women at the centre of its arguments. The introduction to the essay film roots it into the long history of strong Tunisian women throughout the centuries. Attention is paid to several women from as long ago as 218 BC as well as twentieth-century women's leagues and foundations that were set up while the French coloniser was still present.

The first images are of a number of women speaking straight to the camera, pointing out their own importance for the history of Tunisian women. The main actress, Jalila Baccar who also plays protagonist Fatma, gives shape to these women. Wearing different make-up and clothes while moving within the contextual historical surroundings, Fatma embodies historical figures. The first woman to speak to the camera is Sophonisba, daughter of a Carthaginian general who lived during the Second Punic War in 218–201 BC. With her gaze fixed on the camera, she introduces herself, details what she has done for her country, and why this has been important. In fact, Sophonisba has become the subject of many Tunisian stories because of her extraordinary courage during the war. She was used by her family to secure allies, but when she was subsequently captured by the Romans, she refused to be treated as a slave and a victim of war and she decided, with the help of her lover, to commit suicide rather than let herself fall into the hands of the Roman conqueror. Her loyalty to and sacrifice for Carthage gave her an iconic status. The second figure represented by Fatma is Jalajil, a previously enslaved harem woman, who, after being liberated, founded a school for girls in Kairouan. She insists that the lower classes must get access to education. The third woman to introduce herself is Aziza Othmana, a princess of the Beys who died in 1669. After her father's death, she freed her slaves and spent her fortune on charity, set up a hospital and assisted young girls from the lower classes in securing their dowry for a good marriage. She is buried in the medina in Tunis and has her own shrine at the cemetery.

These three historical figures represent a privileged or extraordinary section of Tunisian women in a prelude to a film exploring contemporary paradoxes in women's realities. The fact that these women are speaking directly to the camera through Fatma, asserts their identity as part of a filmic essayistic event. As they address the spectators, they engage them to listen carefully to who they are: they assert not only their subject status by speaking from beyond the grave, they also stress their agency by stating exactly what they have done and why this was so important for the history of Tunisian women. They are defining themselves as part of history. After these three, Fatma also introduces herself to the camera as a student of history exploring the roles of women through the ages. Her voice-over in the film attempts to reach academic objectivity while asserting an individual subjectivity as a woman, and a Tunisian. Fatma's research includes recent events in which women took up important political and social roles. She explores the twentieth century through three additional generations in the 1930s, 1950s and 1970s, which encapsulate three different forms of women's emancipation.

The film essay envisages historical and contemporary intersubjective relationships between different women across the centuries. Fatma draws parallels between different women's situations and illustrates that women have indeed had a much more prominent role in the national struggle for independence and the post-independence turnaround for women's rights than is generally admitted in official discourse. As Gabous says, 'liberation, if it is present in the texts, is still far from being effective in everyday reality for all social classes' (Gabous, 1998: 70).

Fatma 75 was made with the intention of inserting women's agency into Tunisian history, an inherently feminist agenda. This film speaks of women: it is a reinscription of women into a history that had thus far ignored them. Baccar/Fatma create and reveal parallels between women's situations in ancient Tunisia and in the twentieth century. Including her own period, the 1970s, is significant inasmuch as it was the time of the amateur cine clubs, and the club Baccar was a member of in Hammam-Lif was especially open towards women joining. In that club there were four women, all collaborating on an artistic and idealistic scale: Najer Maabouj, Saadia Guellala, Sabah Fattah and Selma Baccar worked together on several productions. At the same time, everything was politicised. Gabous writes about the year in which Baccar made *Fatma 75*:

> In 1975, Tunisia was burning, an intellectual awakening dominated the generation of Selma Baccar, that generation that saw the rise of youth culture within the light of independence in Tunisia, but that youth was disenchanted twenty years later. The university boiled, women organised themselves, and expressed themselves, syndicates became the highlight of their revindications, the processes multiplied, poetry became contestable, the ciné-clubs were politicised and their discourse was often ideological. (Gabous, 1998: 67)

This situation gave Baccar the incentive to take up the camera and start to speak out: 'finally, a woman made a film that spoke of women' (Gabous, 1998: 69).

Like her characters, Baccar is not a representative of the ordinary Tunisian woman who has no voice. Nevertheless, in *Fatma 75* she specifically aims to express the grievances of the Everywoman in Tunisia. While she portrays extraordinary women from history who have influenced the status of women, she also interviews women from the countryside and those working in factories. While these 'ordinary' women remain nameless and without agency, Fatma speaks *with* them, and *of* or *about* them in her essay. Baccar attempts to combine her own and other emancipated women's viewpoints convincingly by means of illustrative instances in which women are treated unequally in reality while the law talks of equality.

Fatma 75 has an overall combative tone, as it defends women's rights fervently and as Fatma's voice-over is often impassioned when talking about inequalities. The fact that it was banned for such a long time in Tunisia (thirty years) resulted in a few clandestine, private screenings. These were enough to create a myth about the film and its film-maker in Tunisia, while it also drew attention from international platforms: French and Dutch film festivals obtained the rights to screen the film outside Tunisia. So while the censor aimed to silence the film's voice, it did not succeed in silencing Baccar's voice completely.[4]

We have seen that women's voices are atypical for documentaries and stand out, attracting attention to themselves. In Baccar's films, the female voices are so dominant that they drown out any male voices. Fatma's voice-over illustrates that in Baccar's films the female voice is the only one that counts. But the relationship between subject and director reflects the film form. There is no direct equality or sympathy from the extraordinary woman for the ordinary. Through Fatma and because of the essay film form, Baccar does not at first sight speak *with* the ordinary women; she attempts to speak *for* the extraordinary. There is too powerful a message to be communicated, a goal to get to and an argument to convince of, to leave space for self-reflexivity. Baccar's films deal with extraordinary women in unusual circumstances in an aesthetically pleasing *mise-en-scène*. Herein lies perhaps the main difference between documentaries and the essay film. *Fatma 75* is very outspoken and passionate about gender issues in society and legislation. The film powerfully asserts its politically inspired voice and its interest in the women's movements through history, in order to provide a counterbalance to the predominantly male point of view on women's rights in the country.

Fatma is twenty-three years old, her father is retired, her mother does not work, and she is a student at the university studying literature. In contrast to the other introductions in the film, her own introduction is not a monologue. She answers unheard but obvious questions in short sentences. During this snappy introduction we hear the sound of a typewriter in the background. This may indicate more about the nature of the questions: Fatma seems harassed by the questions, as if she is being interrogated.

The actress Jalila Baccar gives shape to Fatma, to the three historical figures from the introduction – Sophonisba, Jalajil and Aziza Othmana – and she also embodies the figures of twentieth-century women in later re-enactments. Her presence creates a sense of unity, but Jalila Baccar's shape-shifting dominance also causes uncertainty about whether the embodied women have their own agency. As an extraordinary Everywoman (a contradiction in terms), Fatma represents all Tunisian women's past, present and future. Fatma undergoes an elaborate subjective process in which she finds in herself diverse aspects of a variety of women. The historical perspectives and educational purposes have an outspokenly feminist nature. The nature of the academic paper used as a vehicle through which this message is conveyed enhances the essayistic nature of the film. The film is multi-layered, with a multitude of metafictional references to the past and to the medium of film as a means of education. It firmly places Fatma in her position as the storyteller. The academic paper is the source of this mode. She asks the questions of the interviewees and she passes judgement on what is being said and done. Her point of view is academically informed, but her voice perhaps lacks sympathy for the lower classes and uneducated women.

First, Fatma introduces the spectator to Tahar Haddad, the writer whose theoretical work she uses to conceptualise her paper. Tahar Haddad wrote a book, *The Tunisian Woman, Islam and Society*, in which he presented new and liberal ideas on the position of women in an Islamic society, saying that contemporary interpretations of the Koran inhibited women. Fatma visits the Tahar Haddad Club in Tunis to do her research. She reads pamphlets, looks up photographs and reads slogans from the past, emphasising that the 'Koran grants women the same rights as men. The problems of inheritance and inequality do not have a basis in the Koran. Marriages must be conducted between a man and a woman who are there of their own volition. Polygamy is a crime. Medical checks need to be done before the wedding. Women must not be banned from the home but have the right to a divorce. Education is mandatory for both men and women.'

As Fatma imagines Haddad, the historical re-enactment of a woman's home life in the 1930s also witnesses a demonstration against his writings on the streets of Tunis, which spills into her family's discussion and her father admonishes her for her outspokenness. People call Haddad a heathen who is collaborating with the French. Blurring the lines between her imagination and her reality, Fatma in 1932 fails to align history with her modern point of view, and in the process insults her own mother for being a slave to her husband. She learns several lessons. Here the film shows that anachronisms and misinterpretations of someone's writings can be avoided through contextualisation and a thorough understanding of contemporary attitudes.

Next, Fatma interviews Bouchira Ben Mourad, the woman who instigated the liberation movement for Tunisian women. She inaugurated the Union of Islamic Women in 1936, but the union was only recognised at independence in 1956, by Bourguiba. The interview takes place in Ben Mourad's home, where she answers Fatma's questions. As an interlude during this interview, Fatma's voice-over comments on the past, illustrated with photographic footage: men and women shown demonstrating against colonial rule and for the dawn of a new era. When that day finally came, men and women stood side by side and demanded a Tunisian parliament. Ben Mourad's active bravery is emphasised through other men and women's passivity. She was arrested because she tried to raise awareness among other women of the necessity of independence and Bourguiba's right to power. Ben Mourad spent time in jail and under house arrest.

A historical re-enactment at the end of this part shows the young student Fatma returning home late in the evening without her veil on, after a day of demonstrations against the coloniser in the late 1950s. She tells her mother of the violence that took place in town. Once again, then, the intellectual represents the Tunisian women who took part in these demonstrations, while her mother does not get the chance to express her opinion. There is a danger that the academic tone of Fatma neglects her mother's agency to say something in return. The chapter closes with the question: 'is Tunisian society really ready for these big changes?' This question and Fatma's own attitude are juxtaposed in the next fifteen seconds in the film: older women having coffee discuss marriage as the better option for young women; an education does not serve them. This conservative view serves as another consideration of the question about wider society (not) being ready for change.

The lack of education commented on here is again juxtaposed with a fragment of a sexual education lesson for teenagers. Ostensibly, this was the reason why *Fatma 75* was banned for such a long time in Tunisia, but Baccar used it as an example to illustrate the dangers of ignorance for women specifically. This fragment comes at the centre of the film and seems out of place with the rest of the film: Fatma does not feature, she does not comment on it, and the style of the film here is entirely documentary. In an almost clinical and very objective, serious manner, doctors and professors explain the reproductive organs and virginity. Equally, students remain very serious and ask pointed, practical questions. It could be argued that this is so different and stand-alone, that it is the enfolded centre of the film. This is what the surrounding discourses have been about in essence: the difference between men and women when it comes to the body politic, the oppression of women because they are 'the weaker sex', and the refusal of Fatma and Baccar to accept this conservative stance on nature.

Fatma can come across as judgemental, as a young student and feminist. She states, for example, that 'some women hide behind age old traditions' and 'there are also women that pretend' or 'women who wait on street corners until someone gives them work for the day, they are like slaves waiting for a new master'. Utterances like these place Fatma in a privileged position casting quick glances on poorer women without offering them the chance to really speak. When showing elderly women working hard in the fields, Fatma's voice-over states 'how can you speak with them about anti-conception when their men search for compassion in their bodies after their daily misery, and want children as the sole hope that they will take care of them in old age'. So while the film-maker illustrates the resilience of a certain type of woman, she also emphasises the reticence and passivity of others.

On two occasions in the film, after a succession of strong, independent women has been shown, such as a lawyer, policewoman or a pharmacist, veiled, poor women literally flee from the scene. The voice-over states: 'of course women are part of public modern life in strong positions', at which point the camera turns away from the extraordinary to the ordinary in a street scene showing two veiled women running away from the camera and looking over their shoulders to ensure it does not follow them. The voice-over states 'but there are those who hide behind old traditions'. The camera in fact harasses them, following them too closely so that they have to dive away and hide behind a stationary van. The voice-over continues that the law tells them they remain dependent on men, as the camera focuses on a couple of women on the street corner, veiled from top to toe, passively waiting for a man to offer them work, 'like a slave'. These women are equally suspicious of the camera, readjusting their veils. They are victims of double oppression of gender and class. They are shown to have no choice, as they have the option to be a servant or a prostitute. These women have no voice, no close-up. The presence of these images is significant, and their position juxtaposed to the extraordinary shows the essayistic nature of Fatma's work. Yet it also shows her slightly patronising air. While Baccar's film gives the impression of being outspoken and polemical, it is also (perhaps too) careful when touching on truly contentious issues regarding the subaltern.

The emphasis Baccar places on the voices and what is being said, and her acknowledgement that she retains intense control over the dialogue and the storytelling implies a clear and feminist agenda. The power of her point of view is enhanced at the end of the film. A coda – the conclusion of Fatma's research and academic paper – expresses a political feminist point of view:

> The emancipation of the Tunisian woman did not happen overnight. It is the result of a long and slow process. The actions of Aziza Othmana and many others are historical milestones. Reformers such as Haddad and Bourguiba have consolidated these women's work. The emancipation would not have been possible without the readiness of the Tunisian people and their capacity to make just choices and take the route towards freedom.

The voice-over in this film is a strong political intervention. It draws the spectators in, but at the same time sets them back critically, as women's issues are vastly more complex than what the privileged student claims in her (film) essay. The informed spectator will know about the ineffective attempts by the government to institutionalise women's rights, while in reality women remain second-class citizens on several levels.

The film-maker admits to revelling in the role of the storyteller and ingraining in the stories a moral or didactic element. It is the nature of the storytelling she admires, such as *1001 Nights* or the fables of La Fontaine. For her, stories need to have a goal: they need to be straightforward. She says, 'as a filmmaker you have to take elements from daily life and reality, but they are not enough: so you add imaginary aspects to give it a twist worthy of film. Films need to be accessible to as wide an audience as possible.' Moreover, according to Baccar, storytelling is a female occupation: 'women tell stories to each other, they gossip and they tell stories to the children. Storytelling is also something that has always been of great importance in my family. Stories are ways to transmit memory and knowledge.'

So while it is her self-assigned task to tell moral stories that are simple and clear-cut, their identity and straightforwardness lie in the characters and not necessarily in the structure of the stories. The main characters in Baccar's films are privileged, intellectual and extraordinary women representing passionately feminist politics. At first sight, her subjectivity and agency as an intellectual artist threaten to drown out the voices of the subaltern. But she does not claim to represent or speak for the subaltern. Instead, she focuses on extraordinary women and their voices reflecting her own. Nevertheless, a closer reading of *Fatma 75* reveals instances where the ordinary woman is addressed very subtly. While the film's voice is wary of the censor, and resorts to self-censorship, a closer analysis of the visual aspects of Baccar's films offers another story.

Baccar's Poetics of Detail

The years of research and preparation that go into projects undertaken by Baccar result in films that are overwhelmingly dominated by visual beauty and decoration, in both *mise-en-scène* and costumes. Baccar strongly believes in the power of the re-enactment, as the detail of clothes, make-up and decoration is visually rich. They add to the nature of the essay film and the tactics of the director to suspend the disbelief of the spectators. In this respect the film reflects the fact that the status of Tunisian women is equal and liberal in legal terms, but not so much in reality. Equality is in fact a fiction itself. Today, the film retains its relevance. It also illustrates that imagery and the visual add a crucial layer of meaning and interpretation to that which is expressed with words, for a subtler and perhaps more effective outreach to the spectators: the visual establishes a clearer intersubjectivity that includes the spectators.

As Rachida Ennaifer has said about *Fatma 75*: 'the documentary has won, over the years, authenticity and beauty. *Fatma 75* is different from those films projected onto our small and large screens, pretending to be documentaries' (Gabous, 1998: 71). As a form of art, then, Baccar's film explores the possibilities of beauty while she attempts to embody the eras of the past in order to provide a context. The level of detail explored in the films is impressive. In *Fatma 75*, the costumes worn by actress Jalila Baccar when she embodies Sophonisba, Jalajil or Aziza Othmane are meant to transport the spectator to entirely different eras in Tunisian history, encouraging a further suspension of disbelief.

As Sophonisba, Fatma wears a wig, headdress and a white toga, representing the age-old customs of the Carthaginians. The illustration of her wealth and personality are all the more convincing for being on screen during the explanation of what the woman did for Tunisia in her time. As Jalajil, Fatma is dressed in many layers of veils, surrounded by schoolgirls whom she is teaching. The setting is the rooftops of Tunis, which illustrates the unusual situation: girls being taught by a female ex-slave. Once again, it is an illustration of the era and the situation in which Jalajil existed and acted. When Fatma then dresses up as Aziza Othmane, the princess' status as royalty is obvious in the wealth and beauty displayed in the surroundings as well as in the traditional costumes. Bruzzi, though she says reconstruction is all too often idiosyncratic, also shows that it can perform a liberating function when no archive is available. As she says, it is often unnecessary, or a case of 'reiterating the same idea in fancy dress', but in *Fatma 75* the 'necessary political intent behind the reconstructions' is not absent, and as such warrants belief (Bruzzi, 2000: 45–6). What is being said here is crucial for the camera-eye not to slide into orientalist voyeurism. The fact that Fatma addresses the spectator directly, enables the spectator to steer clear of voyeurism.

On the one hand, the costumes and display of wealth in the details (accessories, decorative pieces, bird cages) enhances the credibility of the women that are speaking: in *Fatma 75* they are authorities on what is happening during their respective epoch. On the other hand, however, the attention to detail and wealth firmly places the women within a category of the extraordinary: they are women with a privileged position and they speak from a certain point of view. As Gabous says: the film saw the light of day precisely to 'revive the famous women and the grand Berber figures' (Gabous, 1998: 69).

Whereas the verbal representation focuses mainly on the voices of privileged, extraordinary women, all women do receive an equally challenging visual treatment: they are all seen from up close. This simultaneously asserts their individuality, their aware performance in the camera's presence; and their authoritative position as informants. The film-maker employs the indirect power of the close-up in order to express that which is impossible to express with words. Baccar likes to portray the unspeakable in the close-up of women's faces, while attempting to incite in the spectator more political awareness of the feminist vigour in these women. Baccar may neglect the difficult task of representing the voice of the subaltern, but does attempt to include the ordinary Tunisian woman in the visual performative side of the film. In order to communicate the unspeakable successfully, Baccar's camera-eye zooms in on the faces of ordinary women in *Fatma 75*.

There are instances of women observed but not acknowledged verbally. These images have a *verfremdung* effect: their inclusion unsettles the spectators and makes them aware of the fact that there is indeed a silenced voice present, for example, in the images of veiled women fleeing the scene. Visually, this subaltern presence questions Fatma's silence, leading to considerations of (self-)censorship. At the same time, as an outspoken woman, Baccar does attempt to include overt political dissent in her films. She does this indirectly: there is no direct or outspoken discourse criticising the government, but the close-up of the women in the film pulls in the spectator as an accomplice in order to reveal and mock governmental bureaucracy, the supremacy of male opinions and the paternalistic manner in which men treat women. Between Fatma's voice-over and the re-enactments of historically important moments for Tunisian women, many voices of dissent are heard. Equally, when it comes to really contentious issues, the faces of women re-enacting historical moments in the 1930s and the 1950s often say more than the dissenting voice of Fatma in 1975 does. At this point then, we could argue that the gazes and facial expressions are enfolded within the discourses, and the spectator is invited to unfold them through implication and sympathy. In spite of the thirty years during which it was banned, in this film hindsight often means all manner of criticisms and mockery that would not have been available earlier.

Fatma is the vehicle through whose eyes the spectator will see the history of Tunisian women. The filmic academic essay and the voice-over are indicative of this. While the essay format attempts to convince of the reality of the situation, it does not hide its feminist vigour. It is therefore also clear that this essay film is not attempting to be objective. It is a self-consciously subjective and reflective essay with conviction voiced by and seen through Fatma's eyes. When it is made clear that she is going to do a presentation on the women's movements throughout Tunisian history, a male colleague teases: 'so, have you joined the women's movement now?', and she responds by smiling at him in an ironic way. Her facial expression says 'I know you are mocking me'. Already, Fatma illustrates that the face can say more than she could with words. Deleuze's 'organ-carrying plate of nerves' is indeed incapable of hiding Fatma's true feelings about this male observation. While it shows Fatma to be a reasonable and confident young woman, it also illustrates the attitude of her male peers. It is this contemporary attitude in men that Baccar wishes to challenge the most.

As mentioned, one of the most important interviews Fatma does is with Bouchira Ben Mourad, of the Union of Islamic Women. In this interview, the camera focuses on Fatma's positions as she is listening and asking questions, and her body language reveals her personal interest in the topic. It also offers close-ups of Bouchira's face and eyes. While she is answering Fatma's questions and the answers are illustrated with archival footage and photographic material from the time, she also looks at the camera at one or two instances. This interaction with the camera reveals the situation as a filmic event: she acknowledges not only the camera, but also the spectator who sees her on the screen during the screening of the film. She breaks the fourth wall, assures herself of the presence of the camera, and through this act ensures the attention of the spectator: she implicates the spectator to make sure her message, which is an important one for women, reaches the intended audience. Her eyes say 'Do you see? Are you listening?'

Next to the portrayal of outstanding women such as Bouchira and the re-enactments of historical circumstances, we also see the archival footage used to illustrate the past. These images illustrate not only what Bouchira is saying, but also the community spirit of women during the struggle for independence period. We see large crowds of veiled and unveiled women, celebrating Bourguiba with their community spirit. These pictures show another side of the privileged position of hindsight. The camera's-eye zooms in on the pictures, revealing women's passionate facial expressions amongst the crowds. It illustrates the crowd having an identity of its own and the women in the demonstrations as having confidence and power individually.[5] The camera also *reads* these pictures ostensibly as testimonies of the past as it moves from left to right and from right to left over the image, in order to demonstrate its value as a historical document and proof of women's powerful collective.

Another instance in which archival footage and re-enactments illustrate more powerfully the confidence of the collective ordinary women is when the film changes momentarily from an educational document to an observational documentary: filming farmers on their land, showing poverty and daily struggle during the colonial period adds a fold of meaning to the previous images of Bourguiba and his heroic return to Tunis upon independence. The voice-over is silent and for a while the camera observes the women on the farm working just as hard as the men. The absence of voice here illustrates how (self-)censorship determines and limits voices but not necessarily images. Likewise, immediately after the sequence with a sex-education course at university,[6] the camera changes its attitude towards the subject: the observational style returns as we observe everyday life in a rural village where women come to the hospital with their children or on their own to receive treatment. The discussion that is observed is one between several doctors and nurses, on the one hand, and a lower-class, veiled woman, requesting contraceptives. These short interruptions in the essay film temporarily prevent the suspension of disbelief and confirm the spectator as a trusted, thinking subject who is asked to see critically. The camera-eye as such reveals issues that self-censorship prevents the filmmaker from addressing verbally.

The interviews not only provide the spectators with factual information, but also with close-ups of the faces of the people being interviewed. Apart from providing an individual subjectivity and identity to the speaker, the close-up also offers the spectator the other, more ambiguous aspects of the close-up: saying something without words and implicating the spectator in the interpretation of what is being communicated visually. The looks on men's and women's faces often say more than actually comes across in the interview. Two striking examples are when Fatma interviews the boss of a factory after she has spoken to his female employees. He confirms that female employees work more and deliver more quality, but earn less. The look on Fatma's face shows us her opinion. While the man speaks *at* her (not *to* or *with* her), she refuses to absorb his arguments by defiant looks on her face. A conspiracy between the film-maker, the subject and the spectator is going on in plain sight. The factory boss's arguments are as follows:

> Even if a woman has earned the same degrees as a man, we cannot give her the same responsibilities. First, the man has to take care of his family. The law is very clear in this. Second, the woman is too often preoccupied with her own problems. That is why we cannot give her a job with serious responsibilities. Third, public opinion claims that men are physically stronger than woman and that is not entirely incorrect. If you ever work in a factory yourself, then you will come across problems like these. Women get pregnant, feel ill easily, or a child gets ill, or she just does not show up at work. There is always something. And you cannot even really blame her.

Instead of over-the-shoulder shots, which could have indicated a dialogue between the two people on screen, Baccar chooses to include what looks like a shot-reverse-shot, but is actually a full focus on the man with inserted emphasised reactions of Fatma. Fatma does not contribute verbally to the conversation at all. We witness a patronising monologue, and Fatma's response is a look that is nearly invisibly sarcastic: with her head resting on her arm, expressing cynical resignation to the patronising speech, she raises an eyebrow, smiles sarcastically, again raises an eyebrow, and slightly moves the corners of her mouth while she shrugs. These very subtle reactions to the absurd arguments of the factory boss shape the conspiracy between Fatma, Baccar and the emancipated spectator. The implication of the spectator is important here, as it establishes the intersubjectivity between the different parties contributing to the interpretations of the film. It is these interpretations that challenge the voices and the absurdity of the contemporary Tunisian reality as Baccar wishes to criticise it.

Apart from the self-confident and outspoken women that face the camera directly and address the spectator, a large number of women

Figure 3.1 A close-up of Fatma's facial expressions when she listens to the monologue of the factory boss in *Fatma 75* © Selma Baccar

from different eras across the twentieth century pass on screen. In historical re-enactments we see middle-class students arguing with their parents, young women standing up to their husbands and daughters confiding in their mothers. In the contemporary sequences we are introduced to ordinary factory workers, mothers, college students and wives wishing to travel abroad with their husbands. These sequences need attention as it is here that Baccar engages intersubjectively with her subjects, visually.

The women Fatma interviews in the factories serve as illustrations of hard-working lower-class women who have managed to create for themselves a niche within the factory that has ensured their relative independence. Yet the men they work with have remained conservative: they cannot, or refuse to, answer the questions that Fatma asks them when she confronts them with the inequality at work. The different women are filmed at first in a larger group: the whole department of this factory seems to be dependent on a female workforce. The logical conclusion would be that they are highly valued staff. One of them, Mabrouka, is a member of the workers' union representing both men and women.

When Fatma interviews them, they continue with their job and multi-task: they package large quantities of pasta and work the machines without interruption. In close-ups we observe their faces as they engage with the questions Fatma is asking, and they provide the student with information on how many hours they work and how much they earn. They do not, however, acknowledge the camera – they keep their eyes fixed on the job at hand or look up at Fatma briefly to engage in the conversation. The camera observes their faces individually and as they refer to one another, they are each given a clear identity. There is an indexicality to the voice here that reminds of Jocelyne Saab's style, which compliments a dominant voice with a concern for the look and the necessity to 'see', or understand, the ordinary. Conversely, when Fatma interviews one of the men, she asks him the same questions but does this outside of the factory. He acknowledges the camera, and looks uneasy, as he admits that the women are treated unfairly. When Fatma later speaks to the women after they have finished their shift, it is in a long-shot that provides an overview of the surroundings, with a voice-over ignoring the dialogue.

The effort to obtain information from the source – the rural lower-class women of Tunisia – shows a commitment to these women. An intersubjective sympathy is carefully constructed, but Baccar and Fatma do reveal the political mechanisms that oppress women and their film-making. The self-reflexive confidence of the educated women in this film stands in contrast to the uncertain (but optimistic) position of the lower classes. An attentive spectator will notice the attempts to raise awareness and the necessity of this when implicated through the facial expressions directed at the camera.

Communication and conviction go beyond words in the essay film. Another manifestation of the close-up in *Fatma 75* lies in the re-enactments of the historical instances. Baccar spends so much time researching and preparing for films that she attaches enormous importance to the clothes and attributes of her actors. She said:

> Even though the message I am trying to get across is a verbal and explicit one, with the stories being transmitted through my words uttered by my actresses, I find the visual aspect of cinema extremely important. I focus often on the faces, the eyes, and the mouths of my actresses. Looks can say even more than words do sometimes. The importance I attach to details like jewellery, makeup, costumes and props is well known among actors and actresses in Tunis. I love beauty and style, I love expressing things that maybe add to the story I am transmitting. As a director as well as a producer I attach the greatest importance to these things. Their dress says so much about them, and it enables the actors to find the character more easily and to find the voice I have in mind. I suppose I guide them in the direction I want through these details. (Interview, 2010a)

The camera's-eye reflects the numerous eyes of the women in the film: not only the more privileged ones such as Fatma and Bouchira, but also the women working on the fields and in factories. Close-ups of their faces and eyes reveal a larger knowledge and insight into their individual and common situations as Tunisian women struggling with the discrepancies between legislation and everyday reality. Moreover, their facial expressions reveal a deeper-seated understanding and criticism of these ambiguities while they attempt to implicate the spectator into understanding these challenges. With her activist, feminist films, Baccar manages to inform spectators as well as put them in a position where passivity is challenged and mocked. The spectators are urged to stretch the limits of their imagination, while at the same time accept that what is revealed in this film is unambiguously true to real life. Women of all levels on the social ladder are included in the film in order to reach a spectatorship that will comprehend the gazes, the looks and the facial expressions that turn them from passive voyeurs into active, dissident spectators.

Conclusion

Whether or not Baccar manages to establish an intersubjective relationship between herself, her actresses and her spectators is a matter that is addressed mostly by the form she chooses for her films. I focused my analysis on *Fatma 75*, as it was a pioneering film in Tunisia not only due to it being the first feature-length film by a woman, but also because of its subject matter and its format. A documentary is highly unusual in the land of fictions, particularly if it is made by a woman. Baccar had to work within the constraints of Tunisian sensibilities and the censor. Baccar has a clear message and her heroines have strong voices and looks. At first sight, the subaltern disappears into the background due to the dominating personalities and voices of the protagonists. Crucially though, it is through extra-textual non-verbal communication strategies that the film really educates the spectator. More than any other film-maker, Baccar counts on the intellect and film-literacy of her spectators to read the self-censorship and indirect criticism on patronising male attitudes and discourses of equality. In the land of fictions, the essay film in Baccar's hands shows a supple and subtle way in which to directly address the transnational spectator, with words and images, with voices and gazes – with stories and facts, on politically sensitive, strongly feminist issues.

Notes

1. This date is an approximation, as the film took a long time to be made and was immediately banned by the government. The film did travel abroad and was screened in Holland in 1978.
2. The film has been lost to the archives, but Baccar owns an old copy on VHS, which I got the chance to see while visiting her.
3. Khochkhach is an infusion of poppies, used as a painkiller for women in labour, but also for newborn babies if they cannot sleep.
4. I have written in more detail about this elsewhere, see Van de Peer (2014a).
5. The parallels between these images and those in more recent news reports on the Jasmine revolution stand out: images of women on the front lines of crowds enter the collective memory. Photographers point out that women present strong and perhaps even unexpected images of defiance.
6. This sexual education sequence was ostensibly why the film was banned for thirty years, however, the feminist, political nature is much more likely to have been the cause.

CHAPTER 4

Assia Djebar: Algerian *Images-son* in Experimental Documentaries

Assia Djebar (1936–2015) is one of the most famous Algerian women authors in history. In this chapter I focus on the only two films she ever made, in the late 1970s and early 1980s, one of which is hardly ever mentioned while the other is revered as a feminist masterpiece of psychoanalytic treatment of historic trauma. Djebar was born Fatima-Zohra Imalayen on 4 August 1936 in Cherchell, a small Berber city in Chenoua, the mountainous region on the northern coast of Algeria, just west of Algiers. As her father was a teacher of French language his children were sent to the French-language school, and Djebar regrets not speaking Berber. Her studies continued in Paris, at the Lycée Fenelon, and she became the first Maghrebi woman to be accepted to the École Normale Supérieure. As a student in Paris in the 1950s, she joined the protests against the occupation of Algeria and for Algerian independence. Her political activism went further, when, during the War for Independence, Djebar collaborated with the Front Libération Nationale (FLN) newspaper *El-Moujahid* (*The Militant*). Personal experiences as a woman involved in the Algerian War for Independence have heavily influenced the subject matter of her stories, novels and papers, as well as of her two films, *La Nouba des femmes du Mont Chenoua* (1978) and *La Zerda, ou les chants de l'oubli* (1982).

Djebar wrote her first novel when she was twenty years old. *La Soif* (*The Mischief*) was published in 1957. She anticipated the controversy that later surrounded the novel and published under the pen name Assia Djebar. With this nom de plume she continued to confront the controversial topic of the relationship between France and its ex-colony, even though it was still taboo in French political and cultural life until well into the 1980s. The disappointment of independence, the role of Muslim women in society, migration and the longing for home are consistent themes in her novels. In 1974, she returned to Algiers to teach French literature and cinema for the French department at the University of

Algiers. It was during this period that Djebar began to consider the role film had played in the political emancipation of Algerian society. The potential of film-making to open up her stories to a newer and wider audience (illiteracy – especially among women – is still a serious issue in Algeria) convinced Djebar to work on two television documentaries. With Radio Télévision Algérie (RTA), she produced *La Nouba* and *La Zerda*, and the idea was to retell history from a women's perspective, reaching an audience of Algerian women as part of the large contingency of television audiences in Algeria.

With *La Nouba*, Djebar not only wished to focus on women's positions in her home country and in Islam, but also to challenge the documentary tradition. As a docudrama, the film transgresses style and form expectations. *La Zerda* is perhaps easier to label as a documentary, using archival footage and voice-over to illustrate the points made. It is a montage of colonial images of Maghrebi festivals, with accusations of appropriation and theft being answered with re-appropriating statements of ownership. It has been edited in such a way as to illustrate that militant cinema (in Algeria this cinema was called *cinéma mujahid*) could also be made by women. Both films are structured around musical principles. A 'Nouba' is a song with five movements, each movement enabling a singer 'to speak in her turn'. *La Zerda* encompasses four movements, each embodying a forgotten song – or a song of oblivion. Both are experimental films by and about women in revolution and war. Djebar considers herself first and foremost an author, and as such her films foreground the power of the spoken word, which includes oral storytelling, poetry, the lyrics of the songs, as well as the testimonies of the women she interviews. At the same time, the failure of the spoken word in history is foregrounded through silences, which highlight the power of the image. Djebar calls her films *images-son*, or image-sounds (or sound-images). My analysis of the gaze in this chapter is in some respects Lacanian and certainly inspired by French psychoanalytic theory, just as the film was. For *La Nouba*, Djebar received the Grand Prix de la Critique Internationale at the Venice Film Festival, and for *La Zerda* the title of Best Historical Film at the Berlin Festival. The book that followed the release of these two films in 1985, *L'Amour, la fantasia* (*Fantasia: An Algerian Cavalcade*), engages with the films, and further explores the roles Algerian women are able to create for themselves in society. Considering the film as *images-son*, it is these two elements of film-making: images and sound (or visuals and the spoken word) that will be considered in more detail in what follows.

Hybrid Identities in *La Nouba*

Algerian cinema has for a long time been defined by its revolutions and its wars. As such, it has also been dominated by male stories, and men making films. Assia Djebar was the first woman to take up the camera and set the record straight. *La Nouba* looks at Algerian women and their social and political status in history, specifically during the War for Independence, rather than portraying women as the symbols of the revered motherland and bearers of the burden of tradition, as was the case in several men's films.[1] Djebar engaged her fellow countrywomen in the debate on emancipation. While the spoken word is of central importance in her poetic films, as we will see, the look is equally a highly politicised notion, addressed explicitly.

As becomes clear in *La Nouba*, women fought a vital part in the war for independence, but afterwards lost their agency, which was put back in the hands of the victorious men. Moreover, Guy Austin writes, testimonies of rural women were extremely rare (2012: 80). *La Nouba* is thus the sum of many firsts: the first film by a woman in Algeria; the first film by Assia Djebar; the first time women's histories are inserted into Algerian history; and the first time rural women are given a voice. In the context of a very complex history, both colonial and post-colonial, of women in the country, this film addresses women's testimonies through their silences. James McDougal explains that nationalism proved to be a new kind of domination after colonialism (2006: i). Its dominating discourse effaced multiple memories and possible futures. McDougal writes that in spite of the ruling nationalist and heroic discourse, there is something that scratches at the surface: memories and pasts must be recovered and saved from oblivion. This is precisely what Djebar sets out to do with *La Nouba*: letting women speak where they have previously been silenced.

Women have been mostly absent from Algerian cinema history. *La Nouba* was not only the first, but also the only one for a long time. The film was, moreover, disliked at its first screening in the Cinemathèque d'Alger, because of its feminist agenda, and was screened only once on Algerian television, because of its perceived inaccessible nature. The film experiments with the visualisation of the repressed, enabling testimonies and memories to resurface through the aid of associative interviews. Djebar's main subject is a fictional woman, Lila, as well as a host of non-fictional women from the Chenoua tribe, who are being interviewed by Lila about their war-time experiences.

Djebar's own transnational identity and migration trajectory determine the characteristics of her protagonists and the overall identity politics.

Arguably due to her own hybrid, transnational identity as both French and Algerian, the female identities in her films are portrayed as inherently fragmentary. In *La Nouba*'s framing story, the protagonist, Lila, looks like and speaks with the voice of Assia Djebar, and can be identified as her mirror image. They both represent someone living on the fringe of two separate societies. As a returnee to the homeland from France, Lila not only straddles two cultures, but has to admit that she might be unable to fully understand either, when she says 'I used to be elsewhere, but now I am elsewhere too. I am a stranger in my own country!' As the perpetual outsider, Lila starts to question her ability to represent the tribeswomen to her audience. She comes to the realisation that 'there are walls in between people, between hearts'. She bemoans the lack of solidarity between cultures and people: 'even now the soldiers' watchtowers are still there, but empty. The walls are there too.' The walls symbolise obstacles and frustration, caused by the inability to really connect with her homeland, the interviewees and her husband.

The relationship between Lila and Ali is extremely strained. The representation of Ali leaves the spectator in no doubt about where the filmmaker's loyalties and interests lie and with whom she identifies. Ali, a vet, has been injured in a work-related accident. Throughout most of the film, he is wheelchair-bound and unable to leave the house. His immobility stands in stark contrast to Lila's increasing desire and ability to roam the countryside in search of the women she wants to interview. The emasculation of Ali is a topic of most of the discussion available on *La Nouba*, and will be touched upon briefly later on.

Apart from Lila, the film listens to the histories of Jamila, Fatma and her mother, Zoulikha and aunt Berkani. We also hear a myth of the seventh wife of a saint, a well as Lila's own grandmother who tells the story of a heroic horseman. The introductory text to the film states:

> This film, in the form of a nouba, is dedicated, posthumously, to Hungarian musician Béla Bartók, who had come to an almost silent Algeria to study its peasant music in 1913. It is also dedicated to Yamina Oudai, known as Zoulikha, who established a resistance network in the city of Cherchell and its mountains in 1955 and 1956. She was arrested in the mountains when she was in her forties. Her name was subsequently added to the list of the missing. Lila – the protagonist of the film – could be Zoulikha's daughter. The six other talking women of the Chenoua tell bits and pieces of their life stories.

Each woman tells her story about sheltering, feeding and working for the resistance fighters in interviews that we *hear*, but do not *witness* taking place. These interviews are conducted in extreme long-shots, or inside the women's homes where Lila, but not the camera, follows. As Florence Martin has said, in a way, Lila is the über-narrator (2011: 54). While we get to know her intimately, the faces of the women remain indistinct from one another, and their identity equally remains obscure. They are a hybrid identity of their own, but are never successfully distinguished from one another. They sacrificed their homes and their food, and some were tortured for assisting the revolutionaries or for being one themselves.

Cherchell is a city by the sea, and the sea is Lila's recurring escape route. She arrives from France by sea, the Mediterranean symbolising a space of exchange and travel. It embodies the freedom to come and go, and it informs a sense of reflection. The sea is where Lila feels she can dream and contemplate leaving. It is therefore in the middle of the film that she takes a small rowing boat and drifts out to sea. This central fold enfolds *and* unfolds the deepest consciousness of Lila. She dreams of events to come and is confronted with her own contested presence in Chenoua. Lila in the dream looks frankly at the dreaming Lila and confronts her with her unclear place among the women of the mountain. This intensely reflexive moment in the film and the realisation that there is an escape route via the sea settle in her the determination to stay. She manages to come to terms with the fact that complete integration between herself, the women of Chenoua and her audience is perhaps unattainable.

In fact, as a fictional character, Lila creates a diversion: the singular point of view, and her initial confusion encourage the spectator to sympathise with her, but her alone. Because she is an outsider, the representation of the voice or the image of the interviewees fails, as we hear Lila's voice and see her face. However, after the boat sequence, Lila changes her approach to the reception of the women, and the film gains confidence. Lila learns during the dream sequence on the rowing boat that she straddles two cultures, that she is a hybrid, and that, by accepting this, she might in fact no longer be the outsider but rather an insider who is also an outsider. She has seen and heard the interviewees, she has learned and absorbed the stories – even if the spectator has not. The audience is now the outsider instead of her. She has established a bond between herself and the interviewees, while preventing the audience from approaching the women as she did.

Historiography has failed to include subaltern Algerian women, and while Djebar set out to include them, Lila's dominant, self-centred presence prevent both the audience and the director from attaining a relationship with the interviewees. Lila says 'I was 15 with a 100 years of suffering,' repeated a couple of times during the film, as a voice-off accompanying a still image of her face. The fact that the camera focuses so closely on Lila's face but not on the other women's faces acknowledges Djebar's struggle with the representation of all the women's stories through the lonely figure of Lila. Lila says: 'I want to see you, you the women of Mont Chenoua!' Yet having a closer look at the women is her privilege, not that of the spectators.

Solidarity is attained in *La Nouba*, only perhaps between Djebar and Lila. Djebar may not have been aware fully of fictional Lila's power in the film until the end. Her mirror image took on her own persona, and made *La Nouba* a docudrama that even incorporates surreal and fantastic elements, specifically through the extensive use of mirrors and shadows. As one another's mirror image, Lila and Djebar recognise in each other a vehicle through which they can learn about themselves. Djebar has admitted that she found it difficult to attain a closeness with the interviewees: she speaks as *close* as possible to, but never truly *with* the subaltern. The 'ego' and 'alter ego' take centre stage. The goal of the film is to question history as a narrative, and instead experiments with a fragmented physicality.

The problem with hybrid, transnational identities, then, is foregrounded in this film. Lila is capable of experiencing simultaneously both nothing and everything at the same time. She experiences the interstitial space between the two cultures and while she struggles with understanding both, she also has the ability to distance herself from both (Bensmaia, 1996: 879). The impossibility of representing the Algerian subaltern and a lack of solidarity between hybrid identities is highlighted, as Djebar shows how self-representation is the closest one can come to any type of representation. As Spivak (1988) has shown, the outsider, the intellectual, the one in a privileged enough position to be able to claim that they are representing the Other, may find it impossible to do so satisfactorily. Exploring their own reactions and recollections by taking in the stories and interviews with the other women, Lila and Djebar both have to deal with their inability to rectify what history has done wrong. A transnational straddling of two cultures, or a double consciousness, leads to an incomplete understanding of both.

In spite of the importance attached to the individual testimonies of the women, they do not receive full agency. Martin (2011) acknowledges that importance is attached to voices, but also to silences. It is in the silences, and their conspicuous presence in the otherwise busy soundtrack, that the gaps in Algerian historiography are foregrounded. Even though the women's stories are situated in reality and in memory, and thus make up the 'documentary' part of the docudrama, they hardly receive any on-screen time. The collectivity of the storytellers – however fragmented – is dismantled.

Djebar's outlook on the problems of her home country and on how to represent herself and the subaltern woman is not only an existential, but also a cinematic struggle. Documentary, as a form of film-making, 'exists along a fact–fiction continuum' (Hight and Roscoe, 2001), and this blurring of boundaries is exploited in *La Nouba*, through its hybrid protagonists as well as its hybrid form and style. As a mix between art film and docudrama, made for television, it revels in its fluidity. Questioning and denouncing the system of narrative cinema, documentary and politics, Djebar, with this film, refuses to give in to a logical, linear aesthetic, thereby asserting her very personal non-conformist feminist film-making style. Docudrama 'engages with reality through a highly personalised line of enquiry' (Chapman, 2009: 16), and this personal touch is emphasised by the fact that Djebar and Lila are established as one another's alter egos. As Khanna wrote about *La Nouba*: 'if a documentary is to have any relation to the real, the director has to know the subjects, and film what she finds representative of those subjects' (2008: 127). In *La Nouba*, the personal relationship with the subjects is extremely important not just for Lila's self-confidence, but also for the relationship between Djebar and her subject.

So, Djebar experiments with documentary, presenting an alternative version of a one-sided, male historiography, which does not necessarily mirror reality. She is exposing the lie of representational politics by playing fact off against fiction. Djebar questions the ethics and limitations of the documentary: as her central question is how to approach the Chenoua women, and how to let them speak in their turn, the film moves between fact and fiction, between the Chenoua tribe and Lila, and between outside and inside. *La Nouba*'s aesthetic pleasure is what drives the film forward, as there is no real linearity of plot or narrative. Khanna agrees that 'the merging of fiction and documentary draws attention to the impossibility of the unmediated presentation of materials on the part of the director, interviewer, and her subjects' (2008: 128) mainly because memory and the subjectivity of representation will always interfere.

If the documentary form intends objectivity through conducting interviews, the fictional aspect assures a more personally engaged approach. The camera-eye gives Djebar the opportunity to reflect on the state of the Algerian nation, and reveals her particular conceptualisation of individual and collective female identity. Mortimer has shown that the 'appropriation of the camera confirms the importance she attributes to women's vision in a Maghrebian society in which patriarchy controls the female gaze' (Mortimer, 2001: 212). As the first woman in Algeria to make a film, Djebar frankly returns the male gaze. At the same time, Lila's personal life comes under scrutiny as her strained relationship with her husband goes through a crisis precisely because of the contestation of the voyeuristic male gaze.

What makes *La Nouba* a unique film in Algerian film history is its female point of view and its anti-heroic and anti-linear narrative. Like the music of the Nouba, the film moves in cyclical movements around topics and around people, instead of towards closure. The amnesia that dominates writing on Algeria's history is described by both Ranjana Khanna (2008) and Guy Austin (2012) as either a remembering to forget (purposefully forgetting as the pain of reality is too hard to accept) or a forgetting to remember (simply forgetting the vital aspects that could change the perception of history). What Djebar is doing with *La Nouba*, is trying to move beyond this status quo of perpetual forgetting. The film acknowledges its own fragmented and incomplete nature. It highlights the subjectivity of testimony and does not deny that representation is always ambiguous. Yet at the same time, in the struggle to clarify that these forgotten aspects of history must be unearthed, Djebar challenges her subjects and her spectators to rethink historiography. The film problematises memory, testimony and the linearity of history as we know it, and adds to it a degree of doubt and scepticism, nurturing subjective thinking.

Images-son: Images and Sounds in *La Nouba*

The deliberately fragmented and fluid structure and narrative of *La Nouba* are paralleled in the 'mixed media' look of the film (Martin, 2011: 46). With archival footage of colonial images of Algeria, Lila's fictional story, the enactment of a myth and a story, and the documentary-style interviews, this is a filmic experience that foregrounds its construction out of fragments and, as such, it also emphasises that unity and coherence are myths of a certain type of history writing. The foregrounding of a multiplicity of voices is rooted in Djebar's experience as a writer. She describes her two films as an inherent part of her (written) oeuvre. As Mortimer has pointed out, 'linking the re-appropriation of the gaze to the word, the right to see (and be seen) to the right to speak (and be heard), the essay marks an important stage in Djebar's personal quest and explains her decision to become a filmmaker' (2001: 216). The orally transmitted stories of illiterate, rural women from Djebar's own region enable a discovery of the female side of Chenoua history, as well as a renewed insight into the author–film-maker's self. Her film-making is in fact literary: she 'regarded cinema as an art form in a rather negative light, as it didn't communicate the feeling of longevity, as certain kinds of books or music do' (Hillauer,

2005: 305). As her last novel was published in 1967, it had been ten years since Djebar had written, and while this has been attributed to writer's block, Djebar herself has admitted that it was mostly due to an uncertainty about writing about Algerians in French, the colonising language. Instead of words and language, then, she wanted to emphasise space and time. She said: 'making films for me it is not abandoning the word in favour of the image. It is making *images-son* [sound-images]. I wanted to return to the sources of language' (Naim, n.d.). Here we enter the structuralist realm: returning to the source of language is looking at Saussurian semiotics, where the word, or sign, refers to an image or a concept, or signifies, through the sound of the word, the signifier. This fits well with Djebar's interest in feminism and psychoanalysis, and her mixing of fiction and reality.

With this idea of mixing the imaginary and the symbolic, the realm of the image with the realm of language, Djebar reveals an interdependence between director and subject, between Djebar and Lila, between ego and alter ego: if she, as a Westernised intellectual, an outsider more than an insider, goes to Chenoua with a recorder and camera to listen to and to see these women, then she must also give them the opportunity to tell their stories their way. While the film is a journey of self-discovery and self-affirmation as Lila searches for her roots, at the same time, it is a history lesson for those who have created the limited, one-sided, male perspective on historically significant instances in which women are the victims of national amnesia.

Djebar has acknowledged the struggle she has with representation: her insistence on 'speaking close to or nearby' asserts the impossibility of speaking *about* the subaltern. 'Letting the women speak in their turn' is a phrase used at the start of the film that first explains the premise of the film, and next determines how the spectator receives the stories. It is time to let the women speak in answer to the overwhelmingly male voice speaking about Algeria. 'In turn' refers to the structure in which this will be done: one by one. But Lila's presence fragments the stories and contests the unified subjectivity. A fractured, fragmented subject position is brought forward, addressing an unidentified and variously interpretable 'you' as in 'you the women of Chenoua': at this early stage in the film, the 'you' stands in stark contrast to the 'I'.

There are two ways in which the film offers alternatives to straightforward narratives: in *La Nouba* songs and stories become corporeal expressions of the author's *écriture féminine*. The writer-director translates voices into music and songs. Traditional Andalusian music of the Nouba, a sort of call-and-response technique, is mixed with Béla Bartók's music, to which Djebar wrote the lyrics that an Algerian musician performed. The music is discordant, experimental and unusual. It expresses the inability of words to express fully the traumatic experience of war and silence. In the vein of *écriture féminine*, songs and stories forgo linearity, working against the realm of the symbolic and logical language, and instead highlight the cyclical nature of the Nouba songs and the repetition of the stories. The voice of the music is female and the music follows a cyclical structure. Songs are – just like stories – means of oral transmission of knowledge from the past. According to Djebar, women are the guardians of this knowledge. Oral literature consists of repetitions, asides, and returning themes and forms rather than logic, linear narrative progression. Film is not just image: it is also sound, orality. The structure of the musical Nouba takes centre stage.

The Nouba is rooted in the musical heritage of the Berber tribes of the Maghreb. It is a type of symphony in classical, medieval, Andalusian music, with seven specific rhythmic movements, one for each woman telling her story. The origin of the term is uncertain, although both Morocco and Algeria have in their heritage traditional music called Noubas, dating back to the time of El Andalus, the medieval Muslim conqueror of the Maghreb and the Spanish Peninsula (as we will see in Chapter 6 on Moroccan documentaries by Izza Génini, who also made a documentary on the Nûba). This was an era of great artistic and philosophical prosperity between the eighth and fifteenth centuries, during which Islam thrived politically, economically and culturally around the Mediterranean. In the Algerian and Moroccan dialects, Nouba means 'turn', referring to musicians and poets awaiting their turn to perform.

In North Africa, storytelling is the privilege of women. As Lila explains, grandmothers repeatedly told their grandchildren the stories of the past: 'as a little girl, in bed, I listened to granny every night tell in her own special way the story of our tribe'. The repetition of the oral stories allowed them to live in the dreams and memories of the children, and gave the women a particular power over these stories and over the children. These voices and stories, Djebar shows, have been drowned out by official history, but were never completely extinguished: 'so it was in a silent Algeria, old women whispering by night and their stories become wonders in the dreams of children. And history is revisited by the fire, in broken words and voices searching for one another.' Broken words and voices searching for one another illustrate the film-maker's realisation that while a narrative is desirable for the medium of film it is also necessarily unattainable for a traumatised Algeria. Nevertheless, individual stories are heard. The voices are beginning to be reclaimed even though they never coalesce to make one single narrative. They are told to Lila in an attempt to instigate a personal recollection of a subjective past. It illustrates that the trauma of the past in Algeria has not quite completely eliminated memory. The presence of these female voices ensures that at least in film-making, artists can show how official narratives of the past are often constructed by the state rather than by the people who lived it.

As we have seen, the simple foregrounding of women's voices in documentary is subversive (Bruzzi, 2000: 64). By including voices that would not normally be heard by official historiography, Djebar ensures that the gaps in memory are (partially) filled through radically new information. Moreover, Djebar's penchant for *écriture féminine* has become more than just writing: it has gained an audible voice that equally refuses Lacanian law and order. As a feminist author, Djebar inscribes the female voice and the physicality of the women into language through the quality of orality. This results in non-linear, cyclical and non-patriarchal texts. Until *La Nouba*, this was the privilege of the author, and in *La Nouba*, Djebar experiments with the voice-over, music and stories in the same way. According to Cixous, *écriture féminine* enables new freedoms and transformations due to its openness and fluidity. Ultimately, Djebar does not see such satisfaction in the form. While associative sounds and images do inscribe women's bodies into the *images-son* of *La Nouba*, the failure to produce consistent meaning between signifier and signified emphasises the fragmented nature of Algerian historiography, where women have been neglected and their stories ignored. The voices in the film are mediated by a traumatised woman who is physically very present in the words she utters. Her language, spoken, refuses the patriarchal language of linearity.

The intention on Djebar's part to speak with new voices explores the possibilities of representation as Spivak has problematised it. Khanna says: 'the semiotic, representative wounding signalled when woman is represented, gives testimony to the specificities of unrepresented crisis that women experience at the moment of the birth of a nation' (Khanna, 2008: 124). The subaltern here is again the woman, and it is the task of the Algerian feminist in Djebar to seek the voice of women to emancipate them and raise awareness of their role in the struggle for independence. The film being made for television, it becomes clear that the intention was to address women, and to encourage the realisation that women had a crucial role to play in independence. She creates a discourse 'within which the figure of woman is structured, and acknowledge a name that is not tied to patrilineal descent' (Khanna, 2008: 14). As Khanna sees it, agency and sovereignty over one's own life incorporate the subject as master and author of her own meaning.

The film is a platform and a receiver of the message of the women. It enables speaking and listening. But it also makes space for silences, highlighting that while amnesia brings silence, silence can also speak. Putting the uncanny centrally on screen in the form of the female subaltern problematises the very concept of representation. 'A representation of subalterns that signals a self-reflexive moment in representation, results in a moment in which self cannot simply speak the memory of trauma, but can enact a space in which silence is recognised as a symbolic space of political non-representation' (Khanna, 2008: 124). This self-reflexivity is shown in Lila's inability to speak on camera directly. Her voice is heard only in monologue, in voice-off, and she never visibly or audibly addresses anyone (except her daughter). What Lila says is uttered in the void of the off-screen non-reality of the film. She addresses no one in particular when she exclaims that she speaks, speaks and speaks. The uncertain identity of her addressee puts Lila in a state between worlds: the one of the listener and the one of the speaker.

We have seen that this hybrid film, an experimental docudrama, identified by Djebar herself as *images-son*, is made by someone with a hyphenated identity as French–Algerian, someone who is both an outsider and an insider. The interstitial nature of her speech parallels her transnational identity. Her hybrid identity and her transnational presence in Chenoua are explored and connected to the absence of voices of women who have been present all through history but whose voices have not been heard or identified. These gaps in Algerian history need to be filled with music, testimonies, recollections and associative storytelling. Djebar has said that 'I found fiction – filling the gaps in the collective memory – essential for me to be able to recreate those times in which I wished to dwell, and to try to put those distant days into their context' (Ringrose, 2006: 221). Moreover, the self-reflexivity of *La Nouba* emphasises the necessity of looking back at oneself critically. Due to the traumatic past and the ensuing amnesia, 'there is a moment in which the self cannot simply speak the memory of trauma but can enact a space in which silence – nonspeech – is recognized as a symbolic space of political nonrepresentation' (Khanna, 2008: 124). These silences foreground the gaps in history: they are 'the driving enigmas around which other narratives circle endlessly, unable to provide any answers' (Martin, 2011: 59). In film, silence points towards the image, the visible. The fact that visual representation gains importance, signals the breakdown of the voice and its inadequacy for the representation of a traumatic past. Gaps in history cannot be filled by stories and testimonies exclusively. The unrepresentable may be expressible only in images: 'the uncanny could become reified on the screen' (Khanna, 2008: 124).

Aiming to let the subaltern speak for herself in this case is not enough. Questioning the ability of the film-maker to represent or speak for the subaltern is a vital task in the post-colonial period in which Djebar was making this film. The stream-of-consciousness-like technique shows how the film-maker–author is not only writing or speaking, but listening and looking as well.

Listening to the Nouba

Djebar creates a female space, with undulating mountains, women roaming the paths of the countryside, and a much-discussed cave sequence where the uteral psychopathology of the cave is foregrounded. In these female spaces, the women in the film can finally speak and listen to one another. Lila mediates through an interior monologue in voice-off. This voice-off is dominant: Lila never speaks directly, 'her voice has an acousmatic-like quality. Although we see whose voice it is, we are seldom given the opportunity to make the visual character coincide with the haunting inner voice we hear' (Martin, 2011: 55). As a result, it feels like a disembodied voice off-screen. The rest of the women tell their story 'in turn', and Lila listens. Through Lila's negotiation, we learn that the interviewed women have a familial bond with her: they are aunts or mothers of friends. Being part of the tribe counts as being a member of the family, as they are so close-knit that Lila says at one point that 'all the women, wandering in the past, become my mother. I am the little girl who once drank from their hands'. The interconnected revelations by the women are made possible by the intimate setting in which they are interviewed. Their collective identity is the mother figure, and the land that they occupy is the motherland. Even though she is an outsider, Lila asserts that she is part of the tribe, by making it a motherland and making the interviewees her 'mothers'. The collectivity and the sense of family are crucial for the trust that needed to be established in order to convince the women to tell their stories: one story leads to another. This carefully constructed trust relationship is rooted in solidarity, and a knowledge and acceptance of interdependence.

Bensmaia explores the idea of lying fallow to describe Lila's sense of self and sense of belonging. Lying fallow, he explains, consists of three conditions: acceptance of the self as a separate person; tolerance of non-communication; and a reduced relatedness to and from the environment. While Lila herself manages to deal with these three conditions, and she eventually learns to experience freedom within the community to which she has now connected, in her egocentric quest she leaves the interviewees and spectators out. Lila stands between interviewees and spectators. Lila is the go-between, while the spectator is excluded from the solidarity triangle. When Lila achieves solidarity with her interviewees, it is through accepting herself as a hyphenated identity and by choosing to lie fallow. It removes Lila, says Bensmaia, from the symbolic terrain that enclosed her, and she gains the freedom to encounter surreality (Bensmaia, 1996: 880). In other words, the suffering from patriarchal oppression and Lacanian symbolic language ends only when her confidence rises as she accepts her own interstitial persona, as an imaginary Chenouan.

In *La Nouba* the reinsertion of voice and look into the history of women is a reaction against the enforced silences of amnesia and trauma. As Mortimer writes, Djebar has ascertained that 'women's cinema – as much in the Third World as in the Old World – begins with the desire for the word' (Mortimer, 2001: 217). While silence is a tool in the film to draw attention to the image, breaking the silence is the central concern. Listening to what is said or sung is the main task for Djebar, Lila and the spectator. Female testimony, sung or spoken, takes the form of two distinct types of expression. On the one hand, we have interviews mediated through an indirect voice-off: the things we hear as spectators. On the other hand, we have direct silences, breaks in the narrative and between the songs. Again, then, we see a consolidation of juxtapositions.

The silence is most oppressive when Lila is filmed inside the house with her husband, while the voice of the collective roams outside among the women in the hills of Chenoua. Yet *La Nouba* is about silences as much as it is about female expression. First, Lila is a very quiet diegetic woman, who hardly ever says anything on screen, even though she is a very talkative extra-diegetic storyteller (Martin, 2011: 58). Moreover, Lila is quiet about certain things that are shown rather than explained: in flashbacks or dream sequences, we witness events and see things that remain unexplained. Secondly, Martin says, the women – while they are ostensibly coaxed out of their silences – still leave out considerable aspects of their stories. The audience is left with additional questions that Lila does not ask, and an explanation is certainly not offered. These silences not only represent the gaps left in history, they also emphasise Lila's intent to just listen, without forcing the interviewees into saying anything that they do not want to. It ensures a fluid development between interviews, where associative tendencies drive the voice-over forward rather than a clear structure. However, these silences are either foregrounded and listened to or broken by women who speak in their turn; women who perform the nouba.

The experimental nature of *La Nouba* reflects the exploration of memory, and the manner in which to fill in the gaps that have been left, or the violence that has been done to memory. The trauma of the event leaves an incomplete memory, as the event is incomprehensible. Trauma theorist Cathy Caruth reveals the implications of trauma for concepts such as temporality and historicity. Caruth claims that the pathology of traumatic experience should not be defined by the event itself nor by the distortion of that event, but by the structure of its experience (Caruth, 1996: 4).

Trauma is a physical and psychological reaction to an event that 'was precisely *not known* in the first instance – [and] returns to haunt the survivor later on' (Caruth, 1996: 4). Caruth says that the victim departs from the traumatic event while it is happening: one experiences the trauma in a numbed state of mind. The victim closes off his or her psyche in order to protect him- or herself and survive the event. Lila is haunted by her own and others' silences and by the gaps in a traumatic history. Equally, her husband Ali is traumatised by war as his dreams are dominated by fragmentary reconstructions of what he has repressed in memory. The traumatic event is not only unknown due to the overwhelming anxiety that it imposes upon the victim, but also because the event was never fully known at all. Trauma is a temporal delay that carries the individual beyond the shock of the first moment. By placing latency *in* the traumatic accident, Caruth claims that the traumatised never fully experience the event and thus can never discover the truth of what happened. Likewise, reality is unknown or unknowable, and very hard to narrate. Silences or gaps in memory and historiography appear. These gaps in memory need to be filled in with a return to the event and recollections that may or may not be the truth, but will be truthful: this makes docudrama the ideal medium. The departure from the traumatic experience itself preserves a literality of the event that strengthens the accuracy of historical facts in memory. The leaving behind of the whole trauma – the event and the recurrence – also contributes to the accumulation of historical knowledge when testifying finally becomes feasible for the traumatised. Filling gaps in reality with stories makes history a narrative, a testimony that can be comprehended.

Accordingly, in *La Nouba* the possibility of narrating and understanding is problematised. Lila, who left behind the trauma of the Algerian war, has accumulated historical knowledge that stretches beyond the locality of Chenoua. Yet the contextualisation in the film is highly complex and presented as an impossibility. The dream-like voice-off and the deeply unsettling egoism of Lila prevent her from narrating history. Instead, she voices fragments of her own and mixes them with mediated testimonies. The inaccessibility of truth provokes a crisis in history: the traumatic event refuses historical boundaries. The trauma is apparent in a time and place other than the one in which it originally occurred. History is no longer straightforwardly referential. The return of Lila/Djebar to Cherchell is a prerequisite for the repressed to return not only within herself, but also for the women of Chenoua.

Caruth suggests that we should resituate history in our understanding and permit '*history* to arise where *immediate understanding* may not' (Caruth, 1996: 11). The traumatised carry a burdensome history with them, or have become part of a history that they cannot possess. 'In the Lacanian view . . . trauma is associated with the Real and is outside and resistant to any symbolic expression. Trauma's initial effect is to disrupt understanding, language, identity – to rip apart the symbolic order, to efface memory' (Berger, 1999: 79). The 'Real' of the traumatic event therefore becomes intangible for narratives, which intrinsically construct a meaningful symbolic order. As Djebar points out, the similarity between the real and the symbolic is never absolute, no representation will ever adequately represent any entity. Entering into as close a relationship as possible with the testimony-teller is the only option for Lila. The seeming impossibility of representation is associated with the notions of testimony and consequently also with memory. 'Testimony tries to approach the unknowable and in doing so, it assists the difficult path of traumatic memory.' If one equates testimony with narrative, then the previous findings by Caruth demonstrate the complication of testimony: 'to speak is impossible, and not to speak is impossible' (Caruth, 1995: 154). The urge to testify is so strong that all eight women tell their stories, but the mediation through a traumatised Lila and the fragmented editing of the film illustrate the precarious status of testimony as truth and history.

Through these stories, songs and testimonies, amnesia ebbs away and memories return. Anne Donadey has used the image of palimpsest (1996) to illustrate the violence done to the past and the gaps that need to be filled in by memory. She claims that the scars of the past can be healed only by over-reading the French past and by breaking the enforced silence, especially women's silence. She says that the narrative in films like *La Nouba* is fragmented and cyclical precisely to indicate the problems with linearity of history. Here, the gaps, or indentations on the page, are over-written with new or returning Algerian, female memories. The reconstitution of history must be achieved through women's testimonies in order to reinstate their agency into the collective memories.

The multiplicity of voices in the film not only includes unofficial fragments of a collective memory, but also serves as an act of collective rectifying a one-sided, patriarchal and heroic national story. The many voices give each other the courage to keep on speaking and testifying in a 'female polyphony' (Donadey, 1996: 52). This polyphony not only explores the submerged, whispering voices, but it also leads the structure (or lack of it) of the musical, cyclical plot. The fragmentary nature and the imprecise identity of the storytellers enable a generalisation of the testimonies, exacerbated by the disorientating lack of action, plot line and logic. While orality and *écriture féminine* ensure that the testimonies are scattered and fragmentary, their imprecise multiplicity, the lack of subjectivity for the interviewees and Lila's mediation offer the possibility of seeing this group of testimonies as an alternative to official historiography.

Apart from speech, the act of listening is emphasised, as Lila is shown to lean in, often with her back to the audience, creating an immediate space for the voices to echo. It is through Lila's listening that the women are encouraged to tell their stories in the first place. Because of the trust relationship, the women manage to tell highly personal stories, and Lila absorbs these in an effort to grasp her family history and a new national history. The testimonies of others are tools that help her to reconstruct a fragmented personal and collective history. From the start, Lila fully intends to listen to the voices of the Chenoua women. She visits the women and stands beside them to listen to them. Her 'desire to (learn to) listen, to ask questions, to glean something from or about others by listening to them' (Bensmaia, 2003: 86) reflects a belief in the ability of the subaltern woman to speak and to represent herself.

However, the challenging value of *La Nouba* lies precisely in Djebar's and Lila's struggles to attain the goal the film-maker has set out for herself at the outset of the film. If *La Nouba* is a film that allows women to speak in their turn, then they speak only when Lila has decided it is their turn. When Lila expresses her tortured chant 'I speak, I speak, I speak' it not only emphasises that she is expressing herself in the voices of others, but also that it is the 'I', Lila, that takes centre stage instead of the other women. Her off-screen monologue dominates and her agency is emphasised. Djebar as well as Lila speak next to and as close as possible to the subaltern women: it often remains uncertain who is speaking and whether they are conscious of their agency, because the main voices can be heard only in voice-off. The women never speak closely enough to the camera for the spectator to *see* them speak. It is an aspect of *La Nouba*'s docudrama form that there is more focus on the fictional character Lila, who is used as a vehicle to interpret and transmit other women's voices to the spectator, but also never speaks on screen. Through the non-synchronous sound, two things are foregrounded: the literary quality of what is being said, as well as the fact that Lila is mediating the testimonies of the other women. In her (not the other women's) facial expressions we can see how she complements her verbal utterances with visual feeling. Djebar's preoccupation with voices and testimonies pushes a visual understanding of the many faces to the background and brings Lila's individuality to the foreground in the landscape of women. The struggle with representation is therefore underlined in the film. Self-reflexivity and self-doubt of the hyphenated transnational identity, and the existential struggle with form makes *La Nouba* a film that challenges its spectators, its actors, its interviewees, its director and, more than anything, the amnesia of Algerian history as a whole.

Seeing the Nouba of the Women

It is not only music, songs and voices that work together in *La Nouba*: so do spaces and gazes. Djebar has said that the more space a woman has, the more balanced she is (Hillauer, 2005: 307), and this is illustrated in the film through the relationships between Lila, the interviewees, the camera-eye and the spectator. The gaze is a politicised notion in Algerian cinema, as 'the prohibition against woman seeing and being seen is at the heart of Maghrebian patriarchy, an ideological system in which the master's eye alone exists' (Mortimer, 2001: 214). Djebar attributes much importance to women's space, as a space to gain confidence in also provides the possibility of returning the male gaze. The return of the gaze is the feminist act at the core of her films: Djebar explores the recasting of the female gaze back against the dominating male gaze. Yet it is not only protest against the male gaze that defines her work. Djebar is equally interested in women looking upon one another, especially when considering their individual personalities and the differences between them (class, ethnicity or geography). The network of gazes in *La Nouba* brings into question three ways of ordering the Algerian world: the spatiality of inside versus outside, the gendered gazes of women versus men, and the differences between the protagonist as a transnational woman as opposed to the local collectivity of the women she interviews.

In order to look at the gaze in *La Nouba*, it is necessary to explore the contrast between the gaze of the camera-eye inside (in an enclosed space) or outside (in nature and the hills of Mt Chenoua). We have seen how Lila is free to roam the countryside to interview the Chenoua women, while her husband remains inside, dependent on his wheelchair. The exterior is a beautiful landscape: the sea, dunes, country roads and hills. Panoramic views show in travelling shots the wide wild ruggedness of the region. Lila encounters musicians on her way, mansions, ruins. She is renewing the contact with her childhood and the region in which she grew up, and rediscovers her family roots. Her gaze is one of awe and a deep longing for remembering. It encompasses the landscape, nature and architecture, as well as the people. She takes in the beauty of nature and the vastness of the Mediterranean, which reflects not only her openness of spirit, but also the vastness of memory. The bright colours and romantic hues suggest nostalgia for the past, as memories resurface and her confused state of mind attempts to gain more clarity.

In contrast, the inside is an enclosed space in which Lila and Ali fail to function as a family. The domestic space is where the male, patriarchal gaze still needs to be challenged most powerfully; and this is where the intricate politics of the male and female gaze are explored in more detail. Her restlessness inside the house is a direct effect of the oppressive domestic atmosphere. Lila's refusal of Ali's gaze is pointed out at the very beginning of the film. She addresses Ali saying 'I don't want to be seen; I don't want you to look at me,' as she is turned towards the wall in a room. She closes her eyes and hits the wall in frustration. Djebar explores Lila's state of mind by filming her with her back against the wall, while the voice-off expresses her anxiety. The camera stays close to Lila's skin, making the suffocation palpable. From this point of view, a remarkable semiotic filmic language explores walls, windows and doorways. 'Doorways frame a fragmented subject whose form appears almost indistinguishable from her shadow' (Khanna, 2008: 127). Their frames often surround Lila, her husband and their daughter. The static nature of the shots inside the small house enhances the effect of the frames: inertia, solitude and confinement stand in stark contrast to windows and doors that suggest an escape to the outside. White walls and dark shadows reveal a chiaroscuro that feels threatening and nightmarish. Inside, Lila is only a shadow of her outside self: as she searches for her identity, she is a dark shadow on the walls of a small house, a prisoner of her unknown past.

The chiaroscuro also illustrates the highly uncomfortable relationship between husband and wife. For Lila doors and windows offer the opportunity to flee the darkness and tension inside the house, but for Ali the bars in front of the window emphasise his immobility and confinement. Lila's constant gazing out of the door or the window mirror her rebellion against the stifling atmosphere. Her husband barely speaks and only moves a few metres within the house. Lila flees this state of inertia. Here, she is perhaps not lying fallow (as Bensmaia argued), but rather actively trying to escape that fallowness, searching for herself by approaching the women outside. Her voyage inward, then, is contrasted to her ability to really explore the outside. However, the camera does not engage with the surroundings *unless* it is in function of Lila's exploration of her inner state of mind.

Figure 4.1 Ali, framed by the door to Lila's room can gaze upon his wife, but cannot approach her, in *La Nouba* (1978) © Assia Djebar

Walls and shadows reflect a tense atmosphere between husband and wife. Doorways in the walls separate them physically, but enable Ali to consistently keep his gaze focused on Lila's body. Their communication skills are problematic. Even in close-ups their faces are non-communicative. While Ali's facial expressions remain literally in the dark, Lila's face is so expressive in her frustrated and pained expressions that it becomes almost unbearable to watch closely the play of shadows on her face. The turmoil she experiences is visualised through numerous close-ups. She almost uses the camera as a mirror to see herself, instead of as a window through which to connect to other women. When this proves to be fruitless, she closes her eyes and turns towards the wall.

Where men stereotypically occupy the outside world as well as the domestic sphere, and women's roles are limited to staying inside, in *La Nouba* these roles are reversed. Lila challenges the patriarchal system by refusing Ali's voyeuristic gaze, on the one hand, and reappropriating and frankly returning the gaze, on the other hand. The male patriarchal gaze is subverted. Djebar's revolt against the voyeur, against the dominatingly male gaze 'charts woman's transformation from passive object under patriarchal and colonial rule to active subject of her own discourse' (Mortimer, 2001: 214). Ali's immobility and muteness put him firmly in the domestic sphere, as if Djebar is showing him what it is like to suffer from typically patriarchal limitations. Lila flees Ali's gaze, both in the filmic present and in flashbacks that explain their relationship and Ali's accident (and even in these flashbacks, the communication between Lila and her husband is non-existent. They gaze upon one another, usually when the other is not looking).

As spectators, we watch Ali watching women. The voyeuristic gaze is central here. Ali is always seen inside, in his wheelchair, dozing off in semi-darkness, with a dark look on his face. He never speaks but is constantly gazing, through barred windows, at his wife, at the women in the courtyard and at visitors, until a little girl closes the window shutters on him. The child temporarily suspends his ability to gaze. The film is 'subversive of the voyeuristic pleasures that characterize narrative cinema' (Khannous, 2001: 45). The fact that a young girl closes the shutters indicates that Ali's gaze is obvious to all, and that it is intrusive. Lila's shadow and the light and darkness in the room play a vital role in this scene: she notices the girl closing the shutters, and Ali is caught out in his voyeuristic act. Again, they do not look at each other: Ali sees her shadow and looks down, guiltily.

The male gaze is further subverted through the woman director's eye behind the camera. Djebar sees her camera as a camera-eye specifically of the veiled, oppressed woman. She takes the voyeuristic gaze, colonialist and orientalist, and appropriates it: the omnipresent Algerian woman is unseen but she can see, from behind her veil. The haik, the white veil worn in Algeria, is draped in such a way as to leave only one small opening for the eye looking out. Djebar uses this image in the film, in free association during an extended sequence of edits showing city life in Cherchell at the start of the film, and thus emphasises the woman's eye, the camera-eye, looking back. In an important scene inside the house, Ali is at the bedroom door gazing at a sleeping Lila. She is unaware of his gaze and of his attempts to rise from his wheelchair to approach her. Whereas the camera is usually static inside the house, at this point it becomes animated, a shadow taunting Ali. Djebar reveals herself and her camera-eye here, and she subverts the male voyeuristic gaze:

> turning slowly around the room, [the camera's] eye envelops the sleeping woman. In this way, the camera affects an important transfer of power, appropriating the control that eludes Ali. Her eye behind the lens, the woman filmmaker successfully challenges the patriarchal gaze. (Mortimer, 2001: 218)

The camera first zooms in twice on Lila's sleeping face, deliberately. Then it turns back to Ali, who is out of focus and dared to try to do the same.

The camera-eye moves, hand-held, expressing someone approaching Lila, building up tension, questioning who will be able to claim ownership of the sleeping woman. When the camera turns back to see what Ali is doing, it is mocking his inability to move and ensuring that he, defeated, sits back down again in the wheelchair. This is repeated when Lila takes a bath. Ali again gazes at her. The camera-eye turns from Lila to Ali, as in a contest of gazes. But this time Lila is aware of his eyes on her. She deliberately turns her back on him and continues bathing, talking to her daughter and ignoring him, denying him the satisfaction of seeing her nudity while still suggestively allowing him to gaze in her direction in her presence. The camera-eye joins the two women, again mocking Ali's passivity. There is no active involvement of Ali in the gazes that he casts upon Lila.

At the same time, Lila is also learning to gaze upon herself and to find freedom in that self-reflexivity. While doors and windows offer ways to move outside, a number of mirrors confront Lila with her own image, which inside is still subject to the male gaze. Her mirror image makes her realise that she is an entity in her self, like the child learning to associate its mirror image with his or herself. She learns to look at herself. However, Lila fails to fully understand her identity: she cannot detach herself from the two mother countries and especially not from the women in her tribe, her mother figures. The source of this insecurity might be the loss of her mother at an early age. Towards the end of the film, however, this mirror image gains confidence, as Lila combs her hair and looks satisfied with what she sees. Her look outward has helped her with how to look inward, to restore a broken or forgotten identity.

The network of gazes goes further than the domestic sphere, it is not only husband and wife who gaze upon one another, but also a network of women, interviewer and interviewees, who see each other. However, in the open space of Mt Chenoua, where Lila interviews the women, the camera keeps its distance. We hardly ever see the interviewees in close-up, and, mostly, their subjectivities blur into one. Even though she set out to provide Algerian women with a voice, she struggles, like Spivak, with subjective representation. The camera remains at such a distance from the contributors that it leaves no room even for 'speaking nearby'. As such, Lila fails to speak *with* or *close to*, and instead speaks *for* the women, *instead of*. As pointed out before, all stories told in the film are told in function of reconstructing Lila's agency.

Djebar battles with feminist activist theories and, in a way, proves that even filmic language and *écriture féminine* are subject to the patriarchal rule of the Lacanian symbolic order. She problematises identification and individuality. The identity of the women, their faces and individualities are blurred, as the camera does not focus on their faces or bodies while they are speaking. Perhaps this illustrates again the veiled camera-eye, which can explore intimacy inside in the private sphere, but fails to do so in public. The eye, able to see past or out of the veil, is the one Djebar uses to see through the camera-eye. Appropriating the male gaze, they return it rather than being the centre of it. The film then negates the all-encompassing power of the male gaze through the collective of the female gaze returned to the camera. A focus on Djebar and Lila instead of on her interviewees, highlights the non-synchronicity between image and sound in this experimental film.

The lack of close-ups in *La Nouba* does create a distance between the subject and the spectator even as it creates more freedom for the interviewees to speak. As there is no intrusive camera that could potentially influence behaviour, and because Lila is regarded as a member of the extended family, she has the potential of gaining better access to the stories and the intimate details of the past lives of the women from her tribe if the documentary camera does not intrude. As such, Lila can create a more intimate, personal atmosphere. That this is not shared with the spectator is, again, an indication that representation is complex and problematised in this film. While Lila gets the whole story, as she would be able to interpret extra-textual, visual, facial expressions, the spectator is left with only the words, as Lila makes no attempt to share or discuss the circumstances of the interviews with the spectator. The context in which the interviews are conducted remains a mystery, while it is potentially crucial for the interpretation and transmission of certain liminal experiences. Where understanding and listening are central to the premise of the film, a true solidarity is made impossible. Djebar's preoccupation with voices and testimonies pushes the visual quality of these women's faces to the background, at least for the spectator.

The ending of *La Nouba* further reinforces Lila's subjectivity and centrality. Lila addresses the spectator directly and places herself firmly in the presence of the women of Chenoua. She says 'You the spectator, you hide yourself. But we shall look at ourselves in the pure light of day. All that was difficult, it will become easy. Leave the land of exile behind, we will reign in freedom and joy.' This is the acknowledgement of a turning point for Lila. She is finally able to identify with the Chenoua women. The 'I' and the 'you' (the first and third person) from the start of the film have changed into a 'we' and a 'you', and so a more communal understanding of her own belonging to the Chenoua mountains has been established. As a history of women who speak in their turn, the film emphasises the strength of the female voice and the importance attached to it by the film-maker. For Djebar, it is important to express the voices of women, speaking in the first or third person and bringing the living word and the lived experience onto the page [or screen]. These are voices which, by speaking for themselves, have escaped the objectifying hold of the historian's pen. [I want to] recapture its presence through the multiple, polyphonic voices of women speaking history. (Ringrose, 2006: 224)

Lila changes and with her, her relationship with the women she interviews transforms significantly. From a confused, singular woman failing to represent the women of Chenoua, she becomes their child able to represent herself. She starts to see her mother in all of them, and eventually manages to become one of them, once she has been able to accept herself as an interstitial person. From being the only individual with agency in the film, she becomes more critical of her observation of the women until she realises that all she requires to understand them is to accept herself.

La Zerda, ou les chants de l'oubli (1982)

After *La Nouba*, Djebar made a second, less well-known film in 1982, *La Zerda*. Like *La Nouba*, it is inherently connected to music and testimony, but it is very different in form and style. *La Zerda* is much more clearly made in the Third Cinema tradition of militant cinema, a straightforward documentary with an agenda for reassessing French colonial impact on Algerian life. One of the reasons the film is never discussed is that *La Zerda* is hard to find, and almost never shown in public, perhaps because it is, more than *La Nouba*, a product of its time that has not aged as well as the experimental nature of *La Nouba*. Like *La Nouba*, it was made for RTA, and it won the Special Prize for best historical film at the 1983 Berlin International Film Festival, but apart from a one-off private screening by and for Le Cercle des Amis d'Assia Djebar in 2011 in Paris and Haus der Kulturen der Welt (HKW) in Berlin in 2014, I know of no other occasions on which this film has been screened in public. It is archived in the Centre Culturel Algérien in Paris. Half of the film (25 minutes of 58 minutes) is, since 2012, also available on YouTube, in Arabic and without subtitles.

La Zerda is a poetic-political film-essay, showcasing a montage of photographic images and cinematic footage shot by colonial film-makers, of a Maghreb under submission of the French. A collaboration with her then-husband, poet Malek Alloula, it analyses the colonial gaze, which is challenged in the poetic, forceful voice-over. A contemplative montage of black-and-white images shot between 1912 and 1942, is edited together in such a way as to tease out cinematic and political injustices and accuse the coloniser of voyeuristically gazing upon the peoples of North Africa.

Its montage of colonial images combined with rapid zooms, pans and diagonally shot slogans really place it within the purview of Third Cinema in Algeria. As in *La Nouba*, the clash between sound and images, and the non-synchronous sound, makes what is being said and shown important separately as well as together. The discord is not just apparent in the non-synchronicity, but also in the clash between the apparent content of the images and the explicit content of the spoken words.

The Zerda is a feast, a celebration, which, as the voice-over states at the start of the film, is being gazed upon by the French, and under scrutiny of the exoticist gaze, loses its power. As a ceremony, the Zerda was and remained for a long time a mystery to the coloniser. The images we see in the film are of Berber men and women dancing at moussems, or festivals, in traditional dress. The Berber culture is known for its celebratory lifestyle, with moussems being of vital importance for the continuation of particular rituals and traditions in the Maghreb. Songs and dances are an inherent part of these testimonies of the past, but the anthropological gaze of the coloniser, appropriating the rituals and de-mystifying them, is seen to have stolen the particularity of the rituals.

So what we see on the screen are images that are intended to show how the coloniser is gaining knowledge and power over the colonised in North Africa. Consequently, these images ostensibly show collaboration, mutual respect, and efforts on both French and Algerian sides towards mutual understanding and peaceful togetherness. However, what the voice-overs underline is discordance. The voices contradict what is happening on the screen, and accuse the coloniser rather than acknowledging the mutual efforts. The voice-over consists of performance poetry in French and Arabic, some of it performed by Djebar herself. It is experimental, tonal poetry, where the subjectivity of the performer is highlighted and assimilated into a returning 'we' and 'our'. As in *La Nouba*, this 'we' contrasts to a 'them', which can be said to refer to a non-Maghreb coloniser or a French audience. The introduction of the film immediately places the speaker in the centre of the narrative:

> Photographers and filmmakers have flocked to a Maghreb totally submissive and silenced, to take pictures . . . *La Zerda* is a feast that they have seized from us. Despite their images, and from beyond the scope of their shooting eyes, we tried to remove other images, fragments of a despised average . . . Behind the veil of this exposed reality woke anonymous voices that re-collected or re-imagined the soul of a unified Maghreb, our past.

However, the speaker is impossible to identify. More than in *La Nouba*, it is a collective voice, people agreeing with and expanding on one another's anti-colonial statements. But these voices remain anonymous, apart from the fact that they identify very strongly as Maghrebin, or North African. The voice-over in this introductory statement explicates this unified Maghreb as a reflection of the anonymous voices. And we do not just have unidentified voices: because of the rejection of synchronous sound in this film, also comparable to the non-synchronous sound and voice-off in *La Nouba*, the faces remain unidentified. We cannot link voices on the soundtrack to faces on the screen. Instead of identification, spectators are encouraged to explore their capacity for solidarity. This suits the political nature of the film: militant Third Cinema aimed to incite solidarity in its audiences in order to gain active supporters for a cause, rather than passive sympathisers.

It is also within this spirit of Third Cinema aesthetic that the film really explores the power of melancholia. Brisley, in her research on Algerian literature, has argued for a de-pathologisation of melancholia, and has explored the reconceptualisation of melancholia as an 'ethico-political model of remembrance that safeguards the memory of the lost or margin-alised other' (2012: 61), rather than a pathological response to loss in the Freudian sense. While there is undoubtedly a sense of mourning and loss, and of accusations and acknowledgement of responsibility that lies with the coloniser, *La Zerda* also offers a sense of empowerment through the bringing together of certain types of image and text or sound.

Like the voices, the images are not credited. We do, however, get infor-mation on the location of the shots: we travel from Fez in Morocco, to Tunis, Cairo, Algiers and Paris, as well as a host of other strategic cities in Algeria, such as Ghardaia, Constantine, Oran and Biskra. The images are presented in a chronological fashion, from Fez in 1911, 'still independent for a few months', to 1942, again in Morocco, when the Allied Forces are stationed in North Africa. In between, images of French entry into the cities are shown to be triumphalist – the French are 'reçu un peu partout' – but ultimately ridiculed, especially in parallel shots of a mosque being inaugurated in Paris while the church arrives in Algiers. The voice-over explains that the mosque is planned in the wake of the First World War, when over 50,000 Algerians died for France. The juxtaposition of this image and voice-over with the image of the French colonialists arriving in Algiers to the sound of French marching music for the inauguration of the church, really illustrates the irony in the montage.

This irony is equally reflected in the titles of the 'chants', or songs, of oblivion. The first song is 'Chant de l'insoumission', or 'The Song of Disobedience'. In the part of the film dedicated to this song, the line 'we were the masters yesterday, servants today' is repeated several times, as is

'You beat us like a drum, cut our words.' With these words, Djebar points out the awareness of the consequences of colonial rule and the earlier period of self-rule. She shows how there is no correspondence between coloniser and colonised. Archival material shows women dancing and men riding their horses during the moussems. These festivals are historically very significant to the regional identity of Berber culture, and continue to form an inherent part of Maghrebi cultural celebrations.

In the second song, 'Chant de l'intransigeance et la guerre des guerrillas', or 'Song of Determination and Guerrilla War', the voice-over becomes increasingly forceful and angry, elaborating explicitly on the developments of the French victory over Sultan Abdelkrim in the Rif region in northern Morocco, the presence of the French Resident in Algeria and specifically the visit of Gaston Doumergue, President of the Republic. In May 1930, he visited Constantine to celebrate 100 years of allegiance between Algeria and France. The footage of this event shows the Berber population bidding farewell to the president enthusiastically, with a moussem apparently dedicated to him. The voice-over here is angry and repetitive, unpacking the French exoticist attitude towards these people and images with the phrase 'le ventre vide et les pieds nus', thus pointing out the stark contrast between the imagined celebratory atmosphere of the French president and the underlying reality of poverty of the 'desert people', as they are called in the original footage.

The third song, 'Chant de l'insolation et des siècles couchés dans les sables', or 'Song of Discomfort and Centuries Asleep Under the Sand', starts with images of women in close-up, as well as ancient rock drawings. These act as referents to ancient indigenous culture, which is juxtaposed with images of increasing French presence in the heartland of Algeria. Three shoe-shine boys are working on one man's boots, beggars stare into the camera, while soldiers march triumphantly and French women frivolously go swimming in the afternoon sun. The voice-over states that these images establish themselves as further 'punches in the nose, the throat and the knees'. The increasingly intense 'regard' of the French intimidates the people on the screen and offends the female voice-over, again increasingly angry and incensed. In Touggourt, in 1935, we witness the Feast of the Date, and the voice-over states how those celebrating suffer under the gaze of the coloniser: 'What will remain of our feasts one day? We no longer dance for our joy but for mourning.' This line directly points out the link between the colonisers' gaze and their appropriating power, as it associates celebrations with melancholia. The more the coloniser gazes, the more the Algerian/Berber will hide self-consciously. Djebar compares these images of Algeria with images of Morocco, and focuses on the tanners of Fes, who are also burdened by the colonisers' relentless gaze, but 'Morocco abides with its ancient cities and the ardour of its people', thus pointing out the difference in colonial history and confidence between Morocco and Algeria.[2] Djebar finishes this chant with images of people on the move, migrating: in Algiers in 1936 'a whole population moves: farmers to cities, the young abroad, the old become pilgrims and go to Mecca'. The melancholia and mourning in this chant are palpable in the contrasts between what is being shown and what is being said. The irony in the juxtaposition of visuals and voice-overs is not humorous but painful, and really shows the power of montage for Third Cinema film-makers.

The fourth and final song, 'Chant de l'émigration et de ceux qui partent en esclaves des peuples du Nord', or 'Song of Emigration and of Those Who Leave to Become Slaves of the People of the North', starts from this premise of a Third Cinema militant cinematic style. We see still images of children and women, zooming in and out, and panning over the surface diagonally. We see those that have arrived in France, and are looking for a place to live and for a job to sustain them. However, this is not seen as immigration or integration: the title of the song explicitly states that those arriving in France from the Maghreb are doing so in order to become enslaved by the people of the North. The pessimism of the title of the chant, and of these images, however, is now contrasted to the assertive statement that 'North Africa, on the eve of the war, rediscovers its strategic importance.' This phrase, of course, refers to a regaining of consciousness and confidence. The German and French troops fighting over control of the Mediterranean and North African trade routes and the Suez Canal, asserted the strategic importance of the region. Djebar here points out the ambiguity of this fact: on the one hand, it acknowledges the value of the region (for foreign as well as indigenous powers), but, on the other hand, it also shows the continued interest in and desire for this land. Indeed, she states at the end of the film that Maghrebins continued to serve the French for a long time even after colonialism, and points out that the presence of the Americans in Morocco (mainly in Tangier) was just another indication of the inconsiderate occupation of the north of Africa by foreign powers (whether these were military or literary).

The four chants of disobedience, obstinacy, discomfort and emigration, all show that the colonisation of the Maghreb by the French was something to rebel against, especially since images available *to* the people of North Africa reflected fabricated realities that did not correspond with the reality *of* North Africans. Djebar used television to reach an audience and raise awareness through the strategies of Third Cinema, a type of cinema that had taken root with the militant cineastes of the Algerian War for Independence, and continued to be practiced throughout the 1970s and the 1980s. Djebar then was the first woman to employ the strategies of Third Cinema, with visual references to Solanas' and Getino's *Hour of the Furnaces* in the way she edited together images and words. The available images needed to be challenged as inadequate for the representation of Algerian and other North African experiences of colonialism. As the archive perhaps failed to deliver any images that did illustrate that side of (hi)story, Djebar adopted and adapted those images that were available, and appropriated them for her purposes. With the inclusion of rebellious slogans and militant editing techniques, she achieved a film that incites through juxtaposition. Returning phrases such as 'le regard' and 'le ventre vide et les pieds nus' acknowledge her political and cultural agenda of returning the gaze and reappropriating cultural expression through traditional zerdas, in order to enable self-expression and identity formation. That *La Zerda* first stood out at the festival in Berlin and subsequently disappeared off the radar, is one of the many bitter ironies of women's film-making.

Conclusion

As Assia Djebar is best known for her novels, her two films may be read in a literary sense too. They feed off and into her writing. Both *La Nouba* and *La Zerda* are poetic political statements of someone who struggles with a double consciousness. While her preoccupation with women's issues and women's voices has a firm basis in politics and philosophy, the stylistic qualities of the films are rooted in French psychoanalysis, feminism and Third Cinema. Djebar's 'own kind of feminism' exposes and resists an unsatisfactory past, present and future (Ringrose, 2006: 257). Along the lines of Shohat's theorisation of nuances and compromises for the Third World woman film-maker, Cixous says that:

> She who looks with an acknowledging look, who studies, respects, does not take, does not claw, but contemplates and reads attentively, with a soft fury, strokes, bathes, makes the other beam. (cited in Ringrose, 2006: 257)

The aesthetics of subjectivity, solidarity and sympathy fit in with this idea of softness. The films' overt exploration of subjectivity and sympathy as post-Third-Worldist alternatives to the political fighting spirit of Third Cinema, acknowledge the values of sensitivity and negotiation, even in political protest. Nevertheless, Djebar destroyed the naive optimism inherent to Irigaray's sisterhood and Cixous' *écriture féminine*. She experiments with poetic voice-overs, revealing a deep struggle with transnationalism, and a subjective bitterness with the ineffectiveness of representation. In her feminism there was a struggle with the future. Due to the threatening presence of constant war and the continued oppression of women in Algeria, she was disillusioned with the promises of independence. She critiqued a society that under colonial and post-colonial circumstances denied a vast portion of the population its role in the writing of history.

Djebar visualises her problems with (self-)representation, as she is intensely aware of her own position as an insider–outsider and as a transnational. The question is whether she is speaking for, with, near or around her subjects. The relationships between the maker, the subject and the spectator of *La Nouba* and *La Zerda* are transnational, thereby emphasising the problems with Algerian national identity. As Shohat argued, the historical and contemporary national situation needs to be evaluated before a substantial analysis of individual stories in film can contribute to a collective historiography in a transnational context. Djebar worked at the intersection of national and transnational, and a multitude of voices and looks in her films show the complexity of an Algerian post-colonial identity.

Notes

1. See, for example, films by Mohammed Lakhdar-Hamina.
2. Algeria was a département of France, subject to 'assimilation', and remained under colonial rule for much longer than Morocco, which gained independence in 1956, as opposed to Algeria, which became independent in 1962 after a bloody war.

CHAPTER 5

Mai Masri: Mothering Film-makers in Palestinian Revolutionary Cinema

Mai Masri was born to an American mother and Palestinian father in 1959 in Amman, in Jordan. She grew up in Amman, Algiers, Nablus and Beirut, and studied film in San Francisco, graduating in 1981. When she lived in Beirut, she was part of the student movement and was very interested in politics. She said: 'I got the idea to study film because I thought film could be a medium that would combine several of my interests: as a Palestinian exposed to social events and politics, meeting people, the arts, travel, research. I wanted so desperately to escape boredom and normality' (Hillauer, 2005: 224). In 1977, she met Jean Chamoun, a Lebanese film-maker, who, in 1986, became her husband. They founded Nour Productions and have co-directed documentaries for international TV channels such as the BBC, Channel 4, PBS and Al Jazeera Documentaries. They started to make films together during the siege of Beirut in 1982, but decided early on they would not make 'classical documentaries' (Hillauer, 2005: 225). Instead, they were committed to witnessing and testifying through documentaries without preconceived plans, 'because people have short memories'. Mai Masri says about her film style that she likes to pay attention to details, which is reflected in her fondness for close-ups, faces and hands. From her first films *Under the Rubble* (1983) and *War Generation* (1989) onwards, she has focused on children and the influence of continued warfare on their psyches and bodies.

This chapter focuses on how Palestinian documentary film-makers in general, and women in particular, look at and 'use' Palestinian children. The constant question of whether a nation consists of people *and* land, or people *or* land, and the overwhelmingly young demographic of this nation is central to this. 'More than half the population living in the territory administered by the Palestinian National Authority since the signing of the Oslo Treaty are under sixteen years of age' (Hillauer, 2005: 197). Young people and children are central to the political and cultural identity of Palestine, and Palestinian cinema. As a continuation of

Gertz's and Khleifi's work for Palestinian cinema, this chapter intimately links landscape to the child's body, while it investigates how trauma and memory manifest themselves in the representations of Palestinian children in documentary. As Gertz and Khleifi focus on men's film-making and fiction feature film, this chapter broadens the scope of studies in Palestinian cinema somewhat, in order to offer a synthesis of the insights into women's documentaries and the performative role of children in these films. The focus will be on Mai Masri's work. As the first Palestinian woman (living in Beirut) to exclusively focus on documentary,[1] winning international prizes, she is also most consistent in her interest in, and portrayal of, children's lives, both in the Palestinian Territories and in the countless Palestinian refugee camps around the Arab world, and in Lebanon in particular. At the same time, I place her in the context of women's revolutionary film-making, as part of a tendency to think about forgetting and remembering the homeland, justifying and continuing 'the struggle', and holding on to the right to return. 'Seeing' as in understanding the 'Struggle' is crucial in any treatment of the highly complex political and socio-economic situation in Palestine, while listening to women and children once again is a political act in itself. Looking and listening in this chapter are acts of defiance in the most straightforward sense of the word.

Mai Masri is not the only, nor is she the first, Palestinian woman to have been involved in film-making. The reason I have chosen to focus on her work here is because films by Khadija Abu Ali are not available, and because I see Masri as a pioneer of a trend that has become dominant in Palestinian cinema by women: the focus on children. Abu Ali was the wife of Mustafa Abu Ali, one of the heads of the Palestine Film Unit (PFU), run by Fatah under the PLO and set up in 1968 by a cooperative, which included the first Arab camerawoman, Sulafa Jadallah Mirsal. Mirsal was a photographer, who – after studies in cinematography in Cairo's Higher Film Institute – worked for the PLO's Department of Photography and later the PFU. It was her rudimentary studio and darkroom, set up in a kitchen in her own apartment in Amman, that served as a workshop for the first films by the PFU. They borrowed cameras and equipment wherever they could.[2] They made revolutionary documentaries that served the cause of the political party they represented: 'PFU's aim was to document everyday life and the extraordinary events that occurred regularly in Palestine during this time . . . Becoming pivotal elements in the Third Cinema movement, the filmmakers in the PFU were not working as artists, or even as documentarians: they were making films to inspire the revolution' (Buali, 2012). They worked as a collective.

Palestinian Cinema and Documentary

Film-making in Palestine is fractured by war, disaster, oppression and insurgency – and remains largely unrecorded officially, shrouded in taboos and sensationalism. Cinema in Palestine is defined by exile and by permits to enter the Palestinian Territories, thus contributing to the discourse on the *Nakba* (the 1948 Palestinian exodus, literally translated as 'disaster') in fragmentary ways. Hamid Naficy writes that 'Palestinian cinema is one of the rare cinemas in the world that is structurally exilic, as it is made either in the condition of internal exile in the occupied Palestine, or under the erasure and tensions of displacement and external exile in other countries' (Naficy, 2006: 91). However, this fragmentation did not prevent film-makers from contributing to the search for a national identity through film. Made both inside the Palestinian Territories and outside them, in exile, Palestinian film-makers have historically focused on the lived experiences of the Palestinian people, however dispersed geographically and far removed temporally they are from their homeland. This homeland has remained constant in Palestinian cinema.

Khadija Abu Ali has made two films: *Children, But . . .* (1981) and *Women for Palestine* (1982). If she is to be regarded as the first Palestinian woman to make films (disregarding the role of Sulafa Jadallah Mirsal in the PFU), then it is worth noting that from her very first films, the focus has been on women and children to such an extent that they even shape the titles of the film.[3] In *Children, But . . .* Abu Ali contrasts images of Palestinian children who live in the Beirut refugee camps with readings from the UN's Declaration of Children's Rights. Abu Ali Khadija was not only a film-maker, she was also an exhibitor and an archivist. Gertz and Khleifi write that 'more than sixty movies were made before 1982' by the PFU (Gertz and Khleifi, 2008: 26), which screened at international film festivals and special events dedicated to the Palestinian cause. This continued the internationalisation of the cause as conceptualised by the political leadership. However, most films were only seen by Palestinians abroad. 'In addition,' they write, 'each cinematic body had screening units, including mobile ones. Khadija Abu Ali operated one such unit in the PLO's Film Institute' (ibid.).

Khadija Abu Ali was also responsible for the archive. The footage stored in this archive was used by film-makers to edit into their new films, precisely because footage of Palestine and the refugee camps outside Palestine was elusive and needed to be categorised: 'in 1975 the archive was set up in a hall in the Film Institute in the Al Fakihani quarter of West Beirut' (Gertz and Khleifi, 2008: 28). In the early 1980s, due to increased animosities between the factions and Israel within Lebanon, Khadija

Abu Ali feared for the survival of the archive, and so it was entrusted to the PLO. It was moved several times, and 'its whereabouts today remain unknown' (Gertz and Khleifi, 2008: 28). There are many speculations as to its whereabouts, and 'after over twenty years of wandering and inappropriate storage conditions, Khadija Abu Ali is not optimistic as to [its] fate' (Gertz and Khleifi, 2008: 29). One of Azza El Hassan's films, *Kings and Extras* (2004) describes Hassan's own search for the archive, and includes footage from the archive and interviews with people like Khadija and Mustafa Abu Ali. El Hassan shows how the difference between reality and fiction used to be very clear, and how the PFU 'wanted to reorganise their world with a camera', since the 1948 and 1967 disasters. Watching fragments of archive materials that are in individual people's possessions brings 'power and a sense of identity' to those watching, as Hassan turns her camera on the spectators of these fragments. People involved in the PFU testify that 'we lived outside space and time' and 'filming made us feel like we were building a dream'. But the film also has a sense of defeat. Mustafa and Khadija speculate that they divorced because they lost a sense of purpose when they lost the archive. The archive had existed for fifteen years under their leadership, and they both say how special it was to them, but that the leadership as well as other institutions they had hoped would help them move and protect the archive in the 1982 devastation of Beirut had priorities other than film. The end of *Kings and Extras* illustrates this frustration and the uncertainty of the archive's status with abstractions of blurry, colourful images. The films made before 1982, in spite of the fact that they were archived, have been lost, but are slowly resurfacing through new archiving materials and archaeological work in the region. Laura Marks describes the recent (2011) and mysterious rediscovery of PLU footage in Rome by Monahad Yacubi (Marks, 2015: 114). The revolutionary feel of the creation, exhibition, distribution and archiving of the films continues to impact the imagining and re-creation of Palestine worldwide.

The PFU's first film, titled *The Palestinian Right*, was made in 1969.[4] It is nine minutes long, and, as Anastasia Valassopoulos shows, part of the late 1960s aesthetics of political cinema, agitprop. It aims to contribute to the creation of a Palestinian national identity and, inherent to that, an intellectual rhetoric of re-acquisition of the land, 'turning lived conditions into principles for struggle' (Valassopoulos, 2014: 149). Importantly, the film internationalises the issues specific to Palestine, implicating Europe and America in the Zionist programme of the colonisation of Palestine, while maximising international support. This early film already shows children as militants, and uses children's drawings to reveal their reaction to the occupation. One of the PFU's most important films, *They Do Not*

Exist, was made in 1974.[5] This film combines documentary and artistic styles, resulting in an attractive piece of Third Cinema from a period and place forgotten or ignored in history. It takes its title from the remark made by Golda Meir that the Palestinians do not exist (Jacir, 2007). It covers conditions in Lebanon's Palestinian refugee camps, the effects of Israeli bombardments, and the lives of guerrillas in training camps. Among these refugees and guerrilla fighters are, inevitably, children. The opening shot of *They Do Not Exist* shows children eating lollies and focuses on family life, with an emphasis on mothers and children. The setting seems homely and happy. The sun is shining, there is an abundance of food and trees with shade to eat under. For the first ten minutes of the film, we are convinced that everything is fine: people smile and children play. But this also depicts defiance, in the sense that it makes its spectator 'see': we are okay in spite of the horrible conditions of war. 1974 was also the year the PLO was officially recognised by the UN, so this defiance comes at a time of confidence for the PLO. Again, then, instead of showing us the children as victims, the film-makers affirm the Palestinians' strength and perseverance. This is confirmed when a young girl is shown to write a letter to a freedom fighter, in which she praises his courage and sends him her love. From this early film onwards, children in Palestinian cinema often function as a reminder of home, and the homeland is the centre of the conflict. This is why children feature so prominently in these films, and how they are given agency and affect, through their bodies, their materiality and their words.

These are some of the earliest, most political and legendary films from the PFU, made collectively by Mustafa and Khadija Abu Ali, Sulafa Jadallah Mirsal, Hani Jawhariah, Salah Abu Hannood and many others. It is within the context of these film-making practices that we can place both Khadija Abu Ali's and Mai Masri's films. At the same time, they need to be placed in a wider context of international activists and film-makers who have turned Palestine and its children into a cause, the way PFU film-making intended. In 1972, Mona Saudi (Jordan) and Qais Al Zubaidi (Iraq)[6] made *Testimony of Palestinian Children in Wartime*, a film using children's drawings along the lines of *The Palestinian Right*. In 1977, Nabiha Lutfi, an Egyptian-Lebanese documentary maker, made *Because the Roots Will Not Die*, about Tal Al Zatar, a Palestinian refugee camp in Beirut, where she focused on children's lives in the camps and their deaths in 1976 at the hands of the Lebanese Phalangists.

After the age of the Third Cinema rebel film-makers of the PFU, Michel Khleifi became one of the most important and internationally recognised Palestinian film-makers. He is best known for creating the first

full-length feature film inside Palestine, obviously under the most complex
and difficult circumstances (seeking transnational funding for films from
a nation a lot of others had doubts about, and constant harassment from
the authorities, both Palestinian and Israeli). It was in particular his first
film, *Fertile Memory* (1980) that defined the next stage of Palestinian film-
making. His narrative documentary style challenged perceptions, and his
foregrounding of themes such as the land and being exiled from home,
collective memory and culture, admitting to a highly complex Palestinian
history, the common humanity of Jews and Arabs, and the critique of an
archaic Arab society (Kennedy, 2015: 53) laid the groundwork for a new
Palestinian cinema of subjective reality/memory and the balancing act of
insider/outsider knowledge. Perhaps the most interesting aspect of his
cinematic vision was that he highlighted the 'innate strength of women
in Palestinian society' (Kennedy, 2015: 58) – something to which the
freedom fighters had not paid particular attention. In fact, even though
some of the most powerful film-makers had been women, the focus of the
Third Cinema film-makers had been on children and male freedom fighters, patriarchal power structures and the common goal for an independent nation. In contrast, Khleifi starts to really look at different forms of
resistance to oppression, most defiantly through memory and culture, and
most importantly through the individual, subjective and personal lives of
women.

Khleifi is an accented cinema director. He lives and works in Belgium,
and, as Naficy describes, most Palestinian accented films are 'intersti-
tially made and transnationally funded' (Naficy, 2006: 92). Accented
film-makers often integrate autobiographical elements into their films, as
they put themselves in their films as displaced empirical subjects (Naficy,
2006: 94). Naficy has a particular interest in the epistolary mode when he
focuses on Palestinian cinema, and, as we shall see, Mai Masri plays with
letter writing and the voice-over reading letters in her documentaries on
children in the refugee camps inside Palestine and in Lebanon.

As Michel Khleifi pointed out in his film *Fertile Memory*, and particularly in explanations of the process of making the film, just as the Israeli
army, the Palestinian Authorities are guilty of stifling freedom of speech
and the press. Indeed, women's rights regressed considerably after the
second intifada, as it came to be seen as a secondary issue after freedom
and independence. Critics point out that women started wearing the hijab
again, as the Islamists gained power during the two intifadas. Women's
rights were seen as a luxury (Hillauer, 2005: 199). At the same time,
this was an impetus for Palestinian women directors living outside the
Palestinian Territories to really start to examine Palestinian history, their

own exile and political conditions in their homeland (Hillauer, 2005: 200). Like Khleifi in 1980, most of these women portrayed an acute artistic closeness to their subjects, to make up psychologically and emotionally for the physical distance from their homeland (Shafik, 2005a: 205). With the PFU, Palestinian cinema in the diaspora had developed as a contribution to the liberation. Most of the Palestinian film-makers had been able to gain technical expertise working in the film branches of various Arab host countries. However, their subject matter found little interest abroad, and funding the cinema of their home country has remained a thorny issue. Often the films were funded by NGOs with their own political agenda, or political groups who had specific ideologies. In order to be able to make the films they wanted, Palestinians living abroad and making films about the homeland had to work independently, which required inventive ways of finding funding.

Roy Armes shows that Nizar Hassan is 'one of the first Arab filmmakers of the 1960s generation to make a breakthrough into feature-length documentary filmmaking in the 1990s' (2015: 30). Gertz and Khleifi agree that he is the 'paramount Palestinian documentary film director of our time' (2008: 49). Like Michel Khleifi, he makes personal films, with autobiographical elements, interviewing friends and family, incorporating their opinions on politics into a cinema of Palestine. Where the political had been personal for the PFU film-makers, now the personal becomes political.

A cinema of their own claimed a Palestinian history even if it was 'imagined'. It expressed a desire to use film to document the struggle for independence and the right to return. It also shows a degree of activist film-making, where the impact of the films counted as one of the reasons to make it in the first place. In other words, these film-makers 'gather information and document the suffering' (Neidhardt, 2005: 207). Michel Khleifi's first films, then, contributed to the international breakthrough of independent Palestinian film, as he not only attacks the Israeli occupation but also questions the structures of his own society and government; instead of a broad national identity based on political ideals films were now interested in more personal, subjective experiences; and instead of presenting a common history, present and future for the Palestinian people, films now admitted to the fragmented and hybrid nature of the people and their memories. This we also see very clearly in Mai Masri's films and in the women that have followed in her footsteps.

Children in Palestinian Film

One of the aspects of the continued internationalisation of the lived Palestinian experience is its repeated focus on children, and Mai Masri is one of the most consistent and approachable film-makers to have settled in this trend. Younger film-makers, such as Najwa Najjar, Annemarie Jacir, Azza El Hassan and Dahna Abourahme, continue Masri's, Abu Ali's and the PFU's preoccupation with children. In what follows, I will first describe how Masri conceptualises her obsession with children. I will then synthesise some of the theories on children in film and see how useful these might be for our study of Palestinian documentaries. Then a sustained analysis of three of Mai Masri's most accessible films will demonstrate the Palestinian preoccupation with children.

In 1982, Mai Masri and her husband Jean Chamoun lived near the Palestinian refugee camp of Shatila in Beirut, when the Israeli–allied Lebanese Phalangist militia, with the assistance of the Israeli Defence Force (IDF), perpetrated the massacre there. She says: 'We walked the streets after the carnage. It was eerie. Death was everywhere. Suddenly, I heard sounds of children's laughter. I saw their faces framed by the holes in the bombed-out walls. And I felt the dead were coming back to life. That is what sealed my fate. I decided to become a filmmaker' (Padgaonkar, 2011). They started to make films together. *Under the Rubble* (1983), their first collaboration productively juxtaposes the devastation Palestinians have to suffer internationally, with images that foreground the resilience of young children during war. *War Generation* (1989) continues this initiative, looking at the consequences of protracted war on the psyches of three successive generations of young people as they struggle to survive. From 1990 onwards, Masri has directed on her own films, *Children of Fire* (1990), *Children of Shatila* (1998) and *Frontiers of Dreams and Fears* (2001), all of which focus intensely on children's experiences of war; she makes these documentaries subjective, individual and personal. The revolutionary impetus in Palestinian cinema becomes, in her hands, intertwined with people's personal lives. Instead of the political inciting a collective, activist type of film-making, Masri turns this around and reveals that the personal is already inherently political.

Because of the fragmentation within the political parties and their representations on the screen; because of the circumstances of the refugee camps where Masri was filming; because Palestinian refugees had been stuck in the Lebanese civil war; and because of the perceived abandonment by the PLO and its cameras, people had become suspicious of film-makers. She says: 'In the early 80s when I began filming, people were as suspicious about the camera as they were of spies and planes. This fear was broken during the first Intifada when they began understanding the power of the image' (Padgaonkar, 2011). Junka writes about the first intifada (1987–1991) that 'everyday resistance' and the 'suspension of everyday life' was a successful strategy of collective opposition to the Israeli oppressor. It caused feelings of optimism and confidence for the young generations, which were possible because of the perceived success of the first intifada (Junka, 2006: 426). This look inward in the Palestinian territories at the time made it possible for those in the diaspora and the refugee camps to also start to look inward, away from Palestine and towards their own specific situation. Whereas outsider TV makers had been most active in Beirut, perhaps it was now an opportune time for a fellow Palestinian like Masri to turn the camera on these Palestinians abroad. Mai Masri has made a dozen films about Palestinian refugees in Lebanon. The focus on children and young people is in line with the acknowledgement at the time of the intifada that the younger generations represented the affirmation of life (Junka, 2006: 426).

Masri has indicated that her focus on children in her films is both pragmatic and ideological. On a pragmatic level, 'children are a motor of change. They are spontaneous, unaffected and fun to work with creatively. They are the imagination of the future' (Padgaonkar, 2011). On a more philosophical level, they represent a connection between memory, imagination and identity:

> The young generations construct their sense of identity from their everyday experiences in exile or under Israeli occupation. They also draw from their imagination, which is nurtured by the stories that they hear from their grandparents, many of whom were dispossessed from their homes in Palestine in 1948. I am interested in portraying what these children consider as home and how they re-construct their lack of a home. I am also interested in understanding how their imaginary Palestine contrasts with their everyday lives in the refugee camps. For the third generation of the *Nakba*, Palestine is the memory that nourishes their imagination and the dream that they weave and re-construct as an alternative to the humiliation and deprivation of the camps of exile. This is particularly true in Palestinian children. I am fascinated by their ability to transcend the overwhelming difficulties of their everyday lives through play, imagination, and dream. Their creativity speaks to my own subconscious world and opens new horizons in my cinematic journey. (Masri, 2008)

So, for Masri, children are not only part of a realistic representation of the young demographic of the territories and the camps, they are also inspirational and energetic sources of information and subjects for her documentaries.

As we will see, there is also an element of mothering in her kind of

film-making. Masri does not make what she calls 'classical' documentaries, rather she embarks on projects without preconceived ideas. It is
a natural process, which takes shape as it grows. Motherhood is natural
in a universal understanding of womanhood, while it is political in a
Palestinian context. Julie Peteet shows that while motherhood is seen
as a natural universal identity that every woman needs to embody, in
Palestine it is also a deeply political act (Peteet, 1997). It is my contention
that Masri's preoccupation with children is not only due to the inherent
vitality children bring to the documentary, but also, in the context of her
subjective approach to film-making, a reflection of Palestinian motherhood. In Palestine, Peteet theorises, mothers are bearers of children, thus
replenishing the losses of older human life. They are also mothers for all
combatants and martyrs, as they are givers and savers of life (Peteet, 1997:
123). They participate in the struggle, as the home becomes a site for civil
disobedience and collective resistance (Peteet, 1997: 120), and their and
their children's mere existence defies the perceived Israeli exterminating
practices. Motherhood is a contested identity in Israel–Palestine: 'women
are greatly in demand for their role as childbearers and mothers. Large
families have long been regarded not only as a means of securing the existence of the family but also the state of Palestine' (Hillauer, 2005: 197).
Pregnancy and motherhood therefore become political states of being and
childhood a consequence of a politicised gender. The womb works as a
symbol for this so-called 'war of the womb', where children become part
of a 'demographic bomb'.[7] Mothers' contributions to the continued cycle
of life in defiance of the oppressors makes them a repository and archive
of experiences and people. In a way, I would argue, Masri does the same:
she archives the experiences of the children in the camps; she affirms their
lives and their existence in defiance of what the Israeli, Lebanese and
perhaps also the Palestinian authorities would prefer; and she participates
in the home struggle through invisible civil disobedience. This civil disobedience is made explicit when she says that being a woman film-maker
can have strange consequences, where if she is a Palestinian woman, she is
not perceived as a film-maker and thus not a threat to the IDF (Hillauer,
2005: 226). So, while children are her main focus and topic, her role as
a film-maker could be said to be parallel to that of a Palestinian mother,
where motherhood is a political act.

   Karen Lury (2010) shows how, in fiction film, the child is often represented as the Other, the abject. The presence of a child interrupts the
potential linearity of a story, instead foregrounding and revealing strange-
ness. When it comes to war films, Lury writes, the child is the expression
of the relationship between witness, memory and history. The presence of

children influences the way the war is told, and the way it is remembered. Children can be used as a tool by the director in order to reach a certain audience in a certain way. First, because of their perceived innocence, children will elicit precise emotions in the spectator. In a way, then, they are cyphers for adult anxieties and metonyms for wider suffering. At the same time, children tend to normalise war, as war is simultaneously an exciting and a mundane experience and instead of heightened emotions, they deal with instinct and the routine of the struggle for survival. In both cases, the child in film works counter to the conventional narratives of history. The most interesting aspect of children in war film, then, is their ability to dislocate and trouble linear time. The child reveals how memory will be interrupted and distorted. It can articulate feelings in ways other than speech, in facial expressions and body language, which leads to their embodied experiences. Through emotional affinity, audiences see the materiality of children's bodily presence highlighted, and as such a visceral, haptic confrontation with the violence of war is made possible.

Mai Masri admits to an embodied experience of children on film, when she said that she films people that resemble her, and that the films she has made are episodes in her own life. The subjectivity of the documentaries then assists with the physicality of the war experience in her films, through the bodies of children. She says: 'they have a profound effect on the formation of my identity as a person and filmmaker. Film is about unveiling a world that is composed of many magical layers. It is the art of seeing through other people's eyes, discovering and bringing out the poetry in everyday life' (Masri, 2008). Masri further explains that through her focus on the young generations she sees a strong connection between memory, imagination and identity. While this differs slightly from Lury's witness, memory and history connection embodied by the child, they do have a focus on memory in common, and this parallel can be extended to witness and imagination, and history and identity. As second and third generations of Palestinians in the refugee camps never witnessed Palestinian land, they have to imagine it, something Masri is very interested in. The imagination of children ignites her own and she 'believes that all Palestinians have an imaginary Palestine in their heads that they construct like a film and watch over and over' (Masri, 2008). Valassopoulos' understanding of reacquisition chimes with this idea of having to imagine the homeland. Similarly, history is an inherent part of the Palestinian identity, as the obsession with a time before 1948, and its aftermath, defines the existence and development of a Palestinian national identity. Moreover, the Palestinian memory and thus also Palestinian cinema, as Gertz and Khleifi explain, is defined and scarred by the trauma of war. It is in the conceptualisation of trauma as an interrupted memory that we find another overlap with Lury's theorisation of children in war films. Trauma theory highlights the idea of interrupted memory, illogical remembering and the inability to express those experiences classified as traumatic. The breakdown of logic, linearity and control then link the way children express themselves in film to the way trauma is expressed artistically *as* film. The latency of trauma, and the return of the repressed, are enacted on the body, through embodied encounters and visceral experiences. As the child can be seen as narcissistic, unself-conscious, intuitive, it can also be likened to the return of the repressed.

Mark Cousins' 2013 documentary *A Story of Children and Film* grew out of his earlier *A Story of Film* (2011), but also out of his 2009 film *The First Movie*, set in Iraq. Cousins has a rather dreamy vision of children in film. He says that no art has looked more at children than film has, and he speculates this is precisely because children change so fast, which makes them cinematic. He identifies a number of characteristic elements of children that are attractive for film-makers: they can be wary, shy, stroppy and theatrical; they go on adventures; they have dreams; and they can be very sad. In short, Cousins documents how children's emotions live on the surface, are exaggerated, and therefore make them easy to identify with. This conceptualisation of why children are so attractive to film-makers is very different from Lury's. Lury emphasises the complexity of children and their link to memory and trauma in film; Cousins perhaps reveals a more optimistic, naive view of children as magical creatures. However, both do emphasise children's irrationality, which, on the one hand, makes them theatrical and attractive for film, and, on the other hand, reveals the point of view of the authors of these ideas: they both (unintentionally) acknowledge adults' obsession with children *as* nostalgia. Perhaps the main problem with these theorisations of children in film is that there is little attention paid to the possibility that these children might have agency. The children that feature in the documentaries by Mai Masri are very much their own spokespeople, and they demand the attention of the camera. They are not victims, they are performers, as they were in Jocelyne Saab's films.

Gertz and Khleifi show that new Palestinian films reveal a different subjectivity, where private experiences are embedded in films and different identities come to the foreground. They see children as being one of these new identities, as films take on children's points of view (2008: 146). As Azza El Hassan shows in her documentary *News Time*, Palestinian children are newsworthy. The global media, she says, has an obsession with children from the Palestinian territories and in the refugee camps. El Hassan points out that this opportunistic approach to Palestine's children needs to be addressed and problematised. She says: 'as a collective, children have become empty signifiers on which conflicting values and goals are inscribed – as individuals this abstraction can be challenged by showing complex and conflicted human agents' (Allen, 2004: 160). Indeed, in *News Time*, El Hassan shows four young boys and their very individual agencies. They remain in the neighbourhood of Ramallah where El Hassan is located as well, as some of the only people left. They are bored when they do not throw stones at the Israelis and they talk like adults about the friends they have lost in the struggle. In El Hassan they see a diversion from the mundane life they have in occupation: one of them says 'The thing I like the most is being filmed and talking about my life.' They are used to the cameras, but not to getting the individual attention this film-maker gives them. She shows their intelligence, their insight into their situation and their pragmatism. When she asks them at the end of the film whether she can film them again in a few years' time, they say 'Sure, but we will be different. Maybe we won't be alive then. But if we are still alive we will still be friends and you can come and film us again.' This sequence is filmed in slow motion, which shows an awareness and concentration on the part of the film-maker, which gives the spectators in their turn the opportunity to dwell on the harsh truth of what the boys are saying. They know there is a good chance that they may not have a long life in the circumstances in which they live. El Hassan's camera (different from the news reporters' cameras) and her attention (also very different from the sensationalist reporters) has given them an agency they have never felt on-screen before, and which they will miss when the filming stops. When she eventually does stop 'because the film is making her think too much', the boys become desperate to be filmed and almost harass her at her flat. They need to tell their stories. El Hassan states that 'the film became their only means of entertainment', and I suspect it was a matter of it being a different, awareness-raising assertion for the boys, instead of the mundanity of everyday life under occupation.

The mediated children are re-envisaged by film-makers like Mai Masri. Instead of representing victimhood, as they do in the media, they represent both past, present and future, and they respond to the other obsession of Palestinian film-makers: the land. As Gertz and Khleifi show, the landscape is central to Palestinian film-makers' work of the fourth period (the 1980s), where peasant culture, traditional customs, and the land as a source of livelihood and emotional identification with the lost land looks nostalgically at the past (Gertz and Khleifi, 2006: 472). This past is a pre-traumatic period, and has come to 'replace the present'. Meanwhile, 'the future is perceived as a return to this past' (2006: 466). In a response to this fatalistic stance on the lost landscape of Palestine, films about children look at the future differently and retain the optimism that is necessary to continue the 'struggle'. They 'shape a "correction" of the past: they symbolise the future and hope' (Gertz and Khleifi, 2008: 66), and they embody a rhetoric of belonging through their quests for their origins and an explanation for their current situations. This sort of discourse contributes to national identity formation, and a continued national narrative. Even if children's memories are questioned, their questions about the past and stubborn hope for the future unifies a fragmented society into a shared history.

In eyes of adults, children are simultaneously representatives of the future and the past. That they represent the future is most obvious: they are young and have a long(er) time to live, and collectively will define the future, even if in Palestine this is not self-evident. Indeed, as the films show, children are well aware that they may not live to be very old; the average age in Palestine and in the refugee camps is very low.[8] At the same time, children also represent the past. Even though the child 'does not or cannot provide authority on the facts of war . . . the representation of its experience as visceral, as of and on the body, demonstrates how the interweaving of history, memory and witness can be powerfully affective' (Lury, 2010). Children's memories should not be ignored. They embody memory: adults see in children their own past(s) and, as such, the child's body enacts the past. Children are part of the inherent collectivity of the suffering of a people that has not had the opportunity to develop into a nation and where, in parallel, growing up is not guaranteed. Children's memories and adults' memories in these films are often much more similar than expected: memory is not impartial. The past is often represented in nostalgic terms, which is why we look upon children in nostalgic terms as well. In Palestine, the landscape is equally longed for as a fertile memory (for example, by Michel Khleifi) and therefore, film-makers commit children to the landscape of Palestine, whether they are in the Palestinian territories or living in exile in refugee camps. Most importantly, children also represent the present. It is their ability to turn extraordinary circumstances such as war and oppression into everyday life that inspires film-makers to use them, as Lury indicates when she discusses the normalisation of violence in the representation of the child in war films. It is particularly so that when they are enabled to represent the present, they find their agency and manage to represent themselves most productively. As such, they can also act as mouthpieces for the director when it comes to tackling contemporary taboo subjects. Indeed, in Mai Masri's films, children may represent the past and the future: memories of the land and hopes for a return to it. But they also represent the present. Because of Masri's unplanned approach to film-making, the children are able to take charge of the documentary and take a camera when she offers it, enabling them to assert their agency through aligning their look and their voice, demanding that the spectator listens and sees.

Masri's first film in a trilogy on children was *Children of Fire* (1990). It was the first film she directed on her own, with her husband as producer. It was filmed during the first intifada and shows her discovering the city of her early childhood. In an interview with Hillauer, Masri testifies that there were almost no journalists in the city during the intifada, and that people were happy with her presence, as they felt there was an urgent need to document the people's struggle. There was 'a personal bond between me and the city', she says (Hillauer, 2005: 227), and she felt unified through a sense of belonging, self-reliance and hope for the future. Children in the Israeli-occupied territories are shown playing the game they called 'intifada', a Palestinian version of cops and robbers. This first film then already shows Masri's personal, subjective approach to children, her interest in how they approach their situation, and her type of mothering film-making. This continues more confidently in her two following films, *Children of Shatila* (1998) and *Frontiers of Dreams and Fears* (2001).

Children of Shatila (1998)

In *Children of Shatila* (1998), Farah and Issa are two Palestinian children who live in the refugee camp of Shatila, in Beirut. Fifty years after their grandparents fled Palestine, Mai Masri gives them a camera, curious to see how they perceive life and family in a camp that has seen massacre, siege and hunger. The refugee camp here is very different from the one in *They Do Not Exist* in 1974. We are two decades further on and the disillusionment is palpable. Masri shows the camp from a bird's-eye perspective, providing an overview of the size and the devastation of the camp. Once on the ground, she films the ditches, mud, puddles and dirt roads. She also shows bombed buildings and the devastated state in which the camp has been left. The war of the camps and the massacres in Shatila took place in 1982. The film was made in 1998, and the camp still resembles a war-torn battlefield. The first child that was interviewed describes in graphic detail the death of his aunt, whose head was cut off, and whose body, together with many others, was 'dumped in a ditch'. Archival footage and text on the screen confirms the heavy war machinery the Phalangists and Israelis used to enter and destroy the camp. A short explanatory text reads:

6 June 1982, the Israeli army invades Lebanon and besieges Beirut and the Palestinian refugee camps for three months. From 16–18 September 1982, Pro-Israel right-wing Lebanese militias acting in connivance with the Israeli armed forces, massacre hundreds of Palestinian and Lebanese civilians in Sabra and Shatila refugee camps.

The fact that this information is provided in text on the screen rather than in voice-over suggests a belief in the objectivity of facts in written language and preserves a certain distance for Masri in relation to the camp, and her own identity as a Palestinian not present in the camps and not suffering to the extent of her subjects. Indeed, at one point in the film one of the adults interviewed by the children and Masri testifies that there are about fifty to sixty types of jobs that adults in the camps or Palestinians in Lebanon are not allowed to practice.[9] Mai Masri's position is clearly one of privilege, but nevertheless speaks of solidarity with the people in the frame. When Issa and Farah are handed their own cameras, Masri is brought into the story, and both ask the film-maker questions before they ask anyone else their questions. There is a clear affinity between the film-maker and the children, and both Issa and Farah say exactly the same thing to her: after having practised how to handle the machine, they turn their camera on Masri, saying 'I can see very well now.' It almost suggests a revelation, that they are different and yet the same as the director. There is a solidarity between the Palestinians, and Masri identifies very strongly as Palestinian here, but there is also a recognition of their differences, which assist in the storytelling, the testimonies and the question and answer sessions. Like the presence of the camera ensuring a level of performance, as Stella Bruzzi has explained, the presence of a stranger who is familiar enough to trust is an incentive to start to speak to the camera and behind it. Receiving the role of the director of their own film gives them confidence to perform their own life.

Unlike the earlier films about, or with, Palestinian children, the children here do not necessarily represent defiance any more, or at least not as energetically. Once they have the camera in their hands, they ask one another and their friends and family members very specific questions – much more probing and intelligent than one might expect from nine- or ten-year-olds. To their friends they ask questions such as what do you want to be when you grow up? Most of them answer with a profession that one would not imagine coming from an innocent child in a dire situation. But then again, these children are everything but innocent. They perform and repeat what they have heard or seen their parents say and do. As El Hassan said, these Palestinian children are so used to having cameras around that their stories and performances are studied and inspired by

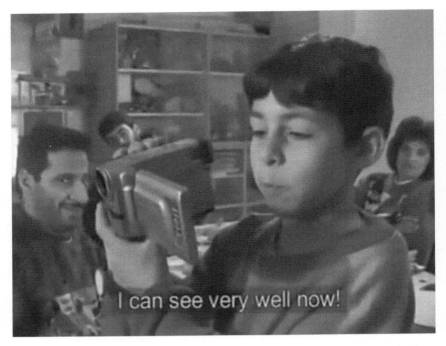

Figure 5.1 Issa receives a camera from Mai Masri and proceeds to film her, saying he can 'see', in *Children of Shatila* (1998) © Mai Masri

stories and performances they have witnessed before. There is a sense of urgency and repetition in their tales and acts. The professions they want are 'engineer', 'spaceman' and 'doctor'. From these utterances and performances comes universal hope and aspirations.

In contrast, the parents and grandparents interviewed instil a static idea of the imagined homeland: they have to dream about it, they must hold on to the idea of return. The adults seem to have lost hope, and testify to their depression, their hopeless situations and the rut they have been stuck in for as long as their children can imagine. One wonders where the children get their inspiration to want to become engineers or astronauts if their parents do not believe in the future. The adults in the film actively discourage the children from aspiring to become the doctors or artists they want to be. Farah's father says: 'I want to lead a normal life and raise my children and educate them well. But faced with reality, you realise how difficult it is.' Her mother continues: 'When my children tell me about their hopes and dreams, like Farah telling me she wants to be a doctor, I feel awkward and afraid to shock them with the truth. I wonder what kind of future lies ahead for us.' Farah's father tells Masri how he is educated in computer science, but works as a street cleaner. Her mother has a degree from the university, but works at a nursery. Azza El Hassan's film *News Time* touches on these issues as well. Shot in Ramallah, the boys in her film say that they are not scared of anything, they are shown to not have a life outside of taunting Israeli soldiers and practising self-defence against them. However, the boys perceptively state that they feel very sorry for parents, as they live in a constant state of anxiety for their children's lives. The children themselves have no fears.

Thus, while the older generations such as the grandparents instil in their grandchildren this deep-seated wish to return to the homeland, the parents and older brothers seem to be more disillusioned with their lives. The stories the children tell almost all start with 'my grandfather told me', or 'my grandmother told me', and we do not hear the actual stories from these grandparents' mouths, we hear them from the children. This reflects perhaps a critical stance on the part of the children or of Masri on these stories and the insistence on the homeland. The children, after all, have never even seen Palestine. They not only seem to repeat their family's stories on automatic pilot, they also imagine the way it looks in the way their stories have shown the land.

However, when Farah and Issa are each given the video camera to film with, the roles are reversed and we are given an insight into the questions that these young minds have, growing up in a war-torn region that has witnessed countless tragedies. These two children are clever and more resourceful than their parents or grandparents give them credit for, as they affirm their agency in defiance of their parents and the other adults around them. Farah and Issa also start filming one another, and their friendship blossoms, as they promise to take care of one another. Farah, a very clever girl who considers herself the smartest of all her sisters and friends, begins to teach Issa how to read and write. Issa has had an accident, as he was hit by an army vehicle, breaking his arm and leg in several places, and fracturing his skull. He has difficulty concentrating, and Farah assists him. They discuss their homeland, which they have never seen, and express their wish to return there, in an echo of what we have heard grandparents say. This illustrates their awareness of the role of Palestinians and especially children: they must continue to 'imagine it, that is the main thing', says Farah. But there is also frustration when their individuality is ignored: Farah, for example, is sad that she can never have a birthday party. Her mother's two brothers were both killed four months before Farah's first birthday, and so she feels unable to celebrate her children's birthdays. 'Every time we ask, she bursts into tears,' Farah says. The camera lingers on her face and she raises her eyebrows and takes a deep breath and lets out a big sigh, not only showing regret about the lack of parties but also a loss of patience with her mother for dwelling on the past rather than looking at the present or the future of her children. As such, the camera takes on a mothering role, allowing the children to express their true individual feelings in uninhibited ways, instead of repeating the studied refrain of nostalgia for a collective past. In a sequence very reminiscent of this one, El Hassan's film, *News Time*, also has a young boy testifying to the fact that he never has a birthday party, 'because of the martyrs'. For them celebrating something Ramallah-style means walking around the city, looking closely at the martyr posters, walking until they are exhausted. The camera lingers on their faces deep in thought. Birthdays are a time of reflection and regret rather than cause for celebration, even for children.

In the last sequence of the film, Issa and Farah are present at an afternoon in a community centre, where Farah's mother is one of the teachers, and they learn folksongs and stories from Palestine. Issa has just explained a recurring dream he has, of him being a knight in armour on a horse, who is handing out money to everyone simply because they tell him they do not believe he is rich. When he wakes up he always thinks 'what a waste of money'. Farah has just told us that she likes to close her eyes just to look at the nice shapes and colours she can see inside her eyelids. These are imaginative dreams and visions revealing a sense of creativity and even humour. And then they are questioned by the teachers about how they imagine their homeland, how they would draw it. They explain very enthusiastically, showing off their knowledge, that 'Palestine is our homeland, it was taken by the Israelis, we have to get it back.' The fact that a young girl who looks about five years old tells it the way she does – rhythmically, glancing at the camera, intimidated by the teachers – shows us that she lacks any direct affiliation with this idea of the land of Palestine. She looks as if she is reeling off a lesson learned by heart. Perhaps though this is so because the children are in group, trying their best to impress the teachers and one another. Indeed, when there is just Farah or Issa on screen, or when they interview each other and the situation is more intimate than communal, they show off their agency, they have ideas and opinions, and especially a lot of questions.

The film does end on an optimistic note, as the children are asked to draw the way they imagine the homeland, and Issa wonders whether the birds have different colours 'there', perhaps even colours that they have never seen before. The children start to enumerate things that they do know: birds, trees, lentils, rice, lemons, vegetables and flowers. From these objects, they make free associations and paint the way children everywhere would imagine a home: colourful, cheery and simple. Their real lives are anything but colourful, cheery and simple: they live in a grey slum, where people suffer from injuries and depression, and where things are highly politicised and complex, but in their voices and hopes and imaginations there is a sense of defiance of the fatalism present in their parents' discourse, and we see a strength in the children that redefines them not as victims but as victors over their fate.

Frontiers of Dreams and Fears (2001)

This film, the 'third in a series of films I made on Palestinian children' (Masri, 2005: 232), introduces us to two young girls, Mona and Manar, thirteen and fourteen years old, respectively. Mona lives in the Shatila refugee camp in Beirut, Lebanon, and Manar lives in Deisha refugee camp near Bethlehem in Palestine. The film-maker meets Mona and discovers that despite the distance, borders and space between them, these two girls have started to communicate through letters and over the Internet. When the news comes in that the Israelis are withdrawing from the southern Lebanese territories after twenty years of occupation, the film-maker plans to have the two girls meet at the border. This is a dramatic meeting at a barbed wire fence, where hundreds of separated families find one another. However, during the making of the film, and soon after the girls meet one another, the second intifada erupts and the young people in the film are confronted with a new level of tragedy and change.

Mona and Manar are precocious and eloquent young girls. They talk to the camera, dominate the voice-over in their reading out of one another's letters to the camera, and are closely observed through close-ups of their faces, hands and bodies. Yet they are also portrayed as typical teenagers, when they discuss boys and love with their girlfriends and are shown giggling and discussing life with the boys in their camps or the boys they have met at the border. They struggle, like any teenager, to find the balance between innocence and wisdom, but their innocence and wisdom is of a different kind compared with other teenagers around the world, precisely due to the locations they inhabit. Their wisdom appears in observations about their own and one another's situations in the refugee camps, and contrasts with the desperation of their innocence. We witness friendships that are intense and strong due to their intense living conditions at war, and the girls often seem much older than their age. They struggle with issues like death and separation surrounding their intense, emotional friendships.

At the start of the film, Mona walks home from school in Shatila camp.

Her voice-over states 'I wish I were a bird, so I could fly back to my home-land, Palestine.' Leaving the camp is central to her thoughts. Returning to Palestine is something ingrained on her mind, as conversations turn to this issue unrelentingly. She is part of a youth organisation for children who have lost a parent: she has lost her father. Her mother does not appear in the film. In fact, very few adults appear in the film, and when they do, they are in the background and do not have a voice. Masri shows with this film that a large portion of the children in Palestine and in the camps are fatherless: 'At least half the Palestinian male population have been in Israeli prisons at least once in their lives. Many have spent several years behind bars. It is common to find households that are run by the women because the men are either missing, in prison, or deceased' (Hillauer, 2005: 234). Motherhood is not only a political act but also a nurturing role. Where the children become adult very early on due to the political cir-cumstances, the mothers are perhaps able to ensure they remain children for a little while longer. The camera in Masri's hands does the same and searches for their agency as individuals and as children. This film focuses on young teenagers and is a follow-up to *Children of Shatila*. Surprisingly, Farah appears in the group of friends discussing love interests.

When Mona hears that the Israeli army has left southern Lebanon, she and her friends from the youth organisation are excited to visit the border and catch a glimpse of the homeland. The soil of the homeland is precious to them. They celebrate and fill all types of receptacles with sand from across the border. Mona and her friend Samar from Shatila describe feeling a very strong pull from their homeland, wanting to destroy the barbed wire at the border and escape to their ancestors' land. There is a big party at the fence, with music and dancing on both sides. Teenagers fall in love, touch, joke and tease each other across the fence.

The film is structured around letter writing. Mona and Manar write one another letters through their youth organisations, and read one another's letters for the voice-over of the film. These intimate conversa-tions show the developing friendship, but also the growing desperation of Palestinian children living in refugee camps and the teenage worries about boys. Epistolary films, Naficy says, are 'characterised by a highly complex style' (2006: 94), as 'epistolarity is a mode of cine-writing that inscribes both as icons and narrative agents the means of communication that links people across time and space' (ibid.). Mona being in Lebanon and Manar in Deisha refugee camp in Palestine share experiences, but also experience wildly different conditions in and about Palestine. Letter writing shows a deep desire 'to close the spatial distance (between here and there) and the temporal gap (between now and then) [that] involves distance, separation, absence, loss, and the desire, however unfulfilled, to bridge the multiple gaps' (Naficy, 2006: 95). Yet these desires remain very unfulfilled: while they meet in the flesh at the border, Mona is unable to return to Palestine, and Manar lives in circumstances of constant oppression and the threat of war.

Naficy also shows that epistolarity is a dialogic mode, between addresser and addressee, and between the film and its audience. It is, moreover, a dialogue with the self, and involves self-evaluation. It invites a complex kind of sympathy. In Palestine, letter writing becomes an 'important strategy for self-expression and self-narrativisation'. It is therefore highly subjective and individualised, but also a social matter, as in exile, one has strong group affiliations or division. Indeed, the letters are read out loud, not just in voice-over, but to friends. Letter reading is a group activity, and the teenagers read one another's letters as much as they read the ones addressed to them. In both camps, for Mona and Manar, the initiative of writing letters came from the youth organisations they are a part of. The writing and reading can be seen as a (group) therapy session, where they read one another's self-narrativisation in order that someone inside Palestine can image the life of someone outside of it, and vice versa. In a way it is nation formation through letters: Palestinians inside and outside are a highly separate group of people, yet the idea of an independent state is at the forefront of their minds. The unfolding of the letters, literally, before the reading, also implies an allegorical unfolding in public of the personal and subjective thoughts of the writer by the collective reader and listener. The personal narrative, enfolded by the writer, is shared and made public in an attempt to 'see', to understand and to really listen to one another. The letters connect teenagers inside and outside of camps, show their similarities and differences, and contrast their experiences: both have better and worse-off aspects; Mona is less of a victim of the second intifada than Manar, but Manar can visit her ancestral land.

Mai Masri is able to build an enormous trust from the girls she interviews, and the groups of friends to which they belong. The people she films let her into their often highly complex and miserable lives, especially in the camps where she chooses to film. The girls are, moreover, teenagers, usually very private and defiant beings, who do not like to talk or share their private feelings with adults. Naficy indeed says that 'in exilic epistolary films, trust between the addresser and the addressee, the subject and the filmmaker, and the film and its audience is crucial' (2006: 100). This is so not only for the creation of the film in the first place, but also for the effect of the film. The film-maker needs to trust that her spectators will unfold the information they receive in a sensitive manner, as we look at children, their feelings and the precarious political situations under which they live. Especially when the film continues while the second intifada starts. The isolation of Manar, inside Palestine, and Mona, outside of it, intensifies, and yet they continue to write letters. Epistolarity under such circumstances is an inherently critical and political act, while it is also a tactic of 'breaking out of the loneliness and isolation that exile imposes' (Naficy, 2006: 104). It is a genre of desire: desire for the other to come closer and the self to find clarity, in Mona's case a desire for her homeland, and in Manar's case a desire to escape from the open-air prison she feels she is in.

Children are brutalised and traumatised by the violence surrounding them. They see endless suffering and experience oppression, incarceration and humiliation as their everyday realities, and that of their parents and friends. Their intimate feelings of despair are recorded in the trust relationship with the director. Manar says: 'Why should we study. We have no future. We are refugees with no rights. Our dreams are dying.' Yet they remain resilient as well, living teenage lives, giggling about boys (or girls), discussing their dreams, and dreaming about love and what the world looks like. Their most important dream is perhaps of their homeland, where they imagine what it looks like. In spite of the knowledge that returning might be an impossibility, they retain hopes. They experience this melancholy, but due simply to their lived experience as teenagers they also know how to not stop hoping. The children and teenagers are, as Jim Quilty says, perhaps too young for cynicism and numbness (Quilty, 2005: 235). They experience powerful emotions and show these more openly.

Next to the film's attention to the voice in the voice-over readings of letters, emails and the conversations between the girls, the camera also focuses on the visual layout of the camps, the lack of a landscape, and the differences between the spaces: Deisha camp has a very distinct look as opposed to the Shatila camp in Beirut. Masri testifies:

> The first time I filmed in Shatila camp was after the horrific massacre of 1982. Since then, I have witnessed its destruction and reconstruction three times . . . The camp consists of a maze of tight alleyways packed into a single square mile with families as large as ten sharing a room. The fathers are unemployed and the children end up dropping out of school at the age of eleven or twelve to help support their families . . . Deisha camp is home to 14,000 Palestinian refugees. Many of the young people are university graduates. I started filming in Deisha camp in August 2000, a month before the beginning of the second intifada. When I was filming I noticed that the living conditions seemed slightly better than in Shatila camp. (Masri, 2001: 233)

The retreat of Israel out of southern Lebanon is a major event in the history of Lebanese and Palestinian refugees. It was both a political historical triumph for the homeland, but also a personal milestone in the lives of many separated families and in particular for the many refugees living in Lebanon. They could now visit the border. Unable to cross the border, Palestinians living in Lebanon could 'see' their homeland, even if it was from a distance, a distance that constantly increases the desire for the homeland. This is also the case for Mona and Manar in *Frontiers of Dreams and Fears*. They both visit the border, with their youth organisations, and Mai Masri makes use of this situation to ensure that the girls meet physically. There is a lot of kissing, touching, hand-holding, singing and hugging at the border between families, but also between these two girls and their friends. Infatuations take shape, and boys now fall in love with the looks of some of the girls with whom they have been corresponding. Yet the most touching moment is when one of the smaller boys half crawls between the barbed wire to be able to touch Palestinian soil, and fills his bottle with it. This visiting of the border event is always seen from the perspective of the Lebanese side of the border.

In total, the film travels to the border four times, always in different atmospheres and moods. The first time Masri is accompanied by loud and ecstatic singing, celebrating that the Israelis have retreated: a spontaneous party across borders ensues. The second time Mona meets Manar for the first time, and the youth organisations meet one another, exchanging t-shirts and other presents: a prepared visit with a clear goal of getting to know one another in a physical rather than an epistolary manner. Again there is singing and dancing, but this time performances are meant to impress those on the other side of the fence; it is not merely a spontaneous party. The third time Masri visits the border, it is without the girls: the second intifada has erupted and the boys have travelled to the border to show their solidarity with the Palestinians in Palestine, throwing stones across the border at Israeli soldiers. They say 'we feel we had to do something', and throw stones for their friends in Deisha, shouting out 'this one is for Manar'. The border is now a space of defiance, but also of devastation: two people were killed, among them a neighbour of one of the boys. He testifies: 'we saw his bloodstained corpse'. The border is no longer an attractive space of desire, but a place to mourn their friends inside the Palestinian territories and people that have gone there in solidarity. The fourth time the film crew returns to the border area, we again witness a larger group of refugees expressing their solidarity with one another, but instead of the initial celebratory atmosphere, there is now outrage, devastation, sadness and crying. The soldiers are back as well, patrolling and harassing the Palestinians on the Palestinian side. The contrast to their first visit to the barbed wire fences could not be greater. In the beginning people hugged, celebrated and laughed, collecting soil from the other side of the fence. Touching and being close to one another was crucial. At this point, the oppressive atmosphere has returned with an increasing sense of distance, desperation and desire for the homeland.

Not only these visits, but also the letters express desire: 'the desire to be with another and to re-imagine elsewhere and other times' (Naficy, 2006: 95). For example, Manar visits Mona's ancestral home in Palestine. She acts as her eyes and describes the experience to her in words. She writes about how beautiful it is. Nevertheless, as spectators we are aligned with Mona. We only witness Manar visiting her own ancestral home with her grandfather, we do not see Mona's homeland. The overlap between Manar and Mona then is complete: they are the same but different. Their epistolary conversations make us (and them) see things in our (and their) imagination. It is also a symbolic intervention by the film-maker to show how cut off from her homeland Mona actually is, as she cannot return to Palestine, while Manar is inside Palestine and has the one 'advantage' that she can touch her homeland's soil and see the places where they used to live.

When the intifada starts, they continue to correspond, and Mona asks about Manar's situation. Manar explains that they cannot go to school now as it is in a war zone, that she cannot sleep anymore, and that she is an emotional mess because she feels like she lives in a prison. She is shown throwing stones, saying in voice-over that throwing stones means she is rejecting injustice, and that life is perhaps not worth living if you are not free. These sentiments are not only very mature, but they also elicit an enormous flood of sympathy from Mona, as she cries and gets frustrated for her friend. These girls, while they have only met in person once, have an unseen but enormous capacity for solidarity, as they live different lives but have so much in common.

One of the most impactful events in Mona's life is when her best friend, Samar leaves Lebanon and the refugee camp. Mona writes a letter to Manar in Deisha, telling her that Samar has left without saying goodbye. 'They tore up their IDs and applied for asylum in London. I know she thinks about us. We think about her too. I have come to hate the word *travel*. Manar, I wish I could see you again. If you were a bird we could fly off and bring Samar back to Palestine,' thus returning to her dream of being a bird and flying home. Travel and space is just not possible in Palestine, but even when a refugee escapes the refugee camps, they remain a refugee, displaced and at an ever greater distance from the homeland. Samar expresses this in her turn, in her letter to Mona. The letter is heart-breaking, in particular as Mona reads it out to her friends, and she sobs and shakes but continues to read it out so that everyone of her friends can hear it. Samar is saying she is sorry, she is expressing the trauma of the ones who got away, the escapees, leaving behind their friends who continue to suffer:

> I lived with you and our friends in our own little world. We shared happiness and sadness. This was my own little kingdom, far better than any kingdom in the world. Now I don't know what I am going to do without you. You taught me the meaning of life. But there are things in life we cannot control. We had to escape. I did not realise then what it meant to leave everyone behind. It hit me the day I left. I felt my heart would stop beating. On the bus I stared at the streets, the sea, the people and the sky. I thought how can I leave, you are part of my life. Why am I a refugee. Why don't we have our own country to go to? I am a refugee wherever I am. I will be lonely without you. I love you very much. I shall never forget you. Please forgive me.

Masri shows Mona reading the letter, as she reads it out loud to her friends in Shatila. Seeing and hearing collide. At first Mona is ecstatic to have received a letter from her friend who escaped, but then their mutual suffering catches up with her and everyone sobs. Here Masri shows Mona intermittently in extreme close-up and in long-shot surrounded by friends, illustrating the personal emotions she is undergoing in close-up on the face, tears and eyes, while also revealing the solidarity between the group of friends and the common suffering as witnessed in everyone's faces and hands. The switching between close-ups and long-shots illustrate how, in unfolding the letter and unfolding its emotional content, the personal and the dialogue have become political and relevant to the whole community.

These sentiments are also expressed in the title of the film. Every teenager across the world has dreams and fears, yet these sentiments are more intense for the Palestinian teenagers we see here. This is largely because of the frontiers they have to deal with, and the limits they get imposed onto their dreams. The frontier is also a physical frontier between the girls: the barbed wire between their spaces is imaginatively destroyed through their letter writing, yet there are limits to how much they are allowed to desire one another and the spaces they inhabit. The film does not end on a note of hope. Instead, it emphasises the continuation of desperate situations and the harsh limits to these children's dreams: they live in increasingly precarious situations, and the adults in their lives cannot change this. They are resourceful but increasingly embittered young people caught in limited liminal spaces which they attempt to transgress through the epistolary crossing of borders.

Conclusion

Palestinian film-makers need children. The older generation of the PFU in the 1960s and 1970s filmed children out of necessity: the conflicts had killed many adults, and the children represented defiance of the Israeli programme to extinguish Palestinians in Palestine and in Lebanon. The film-makers in the 1980s and 1990s feared memory loss and loss of heritage, which were both represented by the children, but also defied by them, as it became obvious that the children retained a collective memory, sometimes different, but it was there. The Palestinian children represented and embodied the homeland, where their presence functioned as a reminder that the homeland needed to be won back in order for them to have a future, but also as their bodies were the homeland, they represent the continuation of the Palestinian identity, which is rooted in the land.

The younger generation of female film-makers in the 2000s continues these impulses in the representation and giving of a platform to children, but now there is a change in at whom the defiance is aimed. While the children continue to embody the homeland, the majority of adults live in fatalistic conditions and fail to hope or dream of a future in Palestine. The children, however, refuse to give in to the fear of no future, and they take charge of their lives and continue to imagine the homeland. Imagination and hope are close allies for them. Epistolarity enables the children to cross borders in their imagination, and the exilic experience becomes one in which they continue to describe to one another the homeland, so that they can imagine and embody it. Similarly, while they may have different visions of the homeland, and have to imagine it instead of being able to remember it, they play a vital role in the continuation of a collective exilic Palestinian memory. So Mai Masri and 'mothering film-makers' like her, such as Azza El Hassan and Dahna Abourahme, now need the children precisely because of their own faltering faith in, and hope for the return to, that homeland.

Notes

1. In 2016, Mai Masri's first fiction feature, *3000 Nights*, appeared. It looks at Palestinian motherhood in an Israeli prison.
2. They also received gifts; one was a 16-mm camera given to them by Jean-Luc Godard after he made *Ici et ailleurs* (1976). Annemarie Jacir writes that the PFU 'worked with Jean-Luc Godard, who always said his soul is Palestinian, on the acclaimed film *Ici et ailleurs*. Godard is "a great filmmaker; dedicated, creative and imaginative. We were both concerned to find the right film lan-

guage appropriate to the struggle for freedom," says Mustafa Abu Ali' (Jacir, 2007).

3. Hillauer also disregards the fact that Khadija Abu Ali made *two* films, as recorded by Gertz and Khleifi, claiming she only made *Children, But . . .*

4. The film is available on YouTube, see at: https://www.youtube.com/watch?v=ulfGiF6jSwY. It was rediscovered in Jordan in 2009 and is one of the films identified through crowdsourcing, by http://afilmarchive.net. It has been digitised, but because the online video has no title, it is difficult to find unless through the website of A Film Archive.

5. *They Do Not Exist* is on YouTube at: https://www.youtube.com/watch?v=2WZ_7Z6vbsg.

6. More information on the screening of Qais Al Zubaidi's films during the first festival of film in Palestine, organised by Annemarie Jacir, can be found on the website of *The Electronic Intifada* at: https://electronicintifada.net.

7. I have written about the assonance of 'bomb' and 'womb' elsewhere, see Scott and Van de Peer (2016).

8. The UN Relief and Works Agency estimates it to be around thirty years, see Chaaban et al. (2010).

9. The rights of Palestinian refugees to work in Lebanon have changed over the decades, but are still not up to the International Labour Organisation (ILO) standards: in 1982, seventy commercial and administrative professions were forbidden to Palestinians in Lebanon. This effectively meant that they were only allowed to work in construction and farming. In 1995, this law was amended and if Palestinians were born in Lebanon or married to a Lebanese woman, they were exempted from these seventy restrictions, but a work permit was still impossible to come by. In 2005, the law was again amended so that Palestinians could pay to get a work permit, but this was prohibitively expensive and still did not allow them to work in medicine or in law or benefit from the social security system while they did have to contribute to the payments. In 2010, then the law was amended once again and now states that Palestinians do not need to pay for their work permit if they have been born in Lebanon or are married to a Lebanese person, and while they have to make contributions to the social security system, they have rights only to some social security rights such as end-of-service compensation and compensation for work-related injuries, but not maternity benefits or family allowances. Palestinians can still not practice syndicated professions such as doctor or lawyer. For more detailed information, see Al-Nashif and El-Khoury (2012).

CHAPTER 6

Izza Génini: The Performance of Heritage in Moroccan Music Documentaries

Documentary was an unpopular form of film-making in an already meagre film industry dominated by men in Morocco in the 1970s and 1980s. Together with Farida Bourquia, who made television documentaries, Izza Génini was the first Moroccan woman truly devoted to the documentary. Génini produced *Transes* by Ahmed El Maanouni in 1981 and from then on directed her own documentaries, mostly concerned with music and performances, starting with the ethnographic *Aita* in 1987. *Transes* is a concert film about Nass El Ghiwane, a popular Moroccan folk rock band, and marks Génini's initial steps in a reappraisal of her home country and exploration of her musical inheritance. During the French Protectorate, Génini explains, many educated Moroccans, including herself, turned their backs on their own culture, preferring instead to direct their gaze towards France. 'Like others in my generation I rejected Moroccan culture because I thought it was inferior to the French. Our dreams of emancipation were directed towards the West' (Hillauer, 2005: 349). When she finally started to look back at Morocco, she experienced an emotional reconnection with the country's musical heritage. This personal journey has continued to define her film-making practice.

Born in 1942 in Casablanca, her parents took her with them to France in 1960, where she studied literature at the Sorbonne and became involved in festivals and the exhibition of films. Génini has made over twenty films, most of which deal with Moroccan music and its multicultural origins or the intercultural exchange that has defined Moroccan music, and Jewish–Arab relationships in Morocco. Most of her documentaries deal with women performers, and the very particular role these performers take up in the wider societal context. This chapter concentrates on Génini's first of her more than twenty films, *Aita* (1987) and her last one, *La Nûba d'Or et de Lumière* (2007). As she has been based in Paris for such a long time, for some her transnational identity excludes her from Moroccan cinema history as a diasporic film-maker. However, as I will illustrate, Moroccan cinema is an inherently transnational experience, and Génini's experience of Morocco revolves around the heritage as well as the diversity of the country.

Documentary in Morocco

In spite of the exceptionally well-organised infrastructure left behind by the French, post-colonial Moroccan cinema developed slowly. During King Hassan II's despotic rule (1961–1999), a period later referred to as *les années de plomb* or 'Years of Lead', film-makers often resorted to self-censorship to survive in the hostile climate. Censorship was widespread, and state-controlled production was limited to propaganda, educational and didactic films. Coupled with a lack of funding, these conditions prompted many film-makers to leave the country.

Under Hassan II, Moroccan nationalism was defined in terms of loyalty to both the king and Islam. Hassan's dictatorial tendencies became obvious in the 1960s, as social unrest, economic problems and student riots in Casablanca in 1965 led him to declare a state of emergency. Throughout *les années de plomb*, Hassan's regime took harsh measures against dissidents and was responsible for forced disappearances, extrajudicial killings and the imprisonment of political opponents. Consolidating its power, in 1965 Hassan's government seized control of the media. The Ministry of Information gained the right to suspend and close newspapers, film production was limited, and training and support for aspiring film-makers largely unavailable. Artists supporting revolutionary ideas such as Marxism (or any other antimonarchical movements) were arrested, tortured and sometimes killed. Films that attempted to show aspects of contemporary reality and departed from the regime's official message were boycotted, because, according to state officials, poverty, underdevelopment and even cultural diversity did not exist in Morocco (Carter, 2009: 121). Moroccan film-makers were compelled to either apprentice themselves to foreign productions or flee the country, becoming part of the *Beur Cinema* movement.[1] The role of France in contributing to Moroccan cinema cannot be ignored: *Beur Cinema* and transnational co-productions continue to dominate a European understanding of Maghrebi cinema.

Even when Souheil Benbarka, a film-maker himself, became the head of the government-funded Centre Cinématographique de Maroc (CCM) in 1986, the situation failed to improve. Censorship was imposed inconsistently and production money was divided unfairly: epic films celebrating Morocco's rule and history or documentaries instructing people on their duties were privileged for funding over projects that demonstrated creative inventiveness or an impulse towards realism. Benbarka's main goal was to establish Morocco as a centre for foreign film production, making the country's beauty and mystery strong selling points. Government policy focused on film as a tool for influencing perceptions of the newly formed nation and supporting its illusionary uniform national identity (Carter, 2008: 538). By investing only in films that confirmed this vision of Morocco, the CCM limited itself to a meagre cinematic output.

Bowing to external (human rights issues) and internal (demographic changes) pressure, in the 1990s, Hassan II began the slow process of democratisation. Upon his death in 1999, his son Mohammed VI succeeded him. The young king's understanding of the role of the arts in constructing a unified national identity led to increased artistic freedom. The CCM was placed under a new leadership whose international ambitions secured the country's position on the post-colonial francophone film map.

Since the 1990s, two distinct tendencies can be identified in Moroccan cinema, both directly related to Morocco's contemporary cultural identity as a globalising country. First, the CCM decreed that in order to raise money to invest in Moroccan cinema, it was necessary to attract foreign production to Morocco. The country was (and still is) actively marketed for its potential as the location for epic international films. As it had been in colonial times, Morocco became once again attractive to foreign film-makers on account of its cheap labour, established infrastructure and dramatic landscapes. At the same time, the CCM encouraged exiled Moroccan film-makers to return home after three decades of oppression. Central to this campaign was the annual Festival National du Film de Tanger. Although first held in 1982, the festival's organisation was sporadic until the mid-1990s. With the CCM's backing, the festival was re-envisioned as a showcase for Moroccan creativity, reflecting a new understanding of the importance of national and transnational productions in forging a new modern national identity. In contrast to the repressive cultural policies of the early Hassan II government, which enforced a false vision of linguistic, ethnic and religious unity, Morocco's new openness to diversity under the later government of Hassan II and then that of Mohammed VI encouraged more self-reflexive productions. Jamal Bahmad explains how the 1995 National Film Festival in Tangier was a watershed event in Moroccan cinema:

> New directors from the diaspora, second-generation Moroccan immigrants in Europe in the majority, were invited to screen their short films in the festival. The new cineastes met their old compatriots, discussions flourished about the state of national cinema, and the Moroccan Cinema Centre promised to cast the net of its funding recipients wider to incorporate the new filmmakers. (Bahmad, 2013: 77)

Also in 1995, a *Cinemathèque* or national film archive was established with the aim of conserving the nation's cinematic patrimony and acquiring new titles in world cinema (Carter, 2009: 202). Moreover, film-makers discovered, through the influx of Moroccans from abroad, the potential of international co-productions was a way through which to secure new (independent) funds. These factors, together with a growing domestic audience, revealed the potential for film-makers of Moroccan descent to return to Morocco and produce and exhibit films there.

Since the early 1990s, exiled and diasporic Moroccan film-makers have started to look back at Morocco for their cultural identity. The inward gaze replacing an outlook steadily fixed on Europe was the signature of a new artistic process. Bahmad shows that Moroccan cities are foregrounded both visually and in terms of film narrative; Casablanca and Marrakech are prominent influences on the spatial, social and political context of many recent films. An urban, neo-liberal reality is the core of a growing cultural consciousness and development. Most importantly, film-makers seek to establish a more intimate relationship with an urban, young Moroccan audience, resulting in more accessible films anchored in a recognisable Moroccan reality mixed with elements of popular cinema.

The history of cinema in Morocco delineates the struggle with national and cultural identity, mainly due to the country's colonial experience as a Protectorate of France and Spain, but also due to post-colonial circumstances dependent on the monarchy and religion. Its position as a crossroads nation has perpetuated this duality of identity: Morocco occupies a unique position between the Arab world, Africa and Europe, and as such its national identity has never been settled or homogeneous. This developing transcultural identity is finding full expression in the country's cinema; while for most of the twentieth century, Morocco had by far the lowest film production levels in the Maghreb, since the late 1990s, production levels have surged as Moroccan cinema found its domestic and transnational audience, ushering in a true revolution in film-making.

Moroccan Women and Documentary

Reflecting the country's struggles with conflicting visions of its national identity, the representation and presence of women in the Moroccan film industry has been unbalanced. Very few women have had a significant role in Moroccan cinema. Pisters shows how, until the 2000s, women directors were extremely rare: it was not until then that women started to make 'modern political films' (Pisters, 2007: 77). In the 1970s, one young woman, Farida Bourquia, joined the film-making scene through a variety of roles in administration and production (scriptwriter, assistant director, production manager). Bourquia is especially prolific as a television producer. In 1975, the UN International Year of Women, she created a ground-breaking television documentary series about women in Morocco. This was the same year that Selma Baccar and Assia Djebar started work on their feminist documentary statements as well. In 1988, Farida Benlyazid, following a successful career as a screenwriter, became the first Moroccan woman to direct her own feature film, *Une porte sur le ciel* (*A Door to the Sky*).[2] These two women now dominate the documentary scene in Morocco, with Benlyazid having produced *CasaNayda* and Bourquia directing *Deux Femmes sur la Route* (*Two Women on the Road*), as recently as 2007. In 2003, Leila Kilani joined their documentary ranks with her successful documentaries confronting political and economic inequalities. Her prize-winning documentary oeuvre is representative of the urban, realist trend in recent Moroccan cinema. Génini's films are often neglected in the context of strong political women's films, as they emphasise Morocco's multicultural heritage through music and ritual performances, not so much in direct political or feminist statements. Yet, as the first Moroccan woman dedicated consistently to independent documentary making, she celebrates her own and her country's transnational identity in her films. As we shall see, to 'see' these cultural elements of her interest in music, enfolds an acute interest in women's issues and politics, heavily influenced by a subjective point of view and ethno-musicology.

When Génini started to make films in the late 1980s, Moroccan cinema was undergoing two significant developments. First, a new tendency towards realism connected audiences more directly with the subjects in the films, and, secondly, representations of women slowly became more diverse as women film-makers took up the camera in the North African region. While documentary production was certainly not encouraged by the CCM, Génini's documentaries, mostly nostalgic on the surface, fit in perfectly with these trends. With her outsider look, she was one of those returnees who were in a position to leave as transnational film-makers, and, as such, with their film-making 'helped reconstruct the nation (Pisters, 2007: 87). However, Génini did not wish to cross any boundaries that were drawn by the censorship board. In an interview, she points out that her documentaries were not subject to censorship:

> My relationship with the CCM has existed for several decades, without any problems. For years I was their representative in Paris. With censorship, you have to keep in mind the subject matter of my documentaries; I have never been confronted with it. Moreover, Morocco has since long adopted the principle of freedom of

expression, on the level of press as well as on the level of art. If one does not touch HM the King or Islam one is safe. (Interview, 2011a)

This needs to be put into context, as freedom of expression has not always been as clearly protected as Génini claims. Documentaries in the 1990s remained primarily occupied with national development issues, which through their local focus were meant to encourage national unity. Within these constraints, Génini was making films that, while not politically direct or militant, certainly surprised by their topic: she was mostly interested in intercultural exchange and the multicultural heritage of Berbers, Jews and Arabs in southern Morocco, especially as reflected in the diversity of Moroccan music. This multiculturalism, however, is in her films often taken as a given instead of being explored critically. Her approach favours music above all else: she is vehemently opposed to sociological or ethnographic documentaries and claims her films are not intended to be historical or anthropological. She paints a picture of a Moroccan utopia, where there is peace between different religious denominations, a peace facilitated by music. She films from a subjective point of view, and thus seems to overlook more pressing socio-political issues, which are nevertheless subliminally present in the background in her films.

Génini takes a creative and intuitive approach to the documentary. She relishes the opportunities for creative thinking and spontaneous development:

> I like documentaries. It is a form that I appreciate, as it lets you discover things and people in a very 'physical' way. The heritage of Black Africa and of the Maghreb is not well known and a great many documentaries should be made. There is no lack of subjects or ideas. The documentary is above all an irreplaceable school. The impossibility to foresee events and the limits of writing, make filming an adventure where the quota of risk cannot be calculated. This situation of 'danger' requires suppleness and spontaneity from the filmmaker and makes inventiveness all the more essential at the editing stage but, in return, offers fantastic opportunities for creation. (Deffontaines, 1993: 15)

Her reflections on the CCM, on her subjects and on the form of documentary making confirm that Génini's approach to documentary is didactic, and largely anthropological, in spite of her claims that they are not. Moreover, her words 'suppleness' and 'spontaneity' echo my understanding of negotiation and solidarity.

In 1973, Génini set up SOGEAV, a distribution company (renamed OHRA in 1987 when she made her first film, *Aita*) devoted to the distribution of francophone films throughout Africa. She distributed music films and documentaries, and later focused on bringing African films to the attention of European audiences. The reason she did this is simple: as she acknowledges, distribution is the weak link in the film business, especially in Morocco. It is important for Génini not only to see her own films screened inside as well as outside Morocco, but also to distribute other directors' films more widely.

In 1981, she made *Transes* with Ahmed El Maanouni. Farida Ayari, chief of communications at UNICEF and Génini's friend, explains that the 1970s and early 1980s were a time when world music was still struggling. Together with Génini she discovered Nass El Ghiwane, a Moroccan fusion group. The term 'world music' really emerged as a category in the late 1980s, when a number of independent record labels coined the term (Armstrong, 1987). Nass El Ghiwane was very popular among the youth in Morocco and France, and Génini and Ayari followed them to their concerts across French cities. When she was asked to assist on the making of the film, she jumped at the opportunity.

Until 1981, *Transes* was the only concert and music film from Morocco. It instigated Génini's personal discovery of her home country. It was therefore a very personal and intimate decision for her to follow this route in her own films as well. The film with Maanouni was born out of the passion of a fan for a group, and it determined the rest of her career. In 2007, moreover, *Transes* proved to be an important film for more than just Génini and the Moroccan fans of Nass El Ghiwane: Martin Scorsese's World Cinema Fund restored the film and gave it a new life almost thirty years after it was made. While it took Génini a few years, until 1987, to decide to make *Aita* herself, this period of gestation ensured that she has always had a clear view of what her goal was with her ethno–music documentaries.

Génini's Documentaries

Her first film, *Aita* (1987), set out Génini's artistic programme. The film follows a group of travelling female troubadours, Cheikhat. Cheikha Fatna Bent El Hocine and her troupe travel the festivals of Morocco to perform. They sing the aita: songs about the adventures of tribal men, solitude, the joys and the despair of love and hope. Their itinerant lifestyle brings with it a stigma of the loose woman. The Cheikhat are reviled because their liberal lifestyle does not parallel the stereotypical expectations attached to womanhood in Morocco. They are outsiders, young girls that have run away from home to pursue their ambitions as singers. Génini says in an interview: 'they are not really accepted by society because they are considered too free and independent: they travel, they live with men, they smoke, and they drink' (Hillauer, 2005: 350). Yet it is Génini's firm belief that music connects generations and traditions. She looks at the past being performed in the present and discovers a Moroccan identity in the art of song. Her main message therefore in *Aita* is: these Cheikhat are artists, not prostitutes, and their songs invoke the forgotten past that constructs at least part of a Moroccan cultural identity.

Génini's latest film *La Nûba d'Or et de Lumière* (2007) is another exploration of a musical genre that is popular as well as old-fashioned. Olivier Barlet (2008) said that in Morocco the Nûba is often regarded as old and stilted, while Génini aims to illustrate that the music is, on the contrary, very much alive, with numerous orchestras across Morocco, who in their own manner explore the different influences the Nûba has undergone over the centuries. As I explored in relation to Djebar's film *La Nouba* (1978), the Nouba or Nûba is traditional music from the Maghreb. The origin is uncertain, but what is generally accepted is that the music comes from Andalusia. Unlike Djebar, Génini does spend time explaining the musical genre in the film. Djebar uses it as a structuring device for the film, Génini as a subject. Génini says that the Nûba was invented by a poet from Baghdad who arrived in Cordoba in the ninth century. The word Nouba or Nûba literally means 'taking one's turn', as we saw with Djebar's film. In Génini's explanation, too, different poets took their turn to impress the royal families. In more contemporary translations, it is also worded as 'living it up', or 'partying'. Both translations express the basis of the concept of the Nûba: it is a musical symphony with a very specific rhythmic pattern that in its poetic lyrics celebrates life as well as mourning death. According to the musicians in *La Nûba d'Or et de Lumière*, there were originally twenty-four Nûbas, one for every hour of the day. Most have been lost; eleven remain thanks to El Haik of Tétouan who wrote them down in the eighteenth century. The eleven remaining Nûbas are expressed differently depending on where they are being played and interpreted. The orchestras of Fez, Tangier, Chefchaouen, Ksar El Kébir, Rabat or Safi remain loyal to the original traditions of performance, but the musical interpretation differs depending on the city.

In Djebar's *La Nouba des Femmes du Mont Chenoua*, the sung texts have the function of looking and listening to the women in the film as they are set in their natural environment in reality. Génini's documentary (made two decades later) emphasises the Nûba's contemporary revival in love songs and poetic performances. Her goal is to restore faith in this type of music in modern Morocco. In the title of the film, 'Or et Lumière' refer to the golden age for Arab knowledge and art in enlightened Andalusian times, in medieval Spain and Morocco. She highlights the cultural exchange between the cultures and their importance for the development of the Arab world. Her own transnational identity therefore greatly influences her perception of different art forms and Morocco's heritage in general. She insists on the diversity of Moroccans' identities.

Génini dismisses objectivity in documentary. She emphasises her entirely subjective approach by inserting herself into the narrative. She acknowledges her outsider status and exploits her transnational identity within Morocco. Even the purely informative sequences in the films are built on the love she feels for music and her conviction of its relevance for all subjects in the films. She states in several interviews that her interest in music and national heritage stem from an emotional reconnection with her own past. Music, film and Morocco are inseparable since the making of *Transes*. With *Aita*, for example, it has become clear that through her encounter with Morocco, and with the music of Morocco in particular, she renewed her personal connection to the country and its heritage. She told me:

> The inspiration that led to my production and directing of the series *Maroc, Body and Soul*, is the result of a long process that was instigated in March 1973, when I had returned to Morocco after 13 years of absence. From then on, I really got to know my country of origin, via its culture, its music, its language, its nature, etc. Working in the film world in Paris, I attached myself to the cinema of Morocco, producing and distributing Moroccan films. At the same time, I got to know a musical treasure. I particularly liked Fatna Bent El Hocine, whom I discovered at Essaouira. She was the one to inspire me to make my first film; I had to do it in order to safeguard her talent for the future. (pers. correspondence, 2011a)

Génini's subjective approach is most explicit in *Retrouver Oulad Moumen*.[3] It is a subjective exploration of the migration patterns of her own family: a Jewish-Moroccan family dispersed throughout the world, from Marrakesh to Casablanca, to Boucheron (now El Ghara) and eventually to Paris in France. Some continued their travels to the United States, Mexico and Martinique. From the first few minutes of the film, Génini puts herself centrally in the frame. A slow-motion sequence shows a group of people getting ready to have their group picture taken. They are celebrating Génini's own birthday, the occasion she chose to bring her extended family back to their place of origin: Oulad Moumen. This photographic aspect of the first few sequences continues throughout the film: the source material she uses for an illustration of history is made up of photographs (sepia or black and white) and archival footage, home videos and old family pictures.

The moment Génini decides to return to Oulad Moumen for the first time, she is alone, travelling through Morocco as a tourist. It is her first time in Morocco since she left when she was eighteen years old. On her journey through the country, she meets people in the places to which they had emigrated, who remember her family and with whom she re-establishes an immediate intimate bond. Génini often enters the frame and gets close to family members and old friends. She joins in the family routines when people are singing, talking, eating. The whole film has a very intimate feel, and the subjective approach adds a familiarity to her exploration of Morocco. It shows her emotional, personal reconnection to be intimately entwined with heritage, migration and art, in particular music.

The exchanges between music traditions, she reveals, also entail an exchange between different ethnicities. The wider perspective of the films is not always directly visible. For Génini it is a nostalgic look into the past that inspires her to make creative documentaries. Nevertheless, a closer look at some of the topics and subjects she approaches do reveal a wider political point of view and a critical eye, if one looks further and listens better, a subtle, enfolded central concern with Moroccan women and minorities is revealed, just as Patricia Pisters sees it in more recent women's films (2007). *Aita* questions the status of itinerant women singers; *Retrouver Oulad Moumen* seemingly avoids the questions or answers about emigration, but they are implied precisely because of the personal bond between the family and the spectator; and *La Nûba d'Or et de Lumière* digs deeper into the performances of the women singers and love poetry of an ancient and well-respected art form. The film-maker's personal relationship with women, artists and a multicultural Morocco leads to ambiguous dissident questions, and a trust in the intellectual abilities and unfolding power of the spectator will lead to possible answers through really 'seeing' and listening. The ostensible absence of conflict or tension in her films is not only a political choice but also an aesthetic statement. While she avoids the censor and ensures investment, her style also reveals multiple enfolded layers to the Morocco she represents. Her own transnational knowledge is reflected in this: being an insider and outsider, she can see and reveal that Morocco is a diverse nation. Her transnationality enables her to accept the various individual aspects of the country. Instead of unity, then, she advocates transnationality, het-erogeneity and diversity, like a mosaic that is only truly understood when observed from a relative distance.

In Génini's films, music represents Morocco, and it takes on such an important role that it becomes a character in its own right. She loves music and wants to represent a subaltern type of music that does not, in her view, get the attention it deserves. She told me:

Making these films, I became aware at which point music films are difficult to edit and at which point they remain subjective. The technical difficulty of cutting in the music, the notions of time, rhythm and tempo are personal and at the same time they need to make sense to the spectator. It is a subtle balance to find between listening and seeing. For me, when speaking about music, what is essential to clarify is the pleasure one experiences. (pers. correspondence, 2011a)

The music not only shapes the structure of the film, it is also the subject that needs to be listened to and seen. She films music and performances in their natural settings, bringing the camera into the situation instead of bringing the situation to the camera. Music in these films represents a spirit of freedom and tolerance. To capture music visually, she shows performances and musicians practising. In addition, she captures audiences and visualises their experience. Génini's documentaries therefore visualise sound. On the reason why she chose to make music documentaries, she comments:

Music constitutes a red thread throughout my career. The first feature-length film I produced (*Transes*) was musical. When I became a director myself, I was immediately attracted to making a film about women singers, the Cheikhats . . . The music of Morocco is so rich and diverse that I have never stopped being surprised and I keep discovering: I am always ready to crack a new genre or a new voice. (Jezequel, 2006)

As music ethnologist Deborah Kapchan acknowledges, music is an intercultural, transnational exchange that holds the promise of universal understanding. But even 'a promise is a "performative": it enacts rather than refers and by its very action accomplishes its goal, which is to create an intersubjective contract that is often affective and implicit rather than acknowledged and juridical' (Kapchan, 2008: 470). As a non-verbal means of communication it relies on the solidarity raised by sounds and the common experience of them. It represents the hope that there is a common human experience that can comprehend the other across borders and cultures, and the 'self-selecting festival audience embraces the promise' (Kapchan, 2008: 470). This intersubjective belief in the language of music holds true for Génini's emotional connection to it, and her very subjective approach. The belief in the power of music reflects another, more contemporary hope for transnationalism: that cultural diversity is an urgent theme in a world in which the rise of fundamentalism is so obvious.

An attempt is made to give new life to heritage through the testimony of the protagonists. These protagonists are usually discovered at yearly festivals in Morocco, where she films and interviews them. Kapchan illustrates that Morocco is a country of festivals. She argues that festivals create exceptional circumstances, where the willingness to perform and be heard as well as to perceive ('see') and listen is heightened and out of the ordinary: 'the Moroccan monarchy has many stakes in the spate of yearly festivals. They construct a public discourse of neoliberalism and engage producers in the active creation of Moroccan culture as a product of national and international consumption' (Kapchan, 2008: 471). That the government has high stakes in these festivals does not mean they are not also used for awareness-raising through music and gatherings. This potential for music and festivals to be politically challenging as well as entertaining is nothing new. Génini highlights the wealth of intercultural exchange and its importance for the development of the Arab world.

Aita (1987)

Fatna Bent el Hocine is a Cheikha, the performing and singing protagonist of Génini's first film, and in later films she continues to focus on Moroccan women's identities and performances. Génini said it is easier to gain access to the internal world of the women she encounters than to men. In our correspondence, she admits this is due to 'a natural rapport between women, no doubt. A different way of communicating, simply explicable by a certain modesty inherent to a Moroccan upbringing, that holds on to the sense of hierarchy.' She observes a natural sympathy from woman to woman and is aware of the patriarchal hierarchy that is inherent to society.

Cheikhat travel from festival to festival between the many cities of Morocco that celebrate music and traditional fantasias. At these festivals the Cheikhat perform songs and dances praising the knights. Openly expressing their female lust, they are celebrated for their transgressions at the same time as being stigmatised for them. The Cheikhat approach the guests, their audience, and dance and sing at high volume directly in front of their spectators. Their dancing takes the form of wild hair waving in a trance-like state. This is meant to excite the men in the audience and lure them in to join the trance – usually the privilege of men. Kapchan clarifies what Génini subtly hints at: these women in themselves are controversial subject matter in Moroccan society.

Cheikhat can be celebrated at festivals precisely because these are extraordinary moments. Only in these circumstances can they be accepted. Their marginality in larger society stands in stark contrast to their central-ity at festivals. They challenge moral codes and transgress propriety. They blur boundaries between public and private and cross boundaries between acceptable female and acceptable male behaviour. In other words, they are anomalies (Kapchan, 2002: 88). As Kapchan explains, codes of propriety are central in Moroccan society, and the transgression of Cheikhat is entirely context-dependent. They sing about sexual encounters. The content of the songs and the Cheikhat's subversive performative behaviour have given them the stigmas of prostitutes. The exaggeration of their public persona takes in the stereotypes and enacts expectations, as Judith Butler (1990) has explained in her concept of performativity. The singer becomes a fetishised commodity occupying the margins of Moroccan society with reputations of licentious living (Kapchan, 2002: 83).

Their position on the margins, the stigma attached to their reputation (rightly or wrongly), and the exceptional space of the festival provide these outsiders the possibility to become insiders. Like the film-maker, Cheikhat have an informed, potentially more detached insight into society, as they observe while being observed. The Cheikhat 'represent the inner thoughts of respectable women insofar as they are licensed in the performance context to publicize the private desires and disappointments of the majority of Moroccan women' (Kapchan, 2002: 89). Cheikhat are women with the performative power to divulge women's secrets in public. Génini's choice to portray in her very first film the disenfranchised but extraordinary itinerant woman singer, indicates a preoccupation with women as outsiders. Her wish to portray Fatna as an artist informs our perception of these women as well. It subtly reveals the process of society to control and exclude them. This encourages Fatna to welcome Génini to follow their itinerary so closely, as it offers an opportunity for the singer to portray herself as she wishes, through her knowledge and lifestyle.

Génini's and Fatna's personal relationship adds value to the film in the sense that it emphasises the individual nature of Fatna's performance in front of the camera and in front of her audience at the festivals. The identity of the performer is straightforward due to the relationship between director and subject, while the identity of the spectator is very complex. Fatna and her troupe are identified as the singers/dancers/subjects. They are in charge of what is performed and how. It is also clear from their performance that they are accustomed to being the spectacle and a type of indifference has set in with relation to the spectators: Fatna lets her young dancers take centre stage while she remains in the background, focusing on the songs.

These women's performances are sensual and spiritual, depending on the content of the songs and their purpose. Kapchan calls the Cheikhat's movements 'carnivalesque enactments of the body' (2002: 87). Rhythmical hip movements and the display of a minute control of the lower body directly in front of the audience are extremely daring. The hair tossing during the trance problematises the normal rules of propriety and

Figure 6.1 A close-up of Cheikha Fatna Bent El Hocine singing while her dancers sway centre stage in *Aita* (1987) © Izza Génini

crosses the boundary with what is accepted as typically female behaviour. Turning the social (male) gaze upon aspects of female expression that are taboo except in the context of performance is the subtly and carefully constructed ambition of the Cheikhat. While left unuttered, the quiet rebellion is enacted upon the men with the help of extreme body movements. It is the body that imposes itself upon the spectators and that leaves the most permanent impression. The film is an illustration of the strength and integrity of the female performers, and their status as guardians of the transnational heritage.

In *Aita*, the audience is at least threefold. First, there are the festival goers. They not only watch, they also contribute to the performance at the Moussem. The circumstances and the performance invite a male audience. At first sight there is a clear distance between performers and audience. The audience is seated on long rows of pillows at the edge of the performance areas, while the dancers perform in the middle, on carpets. Next, the guests are approached by the performers, who dance right in front of their faces and sing directly at them. The dancers expect full participation. As the singing and dancing continue, the male audience starts to participate in the trance. With the Cheikhat, they lose themselves in the trance, swaying their bodies, smiling ecstatically and waving their guns around. In terms of Butler's understanding of gender performativity, the men here take on stereotypically male behaviour, responding to the performed female behaviours of the Cheikhat. The men perform for each other as much as for the Cheikhat and the camera. Holding on to the phallic symbol of the gun, performing thrusting movements unconsciously in the trance, the men are just as caught up in the game of seduction as the Cheikhat are. The difference is that the Cheikhat are aware of their performative nature and the men are not. The male audience, then, also becomes performer and receives its own audience, the Cheikhat.

Secondly, Génini and her film crew witness and record both the performance of the Cheikhat as well as the participating audience. The presence of the camera and film crew influences the performance, as the camera becomes a *provocateur*. Nevertheless, the element of repetition between the many performances as well as the repetitive nature of the performances individually ensures a limited attention being paid to the interference of the camera. While the film crew are spectators of the performance and they witness the bond of trance between the singers, dancers and their audience, they do not participate in the trance. As outsiders who are also insiders, they are tolerated and become an object of curiosity. The Cheikhat acknowledge the presence of the camera by looking at it and raising their eyebrows in an intersubjective conspiracy, while their audience of men gaze straight into the camera interested mainly in themselves. The way the camera is a provocateur, the audience also provokes the camera and the implied spectator. In a way they demand an audience for themselves, through their performance. The camera's presence, however minimally it interferes, does provoke a performative event, while at the same time the Cheikhat and their audience are aware of the film crew and become the crew's audience.

Lastly, the spectator of the film watches an amalgam of performances: the Cheikhat singing and dancing, the film being made by Génini and the male audience in rapt trances due to the Cheikhat's performance and the camera *provocateur*. The ritualised performances diminish the meaning of the spectacle, but the spectator of the film as outsider may unfold the trance productively. One question is: who can the film spectator align with? In other words, where is the opportunity for the film spectator to sympathise intersubjectively with the Cheikhat or the film-maker? There are three candidates for identification: Cheikhat, audience or film crew. The complex identity of spectatorship in Génini's films attests to her being a transnational participant/observer. For the spectator it is imperative to

become an active spectator and make a conscious decision about identification. The proximity to and emotional bond the film-maker establishes
with her subject, as well as the close bond between the Cheikhat and their
audience, enable allegiances between all parties. Different perspectives
potentially afford the spectator of the film diverse impulses to negotiate
their own identity and the transnational experience of watching the film.

As anthropologist Combs-Schilling points out, when Génini deals with
more controversial issues there is a visual display of sharply meaningful contrasts that are iconically presented but not verbally explicated
(1991: 517). This is a much more interesting aspect of Génini's artistic
choices. She over-explains the obvious and refuses to explain where she
makes more political observations. Some areas of the films feel didactic,
while others leave the spectator curious. It propels the spectator from the
passive position of being taught to actively having to study and critically
think about certain aspects of the films. This push-and-pull factor is arguably a conscious choice: as the censorship board had a considerable stake
in film-making in the 1980s, it is quite possible that the contrasting voice-
overs and silences are both elements of self-censorship. Emphasising the
self-evident aspects of a performance such as the venue or the time of day
potentially divert attention away from more contentious issues such as the
lyrics or the physical aspects of the performance.

While Génini pushes and pulls the spectator in and out with her voice-
over, she does trust the power of the universal language of music and
the soundtrack to her films to pull in the spectator consistently. Music is
not only a character in her films, it is also a language. It tells the history
of a people through nature, myths, and beliefs and understanding of the
cosmos. It talks of pre-Islamic African influence and the intermingling of
cultures in the Maghreb. In an individual and subjective mode of expression, it tells of migration and of the influences it took with it along the way
– Morocco is a mix of Berber, Arab, Jewish, French, sub-Saharan identities, and the music expresses this. The film shows that Moroccan music
bears witness to the intermingling of cultures and traditions, and it is the
expression of this transcultural aspect of the Moroccan heritage. Génini
testifies: 'I was silent, an outsider, but felt it inside – I recognised it.'
This ephemeral, abstract feeling of understanding music without needing
translations or the knowledge to play it, the ability to simply enjoy and
interpret it is what makes everyone free to understand music in an individual way. In other words, it is the ideal medium to express intersubjective
solidarity, as it becomes a universal language. Moreover, lyrics, consisting
of certain recognisably transgressive motives avoided in normal speech,
or allusions and metaphors, may express the otherwise unutterable. Like

poetry, song lyrics have the ability to insinuate and imply rather than express straightforwardly. Hidden messages are widely understood and not necessarily censored, as they are traditional or ambiguous and subtle.

In the first few transcribed lyrics of the Cheikhat the translation that is given in subtitles is: 'We reached Azzemmour, we saw the crowd. I have come here in my car so I can venerate you.' They announce where they have come from and where they are going, how they move around and even the mode of transportation. At the Moussem of Moulay Abdallah, with which the film opens, it emphasises the Cheikhat's freedom and independence. They announce their autonomy and their choice to come here, and are independent enough to own their own car. Moments later, they describe their current situation at the festival: horses, weapons and knights are ready for the fantasia, and the echo of the party calls them towards it. They sing about the good deeds in history, written down over the years, in which they rejoice.

Yet in Fatna's hotel room, Fatna and her female singers teach Génini about the true nature of the Cheikhat and their passion for the songs and lyrics. The lyrics they present to the film-maker here are quite different to the lyrics of the songs they sang on camera in front of their male audience earlier in the film. The lyrics to the songs they sing privately are diametrically opposed to the venerating ones they sang in public:

> Tell my lover to return to me. He has abandoned me, and nobody has pity on me. My track has closed up, leave me alone. I have poured so many tears that the river has left its bed. Death is treacherous but between us there was no calculated atmosphere, come back. The pain you caused me, I will forgive you. Between us there is no quarrel. I will turn towards God and he will forgive me my sins . . . My burning is so alive. I am finished; my suffering will only get worse. I am alone and a vagabond.

Admitting to sins is quite controversial in itself, and the lyrics have an immediately subversive content as well: 'my track has closed up' can be interpreted in a sexual way, and is meant to be ambiguous. Moreover, if her 'burning is so alive' it refers to the burning inside her body, the lust for the lover who has left her. She is not speaking of a husband but an occasional lover.

In the relaxed atmosphere of her hotel room, Fatna forgets about the camera as she speaks directly to the director. Fatna says: 'the Aita [repertoire of songs] has passionate followers. Some ruin themselves in order to follow a Cheikha'. She explains there are certain Aita classics known by everyone, sung at large festivals, but her favourites are the other, hidden ones. She says: 'of some Aitas, no one knows the origins. They are the ones that elevate me to another state of mind. The best one is the one from

Abda. I went there when I was eighteen and they taught me treasures from that repertoire.' This explanation refers to the song that has more innuendo than the others. Fatna turns to Génini, on her right away from the camera, and repeats that this is her favourite. She has known it since she was eighteen, and this sensual song made her decide to become a Cheikha. She knew and chose a lifestyle on the fringes of society. This is a truly intersubjective moment between director and Fatna, where the Cheikha grabs her opportunity unconsciously to assert her voice.

In her anthropological study of the Cheikhat, Kapchan acknowledges that they overtly sing words that imply and express sexuality, dance, love and pleasure. The lyrics of the Aitas attest to the power of the feminine desire to change lives and circumstances, to break the silence of women – one of the bases of Moroccan civilisation (Kapchan, 2002: 91). As singing artists they juxtapose mournful words, festive voicing and sexualised dancing acts both to define and, at least momentarily, to resolve crises. Their performances often have a therapeutic effect on communities, who can potentially move away from propriety during the performance and freely think or express their woes. The contradiction between the Cheikhat's exclusion from society and their inclusion in performative circumstances is celebrated, embodied and made into a strength by the women themselves.

The apparent lack of commentary in voice-over is compensated by the repeated juxtaposition of particular images. 'The film is a visual exposition of sharply meaningful contrasts and parallels that are ironically presented but not verbally explicated' (Combs-Schilling, 1991: 517). In *Aita*, the performers are compared and contrasted to horses. Two separate sequences are edited together in such a way that it is the film language that makes a point, not the voice-over. With little commentary, the camera's-eye alternates from the women inside one of the buildings, dressed in their glittering gowns and wailing out gusty songs for the crowds of seated men, to the outside scenes of the moussem itself, where men in elegant white robes are seated on prancing horses decked out in glittering trappings that bring to mind the garments the women wear.

The women are inside, performing in their beautiful clothes and waving their long hair, for the pleasure of the men. Outside, the horses are saddled, tossing their manes and paraded before the men. Are these, then, two performances for the benefit of the men, or is there a deeper meaning to the juxtaposition of these images? In succession, the women put on make-up, brush their hair, and put on garments and jewellery. At the same time, horses are saddled and bedecked with jewel-encrusted belts and reins. Next, the women perform: they sing loudly and passionately, and toss their hair from left to right in order to stimulate the men who are (in the fantasia) going into battle. Their song ends abruptly as they stand directly in front of a number of spectators. Simultaneously, the men outside mount their horses and are handed shotguns to partake in a short, intense race. The horses gallop towards the end of the short parcours, and directly in front of the spectators, they are brought to a sudden stop by their riders as they shoot their gun in the air. Both women and horses then are brought to a sudden halt by the men. Metaphorically, men have proved their power over the unbridled passions of both women and horses. It is the combination of images that expresses Génini's commentary, not her voice.

Anthropologically, Kapchan explains, this is not uncommon. Cheikhat all over Morocco are compared with horses, not only during the moussem or the performance of the fantasia. She explains that a fantasia is a dramatic event that engages the spectator as well as the actors in agonistic play (Kapchan, 2002: 86). It is a game of dare that is played with the audience. Show horses are displayed at national and religious festivals, as they give prestige to the owner. They are a source both of pride and of financial obligation. Just like women, they are supporters as well as carriers of men who ride upon them in the capacity of both owner and the one in need of being carried. It represents the cultural construct in Morocco of women as subordinate to men, while it also bears witness to a subtle agency of a being that is strong enough to take risks and support the man. The performance of the Cheikhat is communicative in that the body is communicative where the voice might be stifled. This paradox is revealed and accepted only because of the enactment of it during the fantasia. An unreality is created in which there is space to play with what is socially permissible. The performance space offers an opportunity for self-revelation, ambiguous meanings and subtle resistance to the dominant cultural constructs.

At the end of the film we find the most straightforward non-verbal ironic comment by the director: Cheikha Fatna visits a shrine as she is a devoted worshipper, but she seems a completely different person. She is quiet and submissive, is not allowed to sing and must sit still. She has her eyes downcast while the men around her look at her. The contrast between her performance inside the tent and her stifled voice at the open-air shrine is almost painful. It displays Génini's strongest sense of injustice and protest, and acknowledges that while Génini refuses to admit to a subtle critique of women's subaltern status, she does appear to be concerned with the spatial separation of the genders or the limited freedom Cheikhat can experience in public spaces.

As music and dance require a performance in public, this performance is unlikely in any other context. As the foremost Moroccan feminist Fatima Mernissi said, the modesty and silence of women is what Moroccan society is based on and women are still relegated to the private spheres. Female performances are Moroccan oxymorons. Yet they are an indispensable part of Moroccan celebrations. Their dual existence as wanted and rejected puts them in an enfolded position in between the social layers of society, and outside of society as a whole. Having a foot in the various camps makes female performers insider–outsiders in their society: as the performers gaze upon their audience, it offers the women the opportunity to look in and see what others might not.

La Nûba d'Or et de Lumière (2007)

The complex spectatorship in *Aita* is further explored in Génini's later film, *Nûba d'Or et de Lumière*. In the first few minutes of the feature-length film, Abdelghani Yazimi, a weaver from Fez, is in his shop, looking at footage of himself as an audience member and participant in the performance of a Nûba concert in Fez. On the one hand, Génini shows his intense and real engagement with the music and the musicians, and, on the other hand, she makes a spectacle out of him more than the seated musicians. Moreover, the music is supposed to be spiritual as is seen in the rest of the audience, where most people remain seated and some enjoy the music with eyes closed. Génini illustrates that each experience of the music is individual, while the context shows that it is also communal. The intersubjective experience of the performance between audience and players, between players and camera, and between camera and audience enables the many diverse possible receptions.

As he sees himself on the screen, Yazimi seems content with his performance. In the voice-over, Génini explains that they met at the concert in Fez. This implies that he stood out from the large audience precisely because of his performance. He comments on the footage of himself adopting what at times seems like an apologetic stance: he says he cannot help it, his is a real appreciation of the art of the Nûba. He says it is necessary for an audience member to intimately know and understand the music before one can appreciate it the way he does. His relationship with the camera is a double one: he seems proud of his knowledge and experience of the Nûba, but is also concerned with his own subject-status in the film.

In the bonus features of *Nûba d'Or et de Lumière*, there is an homage to the performance of the Nûba in Chefchaouen, where Génini is present as an audience member and as an artist, as her film on the Nûba is screened in several places throughout the city. The footage of the open-air screenings includes interviews with her about her personal experience of filming the Nûba. It gives her the opportunity to interact with her own audience on different levels. Some of the musicians and artists from her film are present at the screening. She says on film that she likes to receive feedback from the musicians as well as the spectators. But the feedback Génini gets is also feedback for the musicians themselves: as they are on screen performing, their audience more than doubles and they witness different types of feedback: those from the audience members at the performance, and those of the spectators of the film, plus the feedback by Génini. This very complex engagement with the audience and the spectator is what makes Génini's films truly intersubjective experiences. The music has an audience, film has one and together they create a new experience of watching music on screen.

In *La Nûba d'Or et de Lumière*, the voice-over alternates between being overtly didactic and completely absent or silent. It reflects Génini's attempts to balance the straightforward appreciation and beauty of the music with a clearer explanation of what a Nûba is technically and how it should be appreciated. Art and didacticism intermingle again. As it is such a complex form of music, the Nûba requires slightly more guidance for the spectator than another form of music might. In voice-over she explains:

> The tree of modes is a system that classifies the different Nûbas. Being itself structured into five movements, slow, moderate and quick, that are used to accompany the sanaate, poems in the form of a written word. The twenty-four Nûbas, linked to the twenty-four hours of the day, formerly linked the repertory of Andalusian music. Nowadays eleven remain, saved from oblivion by El Haik from Tetouan who was the first to transcribe them in a copy-book, a real breviary for the lovers of this music.

While the fans of the Nûba will know these basic rules and historical facts, an transnational spectatorship would not. Here Génini makes the conscious choice to teach the outsider, and give them an opportunity to become more an insider. At other points in the film, technical explanations are offered through text boxes on the bottom of the screen that do not to interfere with the soundtrack or performance. The text boxes are often quite elaborate, which distracts the spectators' eyes away from the details of the performance itself and observation of the performance's audience. Moreover, it arguably also relegates the spectator into the position of passive consumer of the text instead of an active collaborator in the visual aspects of the performance. It demands that the spectators' eyes should read instead of look or 'see'. The danger is that no intersubjective relationship is possible between director, subject and spectator in *La Nûba*. A true engagement with the performances might therefore be possible only on second viewing.

The voice-over is a slight obstacle for Génini. As her subject matter of music is so specific to the region where she makes her films, it requires explanation for spectators abroad. Yet, at the same time, some of the content of the films, such as the appreciation of the music (audible) and the performance (visible) arguably do not require as much instructive verbal explanation as she provides. Génini's films experiment with the function of the voice-over. At times absent, at times superfluous, at times didactic and always unusual, the voice-over becomes something that makes the spectator question its functionality. The fact that it is a female voice complicates things further as she admits to not being an expert on the types of music she discusses, and not being a musicologist herself, she has to spend a lot of time preparing and studying the genres. In order to be an authority, with the attitude of a didactic voice-over, she needs to gain the trust of the spectator. This she does through the visual accompaniments to the voices in the films.

The director's gaze conforms to her primary goals for her films: Génini wants to portray the immense musical heritage of Morocco and her own love for and experience of this music. The music is what accompanied her on her personal rediscovery of her home country, and in *La Nûba* she mentions that she wants to give something back to the Moroccan people for giving her so many subjects to make films about. The film explores a more difficult and complex type of music that is appreciated widely but is not very well understood. In the film, Génini attempts to balance the enjoyment of the music by its fans with the commentary and explication an audience new to the genre might need. In order to speak to a wide audience, the film has to be entertaining as well as informative. Often no words are capable of expressing the ecstasy of some performers, and it appears unnecessary to do more than offer them the focus in the frame.

This is why the music and dance performances tend to take centre stage. Costumes, instruments, hands and facial expressions add to the experience of the performance. Close-ups of faces and hands dominate. The camera-eye really studies the artists/performers. Facial expressions and hand gestures are natural non-speech additions to conversations by people to emphasise points in their speech and attach importance to certain aspects. In the performative atmosphere of a music concert, then, these gestures and expressions become heightened and gain importance. The director's focus on hands and faces, very intimate body parts in close-ups, illustrates an intimate relationship with the subjects, and a deep wish to comprehend their passion for the music. The mysticism and metaphysical nature of the music, as well as its complexity and the pride connoisseurs take in understanding it completely, bring Génini's look so close. She wants to 'see': she mentions that it took her quite a while to completely understand the music and to feel confident enough to make a film about it. This expresses her intense longing to share her knowledge and love for the music with others who experience it as ecstatically as she does. The intersubjective experience of being a fan, sharing love and appreciation for a certain type of music, bring Génini and her fellow Moroccans closer together. An example of this is when two male musicians attempt to explain to the camera the function of the Nûba and its instruments. They are not well spoken and are easily distracted, but their transformation when they perform instead of inform is exquisite. They are so well versed in the music and their instruments, and have changed into such impressive garments, that their inability to express their knowledge and love for the music is instantly forgotten, and the spectator is trusted to be able to comprehend the universal language of the music.

The performances in *La Nûba* that are staged especially for the benefit of the film are set in appropriately ornate spaces. One particular performance is set behind a large doorway with an open gate decorated with arabesques. In a courtyard to a large mansion a row of chairs are set up. The camera pans across the garden and shows a fountain and trees and flowers. The light comes from a setting sun, throwing its light on the colourful architecture of the house. The beauty of the place adds to the experience of the music, and as the modest musicians do not demand the full attention of the camera, Génini chooses to focus on the colours of plants and the architecture, the sounds of music and birds, the costumes worn by the performers and the sky framed by greenery. It lends a peaceful surrounding to the music that replicates the reflexive and spiritual nature of the Nûba. Moreover, the camera lingers on sunrises and sunsets, on the sea and birds. Génini says that this is a matter of appropriate illustration during the long sequences of music. For example, when the introduction to one of the Nûbas is played, it takes three to four minutes before the lyrics set in, and as this particular Nûba is the one celebrating the morning hour, she decides to focus the camera on the sun rising from behind the hills.

The beauty of women's voices is celebrated the way the music is. The female performer comes to the foreground of the performance and takes centre stage. In *La Nûba* Françoise Atlan interprets famous Nûbas with the most renowned orchestras in Morocco. She smiles at the camera while she sings and confidently accepts that she is the centre of attention. It adds to her charm that she is rather modest in the interviews and that she has an engaging personality in her relationship with the men in the orchestra. Her confidence is in striking contrast to the girls from the women's choir from Tetouan that collaborate with the orchestra of Mohamed Larbi Temsamani. They represent another aspect of femininity in the world of the Nûba music in Morocco. Their voices are appreciated insofar as they interpret the Nûba in collaboration with the head of the orchestra with which they perform. Yet behind the scenes in Tetouan, the women from the choir receive more attention from the camera. Génini parallels the images of the women getting into their costumes and make-up with images of the famous orientalist paintings of harem women and princesses from the nineteenth century. As such, Génini is commenting in an enfolded manner on this perception of Moroccan girls, and emphasises their voices and the way they look back straight into the camera. Their costumes are rich in colour and jewellery, traditional clothes and headdresses, but the girls themselves have a modern attitude towards the camera. They are teenage girls mostly, looking at the camera with coy eyes and bringing their hands to their mouths to indicate a *performed* shyness. The women in orientalist paintings did not make eye contact with the painter: they stare out of windows or have a mysterious air surrounding them, whereas these women or young girls are straightforward and direct with each other and the camera's presence. Génini presents them against the images of the orientalist paintings to show the likeness in performance attire, but the differences in attitude and perspectives. The girls, on the one hand, defy the image of the silent mysterious woman of orientalist paintings while, on the other hand, they appropriate it and reinterpret it in the context of a contemporary performance.

Once again, then, as she did in *Aita* thirty years before, Génini takes time out from filming the concert and the music to focus on the girls behind the scenes in *La Nûba* in 2007. It is in these unplanned shots and in these unusual circumstances where she has gained admittance to private situations that she establishes the closest links with and most intimate portraits of women in Moroccan society. It is also where she is able to observe and indirectly critique the stereotypical portrayal of women, even in performative circumstances. The jump-cuts from young girl to painted woman criticise the persistent Orientalist attitude towards women. While Génini avoids greater political issues in her films, she does manage to insert a subtle, indirect and moderate critique of space between the genders.

Figure 6.2 The girls' choir performs in front of the camera in *La Nûba d'Or et de Lumière* (2007) © Izza Génini

Conclusion

Génini's emotional involvement in the films and with the subjects she approaches reflects her personal and subjective (re)discovery of the Morocco of her youth. Génini is part of a larger contingent of Moroccan film-makers that have accepted a hyphenated identity and a multiple consciousness. Being an integral part of the transnational community of Moroccan film-makers, she exemplifies the obsession with the homeland, and the inability to return permanently. Through the performances of traditional music and home, Génini identifies herself as Moroccan, Jewish and French. This transnational knowledge is obvious: being an outsider, she can see and reveal that Morocco is a complex, diverse nation, but as an insider, she also longs for the clarity of a unified, imagined past. Her transnationality enables her to accept Morocco's real heterogeneity as well as its constructed homogeneity.

While all Génini's films appear at first sight to be insider–outsider observations of the rich Moroccan past, recording Morocco's heritage for the next generation, a closer look at the direction of the look and the intimate relationship between the different actors in the films unfold another engagement altogether. Génini claims not to be politically motivated, recording the music and performances purely out of love and respect for the genres. Nevertheless, she has a proclivity for portraying women over long periods of time and highlights different aspects of a woman's life in Morocco. Establishing a close relationship with the protagonists of her documentaries, Génini smoothes over potentially 'dangerous' topics and points of view with a dominatingly present voice-over that gives the films a slightly anthropological feel. At the same time, the images and the editing reveal a more critical engagement with the music and the performances. Génini's work is far more critical of the Moroccan political climate than she admits. Her films negotiate the look and the voice of a transnational Moroccan from a diverse international background. She is not only observing but also interpreting. She provides a subtle critique, first, of the situation of women in Morocco: they do not speak freely until they are relaxed and surrounded only by women in private spaces. When they are performing on stage or on camera, the women seem modest and retiring instead of confident. They are unrelentingly aware that they are commodities and spectacles, and that certain social stereotypes are attached to their presence. At the same time, and more importantly, the films are occasions where a female director from Morocco, someone with a voice, can express, silently negotiating a dissatisfaction with this stereotype. Where the films arguably lack a critical voice, they compensate with the use of the visual juxtapositions and critiques of female spatial confinement. As a pioneer of documentary film-making by women in Morocco, Génini challenged conventions and inspired the younger generations of women to become more politically outspoken. In a non-verbal way and with a focus on the visual qualities of films, the film-maker provides the sympathising spectator with indications that even oppressed women have strength and integrity, knowledge and talent. Génini's films put women in the important position as guardians of the past.

Notes

1. 'Beur' is the term used for people of Maghrebi descent in France, and in particular in the Parisian suburbs. The term is derived from urban backslang, in which 'Arabe' becomes 'Beur'. For more on this phenomenon, see Bloom (2003); Tarr (2005); Higbee (2013).
2. I have written more about Farida Belyazid and Farida Bourquia in Van de Peer (2015a).
3. I have written in more detail about *Retrouver Oulad Moumen* elsewhere, see Van de Peer (2014b).

CHAPTER 7

Hala Alabdallah Yakoub: Documentary as Poetic Subjective Experience in Syria

Hala Alabdallah Yakoub has been the pivotal element that has held together some of the most important film-makers from the Arab world. She has assisted, co-directed, authored and produced several of the first independent or co-produced films from Syria, by Mohammad Malas, Usama Mohammad and Omar Amiralay. This triumvirate is often written about, their films often appear at Syrian film events, and in most academic discussions on Syrian film-making history theirs are the defining films when it comes to discussing dissident film-making under the Ba'ath Party. They knew each other, filmed one another, and collaborated on projects both in Syria and in exile. While their work is of huge importance for the historiography of Syrian cinema, both in fiction and in documentary films, it is equally important to look in more detail at the woman who inspired them, spurred them on and supported them in various roles behind the scenes. Feature-length fiction films by women are non-existent in Syria, and this pioneering woman of Syrian documentary only made her own first film in 2006, in exile. It is, perhaps surprisingly, mostly in documentary (and animation and other experimental genres) that women have been able to create a platform for themselves in Syrian cinema. This chapter looks at the artistic and specifically the poetic representation of a difficult, traumatic reality in Syria. Hala Alabdallah Yakoub's small filmography shows that negotiations with dissidence and political repression take shape on many different levels, including an experimental and subjective approach to her subjects and a strong belief in the power of art to deal with pain, fear and oppression.

Hala Alabdallah Yakoub was born in Hama in 1956. She studied agricultural engineering in Damascus, and was a fervent member of the local cine club. This is where she realised the power of cinema as she watched Malas' first films. She married artist Youssef Abdelké and became part of one of the many leftist organisations in Damascus. They were imprisoned for their activities, alongside some of her best friends. When they left prison fourteen months later, they decided to move to Beirut, later moving on to Paris, where they settled and continue to live. This exile was more permanent for her husband than for her, as she managed to negotiate re-entry into Syria in order to make her documentaries. She studied sociology and film-making in Paris to achieve her dream of making films that make a difference. She started to produce and co-direct films in France, Lebanon and Syria, which often go unacknowledged.

Alabdallah has made three feature-length documentaries, and some short experimental ones as well. In this chapter, I will pay particular attention to her first documentary, *I Am the One Who Brings Flowers to Her Grave* (2006), as it establishes her as an experimental film-maker interested in the healing power of the arts. It is the most subjective of her documentaries, and highlights solidarity between four women.

The constant thread through Alabdallah's work is the emotional subjectivity and lived experience of political turmoil and exile, and the way one deals with these difficult states of mind through poetry and the arts. Her first film is a lyrical portrait of solidarity between Alabdallah and her three best friends across the ages, between comrades in politics and between arts and politics, as embodied by her artist husband, Youssef Abdelké. The film experiments with representation: defiantly non-linear, personal and subjective, with an emotional and poetic narrative, it prefers to challenge and feel its way through norms and values of politics, art and film-making, rather than explaining or clarifying. The title of the film is a direct reference to Alabdallah's favourite Syrian poet, Daad Haddad, whose poem about suffering for the arts and using art to deal with suffering indicates the film-maker's interest in poetry and the figure of the suffering poet who dies at a young age from an existential crisis.

Hey! Don't Forget the Cumin (2008), her second film, is equally non-linear and experimental, but perhaps more contained, as it looks in detail at three artists Alabdallah is interested in: Jamil Hatmal, a Syrian novelist; Sarah Kane, a British playwright; and Darina Al Joundi, a Lebanese actress. The film tackles the problem of exile and estrangement (Salti, 2010: 176), and how artists deal with this existential crisis. It progresses from sickness and suicide to a strong will to survive by using art as a healing mechanism. Through its references to art and literature, Alabdallah makes a defiantly anti-conformist film about disillusionment, and thus creates a symbolic *and* sharp critique of the oppressive Ba'ath government.

In her third feature documentary, *As if We Were Catching a Cobra* (2012), she looks at a different non-literary art form, but with the same intentions: the art of cartooning and its political inspiration in Egypt and Syria is used not only to express dissent, but also as a valve through which artists and their audiences alike can shape their identity in spite of oppression. She started work on this film immediately before the revolution in Cairo, and as the film progresses, she focuses with more and more fervour on the insurgencies, leading again to a subjective, intimate and emotional study of artists' belief in freedom of expression and social justice. In this film, she develops a relationship with a number of famous and young artists, chief among whom is Syrian Ali Ferzat. The documentary consists once again of a journey alongside three artists, towards the discovery of resilience and the power of artistic expression.

Art is central to Alabdallah's lived experience and her documentaries: her husband is an exiled artist and her films unflinchingly show art's dangers and strengths. The subjectivity and emotions obvious in her films, however, do not result in purely first-person testimonies. Rather, the singular experimental nature of the films and their being steeped in literature and poetry ensures a choir of dissident voices and a vision of dissident images that critique those in power. Most importantly though, art is shown to be a means through which to deal with despair, it functions as a medicine for amnesia and a cure for what Rasha Salti calls the 'dementia' in Syria (Salti, 2010: 167–82). Alabdallah uses documentary as a weapon, because it is necessary to negotiate oppression and taboos in order to find an avenue for self-expression if one wants to be active in and on Syria. As with some of the other film-makers in this book, there is an aspect of nostalgia in the return to the homeland, and here this looking back at Syria comes with the expression of a collective repressed memory and a pessimistic undertone. Women's identity struggles and fight for self-expression are addressed directly in her films, and there is a trust in her global spectators' ability to feel solidarity, as vocal and aural communication methods complement one another to express trauma and dissent.

The National Film Organisation

At the time of writing, Syria is experiencing a violent civil war and mass migration. Documentaries and citizen journalism are omnipresent, and the war has enabled artists and activists to start to address their issues and represent Syria on the screen. This is not to say that war is the necessary inspiration for documentaries, but it does indicate that the Assad governments since the 1960s have prevented this type of film from being made, while their loss of focus on censorship due to political warfare has enabled young activists to make what Syria has lacked for so long: political documentaries. The state of emergency was lifted in April 2011, due to the months-long protests and its escalation into civil war.

In fact, Syria has been in a state of emergency since the Ba'ath Party came to power in the early 1960s, and no country in this book has had an institutional control over film-making as strict and complex as the Syrian National Film Organisation (NFO) under this state of emergency. While many countries in the Arab world have some form of censorship or control over the media, in Syria the NFO is so contradictory and complex that I devote quite some time here to exploring its workings in detail. While Alabdallah was in many ways fiercely independent and remained so consistently throughout her career, many of the films that will be mentioned in this chapter have not been shown in Syria because of the measures taken by the NFO. The NFO has defined Syrian film-making and film screening to such an extent that even an independent film-maker like Alabdallah has not been able to show her films to her Syrian audiences.

After centuries under Ottoman rule and decades of French mandate, Syria gained independence in 1936. Private financiers and producers dominated the film industry of the 1950s, with a focus on producing and distributing commercial genre cinema. This changed drastically in 1963 when the Ba'ath Party installed a one-party system, simultaneously closing all private and independent newspapers and publications. The Syrian press was reshaped to mobilise the public in support of the Ba'ath Party (Lahlali, 2013: 23), and the NFO was created in 1964 as a quasi-independent arm of the Ministry of Culture to regulate film production and distribution, thereby taking film-making out of the commercial sphere and placing it squarely into a nationalist discourse.

Film production, distribution and exhibition in Syria are regulated by the NFO. The first director was Salah Jadid, and his principal aim was to produce propaganda films in favour of Hafez Al Assad and his government. The NFO adhered systematically to the prevailing ideology of the ruling Ba'ath Party. As is the case in many young post-colonial states, the Syrian NFO propagated nationalism by having film-makers document and hail the great achievements of the state, such as construction of roads, highways, dams, agricultural reform, health services, housing and education. This resulted in the initial production of a large number of didactic documentaries, especially suitable for TV, including a film by Syria's most hailed dissenting documentarist, the late Omar Amiralay: *Film-Essay on the Euphrates Dam* (1974). In his young enthusiasm, he filmed the workers and machines in the way his teachers, the Russian formalists had done before him. In his later film, *A Flood in Baath Country* (2003), he looks back on this early film and explains his young socialist idealism and regrets making the film in the atmosphere that he did.

Nevertheless, in spite of the state-run NFO's power over all aspects of film-making and distribution, the NFO was not purely a propaganda tool. They also considered film-making an art form, which resulted in an unprecedented diversity and quality of styles. Although there is a decided dearth of material treating Syrian cinema, what there is at least has critics in agreement as to its paradoxical nature. Lisa Wedeen ([1999] 2011), Rasha Salti (2006), Miriam Cooke (2007) and Kay Dickinson (2016), depict Syrian cinema as a tale of two worlds: on the one hand, the NFO was in control of film-making and distribution, dictating what was appropriate for a local audience; on the other, the organisation also sent its young film-makers abroad to hone their craft, most often to the Soviet Union. The main reason behind this special relationship between the earliest Syrian NFO film-makers and the Russian schools is that Syria and its socialist government had a special interest in the ally of the Soviet Union, and in full Cold War atmosphere Russia was the best and only option to send its film-makers. Salti points out that most film-makers from Syria who came to the attention of global critics were trained in the Soviet Union in the 1970s. The Russian State Institute of Cinematography (VGIK) in Moscow was the place where the NFO had sent a number of film-makers. After their degrees, the artists were brought back to Syria to work for attractive salaries, which, according to many film critics and scholars, resulted in aesthetically beautiful but politically uninspiring films. In practice, this meant that although films critical of the government were made – often as exercises in metaphor and allegory – NFO officials either did not grasp their non-conformity or did realise and shelved them without exhibition options.

Moreover, the NFO inaugurated the biennial Damascus Film Festival in order to promote Syria as a culturally rich country. The Damascus Film Festival gained an interesting reputation in 1968–1969, as young Arab film-makers like Nouri Bouzid used the festival as a platform to launch the manifesto of New Arab Cinema. Arab intellectuals who protested against the stale commercialised nature of the Arab cinema of the past, which failed to truly engage with political and social reality, wanted to lift cinema out of the defeatist realm, and Syria in the late 1960s was the most symbolic stage for this, as it had lost the Golan Heights to Israel during the Six Day War. Over the course of the 1970s, New Arab Cinema was the force behind a realist impetus and women becoming more prominent in film in the Arab world, though ironically not in Syria, at least not on the surface. While intellectual and political films certainly were made by the highly trained film-makers from Syria, the NFO had such power over them that the films were simply shelved and never screened in Syria, not officially anyway. After 1969, the Damascus Film Festival soon resumed its conforming role as a platform for the sloganeering, clean-faced, safe and commercial film and media programme of the Assad government and the NFO's censorial role in film exhibition. Almost none of the aesthetically strong or subversive films by Syria's recognised film-makers were ever screened, and imported or propagandistic films dominated the programme.

Since its inception, the NFO has thus been a site of hegemony, and its role within the film industry in Syria has been reshaped over the decades to accord with the vision of the person at the helm. According to Salti, the directorship of Hamid Merei in the 1970s heralded an important new direction in state-funded film production. Under his stewardship, film-makers such as Nabil Maleh were allowed enough freedom to create films like *Al Fahd* (*The Leopard*, 1972), while documentaries were completely banned, as instructed by Hafez Al Assad in 1974. When Marwan Haddad took over in the 1990s things once again took the opposite direction: both politically and artistically he adhered strongly to Hafez Al Assad's instructions for the depiction of the state.

This scenario was most controversially the case with Nabil Maleh's *Al Kompars* (*The Extras*, 1993), which, like all Maleh's previous films, was funded by the NFO. It deals with a love affair between two poor, young people who work as extras at a local theatre after their long shifts in a gas station and sewing factory. A friend lends them his apartment for two hours as they are otherwise unable to meet anywhere but in public. These two hours are filmed with incredible intensity and delicacy and lead to a devastating denouement. The film, though initially sponsored by the NFO, was later banned by that same institution. Maleh's earlier films such as *Men Under the Sun* (1970), *The Leopard* (1972), *Flash* (1977) and *Fragments* (1979), on the other hand, screened in Syrian cinemas and festivals, including the Damascus Film Festival, to great acclaim, and he has been called the master of Syrian cinema.

In the 2000s, Mohamad Al Ahmad's ongoing tenure as director of the NFO has proved to be very significant in the tightening of control over the production and the boycotting of distribution of new artistic, experimental and political films. When Bashar Al Assad came to power in 2000 he seemed to be a potential reformer with the Damascus Spring, but his inconsistent and wilful behaviour soon resulted in the Damascus Winter in 2001. The Statement of the 99, a manifesto signed by ninety-nine artists and intellectuals, reacted against this toughening of the law and demanded the end of the state of emergency, which had been in place since 1963. The inconsistencies in the directorship of the NFO, the changing tolerances of the Ba'ath government and the resulting confusion of film-makers dependent on the government and the NFO, has resulted in a body of work that can scarcely be called Syrian cinema, but is certainly a film culture worth investigating academically.

Rasha Salti shows most clearly how Syrian cinema is a contradiction in terms. She shows that Syrian cinema is, on the one hand, a 'repository of aspirations and sentiments, a record of lived experience, collective memory and the realm where the saga of collective national traumas and shared canons find expression, representation and signification', but, on the other hand, this repository does not have an audience, is censored and is sponsored by a single-party state actively interested in suppressing dissent and coercing an official dogma (Salti, 2006: 21). As she explains, the central paradox of Syrian cinema is that it is a 'state-sponsored cinema, whose most renowned filmmakers offered an alternative, critical and subversive narrative of the "national" lived experience of traumas that directly contested the official state-enforced discourse' (Salti, 2006: 30). This central paradox consists of a further four paradoxes: that there is no cohesive, national Syrian cinema, but there is a repository of some of the best films in the region; that Syrian audiences never see and barely know of Syrian cinema, while the outside world admires Syrian films; that we deal with a fiercely independent cinema under the sponsorship of the state; and that while this cinema under the state is a national cinema, it is in fact also a cinema of subjective and independent-minded auteurs (Salti, 2006: 22–3). This paints an optimistic as well as a pessimistic view of Syrian cinema in the 1980s and 1990s, most notably when Salti states that Syrian cinema is the 'repository of thwarted aspirations, failed promises and disillusioned citizenship' (Salti, 2006: 33). Salti therefore returns to the phrase 'lived experience' quite often, especially in the work of Hala Alabdallah Yakoub. While the cinema of the 1980s and 1990s for her shows a real struggle to depict lived experience and rather employs allegory and metaphor, especially that of the Palestinian man and family, Alabdallah's work shows a concerted effort to engage with Syrian lived experience, and consistently follows that pessimistic–optimistic line in her films.

Miriam Cooke likewise describes a complex state that silenced artists even while it needed them, using culture and cultural products to shape public opinion and to legitimise its power (Cooke, 2007: 5). The main contradiction she sees is between 'official emphasis on culture and the stifling atmosphere in which the intellectuals need to function' (Cooke, 2007: 20). When it comes to cinema, she says, the NFO is a 'graveyard of cinema and filmmakers' (Cooke, 2007: 115), and a repressed memory that needs to be revived by independent film-makers, such as Mohammad Malas and Omar Amiralay. The paradoxes Salti speaks about in her writings on

Syrian cinema, for Cooke become 'commissioned criticism', as the NFO sponsors and boycotts its own artists, where a state-sponsored cinema exists but its films are never released. For the audience, Cooke writes, 'it was enough to know the films were being made' (Cooke, 2007: 119). Cooke describes a sombre country, with frustrated and frightened artists that have produced but never shown a body of films that were difficult, and that 'function as political critique and a forum for the release of pent-up anger, even as they run the risk of enabling injustice to persist' (Cooke, 2007: 120). The 'dementia' Salti describes with Cooke becomes amnesia – an official amnesia prescribed by the government. In spite of taboos on the discussion of politics, ideology, religion, society and economics, in the late 1960s the Ba'ath Party originally tolerated the publication and staging of works critical of the regime; in the 1970s, the party increased its censorship laws, but by the 1980s had again 'softened its autocratic image to deflect local revolutionary ambitions' (Cooke, 2007: 15). Under a veneer of freedom and democracy, the state let up on some fronts and cracked down on others, resulting in a complicated cultural experience within a discourse that simultaneously emphasised cultural production while it stifled the atmosphere in which artists were permitted to function. Artists had to negotiate the 'permissible' (Cooke, 2007: 17).

Kay Dickinson looks in much detail at the running of the NFO and its power over its film-makers through a 'dialectic' of free versus revolutionary state-sanctioned film-making. The political manifesto of the early Ba'ath Party, she shows, mentioned industrialisation as inherent to the revolution, and film-making as one of its main expressions of cultural and educational impetuses. The NFO, she says, is a 'vertically integrated, protectionist system' where film-makers are safe yet inhibited. She describes the evolution of 'movement' in Syrian cinema under the NFO. The revolutionary output of film-makers returning from their education in film in the Soviet Union was moulded into a revolutionary praxis through movement and a search for knowledge. Artistic elements of the Syrian film are, in this context, a refusal of stasis through the ever-present lateral tracking shot (Dickinson calls the tracking shot 'Syrian cinema's signature', 2016: 41); a formal dexterity; a creativity due to the lack of infrastructure available to the inspired and returning film-makers; a managing of gaps and lacks through collaboration and solidarity, where a lack of intellectual ownership is commonplace (Dickinson, 2016: 61). This last element especially is recognisable in Alabdallah's work in collaborations with the male film-making stars of Syrian cinema. What Dickinson makes clear, then, is that in spite of limitations imposed on the film-makers, they exchange a revolutionary outlook in the service of the disastrous Ba'ath chaos for a revolutionary praxis that functions productively within a repressive system and that makes unhurried, artistic and collaborative works of art that are rarely screened but are universally admired.

Lisa Wedeen elucidates this complex reality somewhat when she compares what she terms 'tolerated parodies' to 'safety valves' (Wedeen, [1999] 2011: 105). Tolerated or authorised critical practices functioned to preserve a repressive regime's dominance rather than undermining it. The controlled venting of dissatisfaction was, in other words, allowed only in order to displace or relieve tensions that otherwise might find expression in political actions. The state permitted comedies, for example, with political parodies and jokes. This was where Syrian politics resided and where critique and oppositional consciousness thrived. However, it is only there that they are allowed, under controlled circumstances. Those programmes and films that passed the censor and were screened or shown on TV were never directly critical of the Ba'ath regime: the criticism of politics was allowed only in scenarios from before the Ba'ath Party came to power. Directors were thus forced to become crafty with the symbols and the language of the regime 'in order to subvert its system of signification' (Wedeen, [1999] 2011: 107). These subterfuges reveal a trust in the spectators' ability to decode the jokes' subversive content and circumvent the internalised censor: 'metaphor undermines the symbolic power of the leader' (Wedeen, [1999] 2011: 110). Wedeen shows how, in film, these authorised critical practices actually preserved the regime's repressive dominance rather than undermined it. Nevertheless, outside of their work for the NFO there is an attitude inherent to all film-makers to refuse to operate within the politics of 'as if' (Wedeen, [1999] 2011: 110).

These politics of 'as if' are also mentioned by Cooke and Lina Khatib (2013), and perhaps form the best description of the 'tolerated parodies', 'commissioned criticism' and 'paradoxes of Syrian cinema': citizens act *as if* they revere their leader. There is, according to Cooke, a 'performative complicity', where the system is resented but not confronted. However, as she also describes, 'although they had to behave as if they believed the mystifications, outsiders should not. I had a moral responsibility to be open and honest' (Cooke, 2007: 66). Khatib (2013) likewise shows how the Ba'ath government and Hafez Al Assad as well as his son Bashar base their whole image on a performance of legitimacy, and a narrative steeped in sloganeering. The government is a performance just as the 'acting as if' one adheres to their rules is, in itself, a performance. In this narrative, then, reality becomes unable to break through or interrupt the general, accepted, willing suspension of disbelief.

In spite of its adversities, Syrian cinema receives respect and recognition all over the world at international film festivals. Festivals screening and awarding prizes to Syrian films include European as well as Middle Eastern film festivals: *The Dupes* won gold in 1972 at Carthage in Tunisia and in 1973 at the Moscow International Film Festival. Nabil Maleh's *The Extras* won in Cairo and he was also presented with an award for his outstanding contribution to cinema at the Dubai International Film Festival. According to Salti (2006), this is due to the originality of the few film-makers that manage to get their films distributed. Their film education in Russia resulted in films that boast a carefully examined aesthetic composition and poetical reflection on the nation. Through symbolism, allegories, careful composition and iconographic shots, film-makers managed to make statements about history and national memory within an oppressive atmosphere. Production was therefore limited but of the highest possible quality.

Salti illustrates that the main theme in Syrian cinema up until the 1970s and 1980s was the occupation of Palestine, often served up as a metaphor for the political situation of repression by and disillusionment with Ba'ath government. Other related themes were the 1967 defeat, the events in Quneitra, the loss of the Golan Heights to Israel and the many military coups. However, these issues needed to be dealt with surreptitiously, and one of the main ways in which this was achieved was through the metaphorical portrayal of the patriarch. Family life served as a metaphor for the state, of which the father was the ruthless patriarch, powerful and unforgiving. The family reflected the state. In the 1970s, these prevalent themes resulted in nostalgic films about the loss of the heroes who fought for the cause of Syria. In the 1980s, however, this changed as auteurs trained in the Soviet Union returned and allowed themselves to be more critical of the government by carving out a site for critique and subversion. Wars became sites of loss and pain, where the young soldiers were stolen from their families, no longer heroes but innocent victims of the state. But as mentioned before, while these films were produced, not many of them were ever screened in public or distributed.[1] The NFO continued to marginalise, demonise and silence political dissent.

Until the late 1980s, the NFO was the only producer and distributor of films in Syria. It offered consistent financial support and social security to film-makers – but in many cases prevented real creative impulses due to the limitations they imposed, and their staunch control over, and the stifling of, releases. Likewise, Usama Mohammad's *Stars in Broad Daylight* (1988) was simply shelved by the NFO and not distributed or exhibited anywhere. Documentaries were avoided altogether. NFO film production dropped drastically in the 1990s to one feature a year, and independent companies carefully started to pop up. Satellite broadcasting and television became vastly more popular in the country, and Syria surpassed Egypt in the production and popularity of TV serials.[2] Although the NFO maintained its monopoly over film production, it also suffered from meagre resources and limited success. And while offering its dependent artists a steady, if limited, income and social security, it also drained their creative energies and stifled their voices. To address this, co-productions between the NFO and private companies began to be permitted around 2000. A younger generation of artists, less daunted by the censor, began to experiment with new media and new forms, while at the same time independent studios offered training grounds, and co-productions became increasingly possible.

Documentary in Syria

Documentary production was actively discouraged if it was not for the heroicisation of the Ba'ath regime or for propaganda purposes. The role and potential of documentary, namely, that it represents reality and that it engages people who watch the film in a direct and political way, is an aspect of the form that instils fear in its opponents. The power of a good documentary is precisely that it can entice political action and the dissemination of certain social or political ideas. The idea of a shared reality that needs to be changed comes to the foreground. After initially making a short film hailing the construction of the great Euphrates Dam, Omar Amiralay became Syria's most famous dissident documentary maker. Due to Assad's and the NFO's objections to his films, he went into exile in France, but he has defined documentary making in Syria to a large extent, and has inspired and trained many young people in the art of documentary making in the Arab world.

Omar Amiralay is widely considered the craftsman of documentary in Syria and he alone represents the counterpoint to Syrian fiction cinema (Salti, 2006: 74). He started his career with a *Film Essay on the Euphrates Dam* (1974), in which he celebrated the early achievements and ideals of the Ba'ath Party. The film is dedicated to the construction of the Euphrates Dam, which was to be the pride of the Ba'ath Party. Thirty years later, the collapse of the Zayzun Dam, which killed dozens of people and ruined thousands of lives, and the revelation of an official report that had predicted the dam's fate, inspired Amiralay to make *A Flood in Ba'ath Country* (2003). This film examines the flood's devastating impact on a Syrian village. In interviews with local dignitaries such as a schoolmaster and a party official he shows the discrepancies between official rhetoric and the effects of such events on real people.

Amiralay's opposition to the Ba'ath Party meant that he had to live in exile in France, though he continued to make politically critical films about Syria with the help of artist friends and fellow activists. In *A Plate of Sardines* (1997), for example, a short documentary, he tells his own story about how he first heard of Israel. Amiralay's criticism of Israeli and Syrian policies in this short made it a very controversial documentary about historical events that those nations wanted to be forgotten. It was banned. Also from 1997, *There are So Many Things Left to Say* examines the ideals of his youth through a portrait of his friend Sa'adallah Wannous; a Syrian journalist, playwright and intellectual. The film is a frank and critical self-reflection, filmed a short time before Wannous' death. He speaks about the disappointments of their generation, the destroyed dreams of pan-Arabism, the Arab–Israeli conflict and the many political frustrations that ensued. As such, Amiralay is often seen as the spokesperson for anti-government organisations that address the collective traumas and ensuing national amnesia.

Alabdallah worked on Amiralay's films *Fateh Moudarres* (1994), *Shadow and Light* (1994), *On a Day of Ordinary Violence, My Friend Michel Seurat* (1995), *A Plate of Sardines – Or the First Time I Heard about Israel* (1997), *There are So Many Things Left to Say* (1997), *The Man with the Golden Soles* (2000). She is still general director of Ramad films, the production company she set up with Amiralay. In addition, she worked on Malas' films *The Night* (1992) and *On the Sand, Under the Sun* (1993), and on Mohammad's films *Stars in Broad Daylight* (1988) and *Sacrifices* (2002), and she has produced many films by French film-makers, made in Lebanon and Syria.

None of Amiralay's films after *Film Essay on the Euphrates Dam* have ever been screened publicly in Syria. Still, he has had an extensive influence on the productivity and reception of documentary film-makers in the Arab world. His influence on the development of documentary production in the region has been instrumental. Since the dawn of the digital age and the developments in high-definition digital video film-making technology, the horizon of possibilities for documentary makers has expanded. Because production budgets have been drastically reduced, film-makers can attempt to avoid the prohibitions of the NFO and produce their films independently. This has created a revolution in film-making in the Middle East. Amiralay himself critiqued what he termed 'bad' documentary making in Syria. He spoke out against the aestheticisation of dissent, and said that there were no decent sound technicians, no good actors and the narration in films was too stilted (Salti, 2006: 64). He claimed Syrians were obsessed with everyday 'reality' instead of having the courage to invent new realities. He referred to a lack of bravery in subverting the censor.

One of his initiatives to address this shortcoming in documentary film-making was the Arab Institute of Film, which existed between 2005 and 2008.[3] Sponsored by the Danish NGO International Media Support, the Arab Institute of Film trained aspiring film-makers in the Middle East in the making of documentary films, because, as the mission statement read:

> The Institute will be filling a gap in the financing of independent documentary film production in the Arab region. Despite positive trends over the last few years, there is no strong tradition of producing independent documentary films in the Arab world. (IMS, 2009)

The IMS statement reads: 'Independent documentary filmmaking often provides an important platform for alternative voices and views because it escapes the confinements placed on regular news production and mainstream media by way of its editorial independence' (IMS, 2009). Amiralay was a driving force behind the Arab Film Institute. They organised workshops and offered other support for young documentary makers. Reem Ali, one of the trainees, told me that Amiralay's influence is present in the artistic feel to her film:

> He gave a lot of attention to the films and their makers, and encouraged discussion around the original ideas of the films. He supported the creative process and assisted with the ways of working through our problems. (Interview with author, 2011b)

Omar Amiralay passed away in February 2011, a few weeks before the uprising started in his country, something he had been lobbying for with fellow artists for a very long time. He had, among other things, signed the 'Declaration of the 99', urging the government to release political prisoners and lift the state of emergency.

Documentary was doing relatively well in Syria before the revolution. After his involvement with the Arab Institute of Film, Amiralay became one of the main advisers and supporters of DoxBox, founded in 2008. DoxBox, an annual documentary film festival in Damascus, changed Syrian perceptions of documentary. Documentaries are no longer seen only as propaganda or news-related pieces of journalism, but have been recognised as art forms in and of themselves. DoxBox encourages young film-makers who have broken with the past of Syrian cinema and who look forward to being empowered by the possibilities of digital technologies. Their self-conscious and deliberate distancing from institutions such as the NFO and the Damascus Film Festival, and their independent initiatives have lead to a new and different impulse in Syrian cinema, so much so that it is estimated that now around eight documentaries are produced in Syria a year.

So, while the Syrian uprisings have had a detrimental influence on the government-run institutes and festivals, smaller, non-government affiliated film festivals like DoxBox have resisted the cultural wipe-out and have taken to heart the new digital shape that film festivals can now assume. While they could not physically take place in Damascus, the DoxBox Global Days, held worldwide since March 2012, exhibit Syrian film-makers actively resisting the government's crackdown and its accompanying censorship. Annually, films are distributed and exhibited online and on DVDs to a worldwide network of volunteers who coordinate two days of screenings dedicated to Syrian cinema. DoxBox remains true to its word in claiming the Global Day would show 'how poverty, oppression and isolation do not prevent humans from being spectacularly brave, stubborn and dignified' (DoxBox, 2012).

This festival has completely embraced the power of social networking and online streaming, which have enabled it to not only programme a festival of documentaries, but also to counter the portrayal of Syria as a country in which film-makers suffer under an unmanageable censorship regime. Global Days screens classics rarely seen anywhere (either in Syria or abroad), clandestinely produces films and films by film-makers in exile, even as the event itself unveiled a film festival in exile. The labelling of the screenings as 'solidarity screenings' is indicative of the political activism that inspires the festival. In 2012, the festival was dedicated to the screening of Amiralay's 'forbidden films'. He was also one of the chief advisers and supporters of DoxBox until his death in February 2011.

DoxBox is dedicated to the promotion of creative documentary from the Arab region, and was inaugurated in 2007 in Damascus by documentary film-maker Diana El Jeiroudi from ProAction Film, an independent documentary production company. It also works in close collaboration with other documentary festivals around the world, such as the International Documentary Film Festival Amsterdam, the European Documentary Network, DocPoint Helsinki and the Copenhagen International Documentary Festival. This innovative, online, cinematic subversion of, and resistance to, government censorship is illustrative of the flexibility and reflexivity of small film festivals, combining as it does the possibilities of online distribution and voluntary labour with idealism and generosity. DoxBox's online resistance utilises access to a global audience with a potential impact that far outstrips the more limited regional audience to which the festival was accustomed. Its online networking skills and successes have encouraged like-minded organisations and individuals worldwide to embrace the event and even claim the festival as their own.

Poetry and Documentary

Hala Alabdallah Yakoub's films generate extreme opinions: many critics love her work for its experimental nature and the political circumstances within which she has worked; other critics think her films are impenetrable, difficult and self-indulgent. Hardly anything academic has been written about her work: Rasha Salti has published a chapter on Alabdallah's first two films in Flavia Laviosa's collection *Visions of Struggle in Women's Filmmaking in the Mediterranean* (2010), and Roy Armes has dedicated two pages to her work in his latest book *New Voices in Arab Cinema* (2015).

Armes describes her as the pioneer of feature-length documentary in Syria. He dismisses her first film as a co-directed experimental video autobiography and as the archetypal exile film, 'clearly targeted not at a Syrian popular audience but at the international festival circuit' (Armes, 2015: 85). It is, according to him, enigmatic, inconclusive and imprecisely located. He appreciates her next two projects much more, and gives the impression of a self-contained, specialised film-maker. However, Alabdallah is, as I mentioned earlier, at the centre of Syrian film-making at large, and has certainly not made films only for the international festival circuit. She is very much a film-maker of the Syrian 'lived experience', as Salti confirms, and speaks directly to her Syrian comrades and fellow sufferers. In an atmosphere that is melancholic and drenched in sadness, the 'enigmatic, inconclusive and imprecisely located films' perhaps speak most directly to a Syrian audience, to people who are aware of what she refers to when she remains imprecise, who understand the enigmatic performances and allegories, and the unknown locations. Salti shows how it is possible to glean from the documentary – made in circumstances located precisely between France and Syria, in exile wherever she is, dependent on her carefully negotiated re-entry into Syria for the purposes of creating dissident art – where Alabdallah is, what she is doing and why. The triptych structure of the documentaries and the melancholic intellectualism enfold a lamented past and an entrenched love for a lost country in disorder and fellow Syrians in distress.

As Laura Marks shows, much of the Arab world's cinema, and specifically Syrian cinema, has been formed onto an understanding of friendships and alliances. Amiralay, she says, has such good networks with other independent professionals in the film world that his exile was overcome through film. She talks of the 'complex, beautiful and remarkably subversive films' that came out of the friendship between Omar Amiralay, Mohammad Malas and Usama Mohammad (Marks, 2015: 39). Hala Alabdallah Yakoub needs to be included in this productive network of friends that displayed a 'profoundly artful cinematic sensibility' (Marks, 2015: 41) that combined politics and film. Her films are poetic documentary essay films, using the aesthetics of the craft, including subjective voices and politics. While some of the Syrian film-makers have been frustrated, cynical and sarcastic, Alabdallah has remained honest and occupied with lived experience in her experimental documentaries. This description fits in beautifully with Marks' own theorisation of enfoldment in experimental Arab cinema. Where censorship rules and amnesia is the norm, one needs to remember, as Alabdallah does, that history is 'not forgotten but enfolded' (Marks, 2015: 69). While, as Salti shows, many film-makers testify to having to deal with dementia and amnesia due to the intense suffering, trauma and censorship, experimental film, Marks says, has the power to reveal that historiography is a process of unfolding and enfolding, growing out of the 'triadic relationship of experience, information and image'. As Alabdallah prefers to deal with lived experience (though fragmented and non-linear), so Marks argues that images are selective unfoldings of experience. In an oppressive atmosphere, an alternative historiography becomes necessary, where the personal, absurd micro-events are brought forward, and become stand-ins for experience. Experimental cinema is a performative art that deals 'craftily and stylishly with homogenizing information' (Marks, 2015: 71–2). As Khatib (2013) shows, much of Syrian culture and media is dependent on the performative qualities of the Al Assad government and their slogans. Equally, Marks says, the censors and the funders of cinema are subject to this sloganeering, and the experimental alternatives to cinema therefore have the potential to 'draw attention to the steely grip of information'. Through micro-focuses of the subjective in experimental films such as those by Alabdallah, the unanticipated makes collective experiences richer. Information disguised as slogans and performances by the government that result in the 'as if' sphere need to be avoided, and film has the ability to use images in addition to words in order to reveal the experience. Alabdallah's films show the power struggles that force images to take the shape of information, while they lift the information curtain so that they and others may feel the breadth of experience itself.

I Am the One Who Brings Flowers to Her Grave (2006)

As her first film, Alabdallah sees *I Am the One Who Brings Flowers to Her Grave* as the most subjective of her films. After having worked with and for other film directors, both from and in Syria, this subjectivity, the first-person singular, however, is not as self-indulgent as it might sound. It does not, for example, undermine the collectivity of a Syrian identity, but it alternates with it (Salti, 2010: 179). Having been in exile in France for over twenty years:

> she is an important inside/outside figure able to transgress the paradox of her position, this is the outcome of her passion for cinema: 'I draw extreme pleasure from contact and exchange with others, to be able to visualise what another filmmaker has inscribed in words is an inspiring challenge. I don't see it like a sacrifice at all, rather an intense training for the brain'. (Salti, 2010: 169)

And these voices and visions of others inspire this film. The lived experience of everyday Syrian life is the main concern of the film. There is a collective voice, a multiplicity of voices that circulate around Alabdallah's, and that weave the stories of their collective past. Alabdallah and her co-director Ammar Albeik work together, they envisage the returns of/to her best friends, her husband, herself. The film is, in the first place, an introspective journey back into traumatic experiences, an attempt to unravel memories and traumas, and a story of several returns to the homeland, whether physically or mentally. Salti explains that the point of the film 'is not to transpose her personal experience only, but rather to wander into worlds that she inhabits or that inhabit her' (Salti, 2010: 179). She returns to the lived experience of the past that has been erased by the official records of history, and the lived experience of the present, where people who are stuck in the past need to confront their own truths. While it might feel like the story of a disillusioned, deceived and defeated generation, Alabdallah also succeeds in showing glimmers of hope and life in the eyes, smiles and intimate relationships with her friends, husband, daughter and co-director. After all the projects she has worked on with other directors, the subjectivity of this film is reflected in her wish to make her own, and for this one film to encompass all the films she had ever wanted to make. In the year that she turned fifty she finally did. She saw the film as a birthday present to herself and her three closest friends from Syria. The film thus enfolds other films, projects, scripts, locations, stories, footage for films that have not seen the light of day and never will: all the films she ever started and never developed far enough. The unfolding process is complex, intense and surprising.

The sparsely used voice-over is Alabdallah's own. She speaks in the first-person singular, and introduces the film as a film about making films that never materialised. Spectators hear her discuss framing and perspectives with her co-director, Ammar Albeik. The much younger, male experimental film-maker was the ideal partner to make this complex project see the light of day, as he improvises uninhibitedly, and contributes constructively to their discussions about the practice of film-making and the meaning of images. This dialogue speaks of her past practice with the other film-makers with whom she has worked, and leads the film forward. This collective film-making unfolds the multiplicity of voices and gazes in the film, and explains perhaps that subjectivity here is not singular but plural and encapsulates a myriad of voices.

Albeik's presence is most deeply felt in the landscape, the scouting sequences and in the sequences with Youssef Abdelké, Alabdallah's artist husband. They fled Syria in 1981, after fourteen months in jail. While she managed to negotiate re-entry for the sake of her work, Abdelké was not allowed to return until 2006, an occasion the film develops towards in a celebratory climax upon his return, with a hero's welcome at the airport and a large exhibition in Damascus. The structure of the film is such that it develops slowly towards this return and this party, although one also senses the carefulness of Alabdallah, Albeik and especially Abdelké and his mother. There is a sense that things could go wrong and that he may not be allowed in due to his continued political activism.

The portrait of Abdelké shows us a calm, ageing man, introspective yet playful, and in love with his wife and daughter. His modesty makes him immensely likeable, and while he says sad and harsh things in conversation with Albeik, and his drawings are dark and ominous standing in the background in the studio, his eyes remain playful and light, and the extreme close-ups of his face reveal a man with a sense of humour, self-deprecating, patient and pragmatic. Albeik not only films him in the intimate setting in the studio while he draws or tells stories; we also see Abdelké at breakfast with his daughter, in a quiet comfortable camaraderie, at a protest rally for democracy in Syria and at arrivals in Damascus Airport, celebrating the homecoming with a large exhibition and a party with dancing and food. Throughout these peaceful but tense moments, Abdelké remains playful and relaxed. He tells Albeik that El Greco is his favourite artist, that a man who used to live in his studio told him the story of what the neighbourhood used to be like (with cherry trees), and how his daughter is slowly becoming a rebellious teenager. He also gives Albeik subtle instructions: 'if you are going to show my art works, I would like you to show this one last', pointing at a large frame of dark colours with frames of different sizes embedded in the frame. This is perhaps an abstract rendering of points of view, perspectives and selective vision. After the very figurative artworks depicting a severed hand in a fist and a dead fish head, this abstract artwork reveals the artist's acute awareness of the subjectivity of art, a symbolic framing of the film in its turn.

Albeik also films Alabdallah and she films him, often both with their cameras in hand. They film one another exploring the island Arwad and other locations of past film projects. He films her on the road, in the car, sleeping. He studies her in close-up and extreme close-up, as if studying her face, relaxed and unaware of the camera. These journeys of scouting locations and exploring which stories will be told in the film, is really a study of Alabdallah's past as a film producer, after her exile from Syria. While it is a return to Syria, and her films are all set in Syria as if film-making is a homecoming, a political statement of an exile, these journeys and explorations are uncertain, unprepared and improvised. We get a sense of 'suspended time, landscapes captured in a captivating palette of greys drenched in melancholia' (Salti, 2010: 174). The hand-held cameras seem searching and almost directionless. Nevertheless, they also feel hopeful, as if behind every corner, in every person or child they meet, therein is enfolded a story worth telling, a person and a place worth seeing. The black-and-white melancholia in the spaces that are filmed (the empty island of Arwad, deserted houses and roads, fields that are barren) are compensated for with an innate playfulness in the people behind the film.

The film is at its most darkly melancholic in the intimate conversations with Alabdalla's three close friends, Fadia Ladkani, Rola Roukbi and Raghida Assaf, who paint a picture of a suspended life, a past of traumatic experiences and regret over lives that feel lost. At this point in the film it is clear that she is behind the camera: a scrutinising camera, perhaps excessive in its close-ups on the women's faces, hand-held, flexible and intimate, remains tender but also probes and evokes tears. Alabdallah is present and not present. Fadia, Rola and Raghida address her, they say her name, but we do not hear the questions or see her in the frame. From their answers we can glean seven topics the film-maker was concerned with in their conversations. These topics are structured throughout the film, editing one answer after another and comparing each woman's answer. Each time a question has been dealt with by all three, we return to an image of the film-maker, alone and silent, in a courtyard, playing solitaire, as if a pause is required to process the difficult trialogue that has just taken place.

The seven steps Alabdallah goes through with her friends are: getting used to the camera; their family's situation; the experience in prison; their current state of mind; any feelings towards Syrian society and fellow activists that stayed behind; any regrets; and, lastly, their age. What returns here is the sense that there is a journey enfolded, a journey to the deepest state of unrest, the most intimate feelings and thoughts, framed by and enfolded within a gentle journey outwards towards family and society, towards prison and towards the film.

The initial stage, at which the women are still getting used to the camera's presence, is one of searching, zooming in and out, moving around the room to find the best spot for the interview, and finding a position on their chair/sofa in which they are comfortable. It is a dual searching. Alabdallah searches the best way to frame her friend, while the friend searches for an attitude to assume towards the camera and the imaginary spectator. They look at Alabdallah, and straight into the camera, addressing both their friend, the director and the audience. She tries to make them feel comfortable with the camera by urging them to say something, anything. She uses as leverage, to convince them to indulge her, the fact that the cassette in the camera is almost full. It is obvious that this is a trick, but it works. As Jean Rouch, Stella Bruzzi and other documentary theorists have shown us, the presence of the camera enables a performance and is a tool to testify to. Fadia is shy: she smiles and looks away from the camera, we follow her gaze and the extreme close-up reveals an introspective, thoughtful woman. Rola is excited about a film she has just seen, about a strong, impressive woman who overcomes adversity. However, we get the sense of an enormous sadness emanating from her when the camera pans out and shows her smoking a cigar as she stares straight into the camera. Raghida is equally urged to say something, but refuses, rubs her eyes and says she is extremely tired and needs a glass of water. She gives the impression of being the most strong-willed one of the group of friends. Fadia is a translator, Rola a housewife and Raghida a gynaecologist. All three confide in Alabdallah, but only after having been made comfortable and urged to speak. This trick indeed indicates that the film-maker has a lot of patience with and understanding for her friends' situation, and perhaps feels the same way as they do, thus involving herself very personally in the film, but it also reveals an immediate urgency and the conviction of the necessity of her film, and her wanting to speak to her friends about their common difficult experiences.

In the second stage, Alabdallah takes her friends on to the topic of family. Only one of her friends has the strength to talk about the family. Fadia mentions the death of her brother: his initial disappearance and that there was never any official information released and no justice. He is presumed dead and while she says she feels no rancour, she does ask the most difficult question: why did this happen? Rola keeps things more general, asking why things are the way they are, how she feels immense sadness, for family and for society in Syria at large. She says she is confused about who she is, that she used to be strong and a rebel as a teenager, but that she now harbours doubt about her past desires and personal choices. Equally, Raghida keeps things more general and laments that there is so much deception. She is silent and sad, and starts to cry when she says she

Figure 7.1 Fadia Ladkani's insecurity as she gets used to the camera in *I Am the One Who Brings Flowers to Her Grave* (2006) © Hala Alabdallah Yakoub

used to have so much energy but now there is nothing but doubt in her mind.

The third topic is their common experience in prison. All three testify to the company of women in prison and that they felt they were able to express themselves to these women, however horrible the circumstances were. Fadia says she was surprised that there were so many women in prison and that she learnt a lot from the company of women, but after she heard of her brother's disappearance she was unable to see anything positive, even in their company. In contrast to Fadia, Rola stares straight into the camera and says nothing with her head heavy on her hand. Her defiance and silence perhaps say more of her pain and suffering than her words could. Likewise, Raghida is completely silent at first, inhaling deeply on her cigarette. She then says she remembers her first day in prison like it was yesterday and that after prison there was extreme solitude as friends fled, were disappeared or stayed in prison. In fact, she emphasises that the time after prison was lonely in contrast to the time inside, and that she was unable to stay in touch with anyone as the government 'dispersed us completely'. The fact that Fadia speaks of the beginning of her time in prison, Rola says nothing and Raghida speaks of the time after prison also suggests that in between the beginning and the end a horrible time was endured ,of which none of them can speak – Rola being the embodiment of that silence.

The innermost fold of the enfolded topics of discussion is their feelings. Alabdallah asks how they feel now, about their past and about the present and how they cope on a daily basis with the pain of the past. Fadia is most lucid here, and open. She does not say a lot, but what she says is very insightful: she says that she experiences a highly complex pain and fails to be objective about it. 'Everything is subjective and personal, and any possible understanding of my state of mind is an illusion I give into sometimes.' As such, she actually does attempt objectivity, talking about herself as if from a remove. Rola is much more emotional, saying she does not know the person called Rola, and that she has nothing to do with what happened twenty-five years ago. She weeps and says she used to be politically engaged and have strong opinions, but that was another person. 'My ambitions were not realised. I wanted to change the world. I had courage and conviction. But life has broken me.' Raghida has again another approach to the question: she smokes and stares at the camera defiantly. We hear Alabdallah interfere and ask 'what are you thinking of?' Raghida responds: 'You want to confiscate my thoughts? They are my private space. We all need a private space to go when we need to.' This innermost circle of questions and answers are guarded, both by the structure of the film and the folds within which these testimonies are wrapped, but also by the defensiveness of Raghida, and her sensitive reproach of her friend with the camera. The solidarity between the film-maker and her subjects here is most obvious then in their ability to refuse the question or Alabdallah's sensitive allowances, where she includes the silences. They say just as much and perhaps even more than the rationalisations of their feelings and thoughts.

Figure 7.2 Rola Roukbi is very emotional and cries in front of the camera, finding it difficult to bear witness in *I Am the One Who Brings Flowers to Her Grave* (2006)
© Hala Alabdallah Yakoub

Returning to the world outside their own minds and bodies in the fifth stage of the interview reveals almost a relief, and talking about the larger consequences for the state of Syria seems to come slightly easier to the three women, although when it comes to their feelings here, they are still very complex. Fadia explains that the fact that she escaped the war makes her feel guilty towards those who died. Echoing Primo Levi, she says she feels that another died to save her: 'My constant nostalgia towards my family and my homeland replaces this guilt.' She struggles with these complex feelings of guilt and nostalgia. Rola again is much more emotional, and talks of the scent of the earth after the rain. 'Once, it intensely reminded me of Hama and made me return, it changed my life. I had to go to Syria.' She pauses and says, 'I did not escape death, I am dead.' Her melodramatic nature combined with an extreme close-up of her eyes enable the spectator to approach her very closely. Spectator solidarity is actually counted on here, as the emotional state of mind unapologetically invites sympathy. Raghida, on the other hand, invites a sudden distance, as she says 'there is so much suffering everywhere, we all have a right to democracy and peace'. She sounds defensive and her scornful hoarse laughter reveals an uneasiness and sarcastic nature. The most sensitive, vulnerable woman is guarded by the pragmatism of the first and the guardedness of the third. This is a small but crucial fold in the film.

It leads to the sixth level of questions, where Alabdallah asks them about regrets. Inspired by Rola's suspended ambitions mentioned before, she digs deeper into their hopes and dreams. Fadia had things she wanted to accomplish, as she liked working with her hands, and since she was eight has never stopped writing, even in prison. But all these projects remain unfinished, and as a translator it can be expected that she is faced with this frustration every day. Though perhaps the film project in which she is collaborating here is a vehicle to inspire her to use these unfinished projects to accomplish something of her own. Likewise, Rola confesses to having always been very ambitious, but never having accomplished what she thought she would. She wanted to do something important in the political field, but she feels she failed and never got there. Again we see her sadness and her wry smile, introspective and using very few words to explain herself. Raghida suddenly changes from her guarded stance earlier on, to an openness about her profession as a gynaecologist, and about bringing people into the world. For her this is the most important thing, although it is tinged with sadness and the intensity of her job: 'I feel connected to all the babies I deliver, not a lot of gynaecologists have this. And it makes me wonder sometimes where my own child is.' She does not elaborate, and we do not get the impression she had an actual baby that is

Figure 7.3 Raghida Assaf's anger in close-up, as she turns inward and is silent in *I Am the One Who Brings Flowers to Her Grave* (2006) © Hala Alabdallah Yakoub

lost, but that it is more of a general melancholia for the position of mother-hood and family. Her insistence on having her own space and her refusal to talk about family are perhaps an indication that she is lonely and adrift, whereas talking about her profession is easier. She is open as long as she can remain professional. Once the conversation drifts towards personal feelings, Raghida is defiantly silent.

Lastly, Alabdallah asks her friends about how old they feel, perhaps to make them aware of their states of mind and the way they have responded to her questions in an indirect way. This question is also directly related to the fact that the film-maker sees this film as a birthday present to her fifty-year-old self, a sort of 'coming of middle-age', as Salti describes it. Fadia admits that she does not feel her own age, and says she feels stuck at twenty-five, the young woman who left Syria twenty-five years ago. This confirms the idea that her life is suspended outside of Syria. The moment her brother disappeared and she fled the country is the moment she stopped working on her ambitions and the moment she stopped living. Her meta-narrative tendencies, talking very intellectually and at a remove from herself testify to this state of mind. Rola says she feels even younger, twelve perhaps, as she is so frightened and unable to recognise herself. This also reveals, at the end of the process of unfolding, that she is emotionally suspended and perhaps even in need of a whole new life. Raghida avoids answering the question and instead turns it around, saying she wants ten more years and 'that'll be enough'. She laughs hoarsely and then unexpectedly sobs into her hands. When Alabdallah sticks close to her in order to reveal this sensitive nature behind the defensive outer shell, Raghida returns to her defensive self, saying 'are you happy now?' In this apparently tough, independent woman, something is broken and immensely sad.

Concerning the schism between the age one feels and the age one actually is, Alabdallah herself, while she is not always present in the film in a physical way, is also concerned with how she looks, evident from a short sequence in which she studies her face in close-up in the mirror. She films herself in her bathroom, a close-up of her face, an early form of a selfie. She studies her face without her glasses on, looks fragile, but smiles when her daughter comes in. This intimate moment makes her a very sensual character in the film. While her presence in the rest of the film is mostly cerebral, she is sometimes in the shot too, and it is always elegant, modest. It is the most intimate moment in the film, and shows us how universal the subjective nature of turning fifty is, and how general the specific testimonies and experiences are of the women interviewed in this documentary.

The development from one question and its answers to another, and the build up to, and coming back from, the central question about the women's feelings, a question enfolded within the others, reveals a careful construction of the subjectivities of these women. Their agency is respected and their intimate relationship with the film-maker is revealed. Fadia gives the impression of being rational and almost able to be meta-narrative, attempting to distance herself from what she says as soon as she has said it. Rola is different, she is overly emotional and lost in her bitterness and anxiety. The depression (or dementia as Salti calls it) has engulfed her. She also is enfolded within the defensive, guarded, distanced, more rational testimonies of Fadia and Raghida, as if her emotional, child-like nature needs protection during the unfolding process. Raghida, in her turn, is guarded and defiant, differently so to Fadia, in a more direct and accusatory way.

The physicality of the three women in the close-ups and in the looks straight into the camera, implicates the spectator and demands that he or she becomes sensitive to their testimonies, as a universal story of suffering in Syria. The personal nature of the interviews and the subjective answers as such enable both a vision of melancholia as a complex state of mind, but also the resilient nature of these women in spite of their sometimes self-pitying, often defensive, and always clever responses to difficult questions. The slow revelation of their hybrid subjectivities as being a reflection of the universal Syrian state of mind under the Ba'ath government, enables the spectator to build up solidarity for, as well as a defence against, the extreme emotions.

The conversations, however open or closed the women are about their experiences, are intimate and private, and make for a highly unconventional artistic documentary. It is so personal that a spectator understands that through the deep sympathy Alabdallah feels for them, as becomes obvious in the extreme close-ups and the intimacy of the conversation, that this is a much larger problem, a collective experience of the Syrian people. The faces, eyes and mouths express contradictory feelings, suspicion of the camera, and a struggle with being probed. But the camera is also perhaps a tool of liberation that ensures that unresolved and unspoken issues are expressed and, as such, these multifaceted interviews, with tears and giggles embedded in them, also achieve something unexpected: sympathy from the spectator, and, most importantly, a platform for an expression of suffering.

While Alabdallah is not often heard, she *is* the dominant presence, as the women do feel slightly pressured into saying certain things. They attempt to protect themselves, but the film-maker succeeds in revealing their innermost, secret feelings and thoughts. We do not hear her voice or her questions, she is a silent but dominant presence. Likewise, the silences, the tears, the smiles, the unsaid as well as whatever was edited out, are as audible as what is heard. What we get is a tremendously melancholic testimony from three women and from the film-maker and the greater community of Syrian women, and a sense of immense depression, whether they are able or unable to cope with everyday life inside or outside Syria, but always linked to Syria. These three women, as well as Alabdallah, give the impression that we see lives, suspended and stifled, of women who have great difficulty moving on and processing the seriousness of their past experiences.

The melancholia inherent to the trauma of these four women's past (Fadia, Rola, Raghida and Hala) and the intensity with which they testify, is balanced out by Alabdallah and Albeik with interludes after each of the seven sets of answers. In each of these parallel sequences we witness Alabdallah in a ruined courtyard, at a small garden table, playing solitaire. Albeik films her through a rusty mirror, and places branches of dead trees around her. This sequence is filmed from different angles after every question posed to her friends, as a self-reflective interlude after intense moments of traumatic recall. The mirror is perhaps a symbolic tool to put Alabdallah herself within these moments too, without testifying to her own trauma. The solitaire playing also alludes to loneliness and independence. The last time Ammar films her like this, he gets closer to Alabdallah, and instead of playing solitaire, we see her going through papers, notes, writings, fragments of information in a bundle resembling a research folder, presumed to be notes for films. This meta-narrative instant, of which there are so many in the film, implicates Alabdallah as a physical presence and a determining power. It accentuates her fragility as it includes her in the trajectory of testimonies, but it also comments on her position as the director who selects, includes and rejects.

In spite of the trauma and the sadness in the testimonies of her three friends, Alabdallah manages to maintain her optimism. When she comes into the frame, she is usually smiling. Photographs of her also show her smiling, and husband Youssef Abdelké confesses to loving her joyful nature. The close-ups of her husband likewise reveal playful twinkles in his eyes, and her friends smile at her, even if these are accusatory smiles. We see her embrace her daughter, her husband and her mother-in-law. One of the most impressive aspects of this film, and her other films, then, is the unrelenting positivity. Most constant is the belief that art can rescue people from amnesia, suspended lives and depression. In *I Am the One who Brings Flowers to Her Grave*, the art forms of choice are poetry and drawing. Several artists (not only Youssef Abdelké) talk about their work. An example is a restorer of ancient icons who describes the process of bringing colour back to an old, black, forgotten icon. This embodies the optimism and the belief that art provides healing. As Salti describes it:

> Hers is the cinema of a generation that was disillusioned, broken, jailed, tortured, humiliated, exiled, silenced; a cinema of the present moment in this sorry *fin de règne*, not captive to the past; a cinema of unfinished sentences, whose chronology or linearity comes undone; a cinema that does not operate as 'a mirror of the world', her world or ours (the spectators), rather hers is a cinema that journeys and transposes a poetic chronicle of journeying in sound and image. She believes that art saves one from succumbing to despair or dementia. Her cinema, she claims, saved her from drifting into the abyss. Hers is the cinema that restores music to sorrow and poetry to despair, cinema as art, an art that saves. (Salti, 2010: 168)

As such, Hala Alabdallah visits an old friend in Syria, Nazih Abouafach. He is a mutual friend of Alabdallah and poet Daad Haddad. Haddad was a young Syrian poet who committed suicide in 1991. Talking of her, Abouafach admits, makes him cry, and he quotes her poetry, lines that also explain the title of the film. The poem contains the phrase 'I am the one who carries flowers to her grave, and suffer from the intensity of poetry', recited here with much emotion by Abouafach. However, Alabdallah interrupts him, asking Ammar Albeik, the co-director of the film, whether he wants to use another camera to film this sequence. Nazih shouts that he is doing his best to build up tension with the recitation, which she deliberately breaks. She apologises, but it is obvious that she has done it on purpose, to move away from the performance and reverence for the poet, and to provide *verfremdung*, showing that we are watching a film, a performance, and that there is a camera present. It is Alabdallah's more grounded approach to poetry that needs to be foregrounded rather than an eulogisation of the poet after her death. She explains to Nazih that with this film she wants to make all the films 'that I dreamt I would make in the last 20 years'. His eulogy of the poet, that she is 'supernatural, majestic' is perhaps too much for Alabdallah. Instead, she is one of the many stories in the film, one of the many films, frames, fragments that enfold the artistic nature of the documentary: one of the meanders in the long return journey to the home country.

Other stories are plenty. One is that of the island of Arwad, donated to the French by the Ottomans. They did not arrive immediately upon the removal of the inhabitants, and one boy remained, in effect becoming the king of the island. This story is linked to a childhood of playing on Arwad, where many Syrian families take their holidays. Another is the story of an Armenian child who, during the genocide, was saved by a Syrian farmer who hid her under his big coat. This story is linked in the editing process to Abdelké's mother, and very slowly it becomes clear that it is her story. There is also the story of the tobacco factory, where women are working in silent harmony behind a big black gate. This story is then linked to an actual tobacco factory, where repetitive movements, looks and silent conversations are witnessed from behind glass. All these and many other stories are embedded in sequences of desolate landscapes, travelling shots of roads and fragments of spectacular starling murmurations traversing the melancholy skies. While many of these stories are melancholic in nature as well, they do also always result in a positive image: a child running on the beach, an icon being restored, a girl saved from a genocide. The art of storytelling, painting, weaving and especially of film-making is proven to have healing powers. Poetry in particular has a strong resonance. The film is woven like a poem, without a necessity for coherence, where metaphors and allegories unravel, one onto the other. The associative nature of the montage, and the lack of a clear outcome, ending, or even climax, shows the openness of art and of Alabdallah's approach to what this film is: an accumulation of ideas and unfinished projects, a present to herself, to be shared with friends, that shows how art can heal. Within the experimental structure, we are led from one sequence to the next following motifs and metaphors that seemingly do not cohere, but do manage to give an overall impression of a Syrian lived experience by a sensitive woman.

The film ends with the recitation of Daad Haddad's poem. Alabdallah recites it in Arabic. In fact, she recites only a fragment of it, in line with the fragmentary nature of the rest of the film and stories.

Here is my translation of the French subtitles:

I am the daughter of Satan
The girl in this crazy night
The daughter of my consciousness
And of my friend . . .

I am the oldest of all beings
My wine runs through my veins
I am the one who brings flowers to her grave
The one who cries for the intensity of poetry . . .

Close your eyes . . .
I walk . . . alone
Like the tip of an arrow
While your tears . . . flow.

The complete poem is (also translated from French):

I am the daughter of Satan
The girl in this crazy night
The daughter of my consciousness
And of my friend . . .

I am the oldest of all beings
My wine runs through my veins
I am the one who brings flowers to her grave
The one who cries for the intensity of poetry . . .

Upon my modesty they raise palaces
Poetry takes a walk in my blood
Poppies are stolen
From the field of my distraction.

The cushions are for maids
Here are my . . . stolen stones
My knives are . . . frozen
Rain flows from my eyes.

The universe is my home

Close your eyes
I walk . . . alone
Like the tip of an arrow
While your tears . . . flow. (Samara, 2010)

The poem is fragmented, as indicated with the ellipses, and non-linear. It lists a number of sensory impressions and strong imagery, but there is no cohesion. The meta-poetic elements – when Haddad talks about what poetry does to her – highlight the loneliness and despair she expresses even more. Yet there is also a comfort in sadness, a beauty in melancholia and a contentment in nostalgia. The sadness in this poem, and by extension in the film, has a beauty to it that could be captured perhaps in an understanding of thanatic drive.

Conclusion

Even if censorship and a complex NFO put enormous pressure on film-makers in Syria, and the state of emergency and civil war have complicated artistic expressions even further, Hala Alabdallah, as the first woman to dedicate herself to the art of documentary, shows the triumph of art over oppression. Working with the Syrian government through negotiating her way back into the country after exile, and against it by working independently and in collaboration with a large number of insiders and outsiders, Alabdallah manages to make the films that she wants to make without compromising on her artistic integrity. While this may have the effect that the films are dense and intense, it also shows a resilience, both as a woman and as a Syrian, to show multifaceted and traumatic experiences on the screen. In addition, it reveals an inherent belief in the spectator's intelligence, that even in dealing with intense and difficult subjects in an experimental manner, spectators can be trusted to unfold the narrative and enfold the vulnerability of its tellers. The film aims to show how sadness, melancholia, nostalgia, pain, amnesia and anxiety in themselves and on the faces of people can be beautiful, and art can assist in healing processes. The making of the film itself quite literally blends with its subject, as it shows the tenacity of Arab artists and the continuing strength of the arts. The result is a focus on art as a vehicle for dissent, and a way to deal with oppression, fear and sadness.

Notes

1. This was the case, for example, with films such as *The Night* (1993) by Mohammad Malas, *Something is Smouldering* (1993) by Ghassan Shmeit, *The Greedy Ones* (1991) and *Exodus* (1997) by Raymond Boutros, *Dreams of the City* (1984) by Mohammad Malas, *Stars in Broad Daylight* (1988) and *Sacrifices* (2002) by Usama Mohammad, *Nights of the Jackal* (1989) and *At Our Listeners' Request* (2003) by Abdellatif Abdul-Hamid.
2. One possible explanation for this could be the repressive measures Assad took against the Muslim Brotherhood in the 1980s. Insurgency was responded to with military violence, and people were unable to go out for entertainment. The growth of television's popularity therefore went hand in hand with a

decreasing freedom, and people stayed at home, where they could watch television.
3. Due to political circumstances in the area, the Arab Institute of Film continues its work only in Lebanon. It was renamed Screen Institute Beirut.

Works Cited

Adorno, T. W. ([1955] 1967), *Prisms* (Cambridge, MA: MIT Press).

Al-Nashif, N. and El-Khoury, S. (2012), 'Palestinian Employment in Lebanon', *ILO*, available online at: http://www.ilo.org/wcmsp5/groups/public/---arab states/---ro-beirut/documents/publication/wcms_236502.pdf, last accessed July 2016.

Allen, L. A. (2004), 'Palestinian Children: Dying to Live', *American Anthropologist*, 106(1): 159–60.

Andrew, J. D. (1976), *The Major Film Theories. An Introduction* (Oxford: Oxford University Press).

Armbrust, W. (1995), 'New Cinema, Commercial Cinema, and the Modernist Tradition in Egypt', *Alif: Journal of Comparative Poetics*, Arab Cinematics: Toward the New and the Alternative, 15: 81–129.

Armes, R. (2005), *Postcolonial Images. Studies in North African Film* (Bloomington, IN: Indiana University Press).

Armes, R. (2006), *African Filmmaking North and South of the Sahara* (Edinburgh: Edinburgh University Press).

Armes, R. (2015), *New Voices in Arab Cinema* (Bloomington, IN: Indiana University Press).

Armes, R. and Malkmus, L. (1991), *Arab and African Filmmaking* (London: Zed Books).

Armstrong, R. (1987), 'Press Release 01: World Music', *froots.com*, GlobeStyle, London, available online at: http://www.frootsmag.com/content/features/world_music_history/minutes/page04.html.

Austin, G. (2012), *Algerian National Cinema* (Manchester: Manchester University Press).

Bahmad, J. (2013), 'Casablanca Unbound. The New Urban Cinema in Morocco', *Francosphères*, 2(1): 73–85.

Barlet, O. (1998), Interview with Férid Boughédir, 'The Forbidden Windows of Black African Film', *Africultures*, No. 5327, available online at: http://www.africultures.com/php/index.php?nav=article&no=5327&texte_recherche=Boughédir.

Barlet, O. (2008), 'Critique *Nûba d'or et de lumière* d'Izza Génini', *Africultures*, available online at: http://www.africultures.com/php/?nav=article&no=8200.

Balázs, B. (1952), *Theory of the Film. Character and Growth of a New Art*, trans. Edith Bone (London: Dennis Dobson).

Bensmaia, R. (1996), 'La Nouba des Femmes du Mont Chenoua: Introduction to the Cinematic Fragment', *World Literature Today*, 70(4): 877–84.

Bensmaia, R. (2003), *Experimental Nations: Or, the Invention of the Maghreb*, trans. A. Waters (Princeton, NJ: Princeton University Press).

Berger, J. (1999), *After the End: Representations of Post-apocalypse* (Minneapolis, MN: University of Minnesota Press).

Bloom, P. (2003), 'Beur Cinema and the Politics of Location: French Immigration Politics and the Naming of a Film Movement', in E. Shohat and S. Robert (eds), *Multiculturalism, Postcoloniality, and Transnational Media* (New Brunswick, NJ: Rutgers University Press), pp. 44–62.

Boughédir, F. (1987), *Caméra Arabe* (Paris: M3M).

Bouzid, N. and El Ezabi, S. (1970), 'New Realism in Arab Cinema: The Defeat-Conscious Cinema', *Alif: Journal of Comparative Poetics*, Arab Cinematics: Toward the New and the Alternative, 15: 242–50.

Brenez, N. and Hadouchi, O. (2005), 'Jocelyne Saab Dossier', *La Furia Umana*, 7: 205–93, available online at: http://lemagazine.jeudepaume.org/blogs/each-dawn-a-censor-dies-by-nicole-brenez/2016/02/05/jocelyne-saab-the-price-of-freedom-is-high, last accessed 8 February 2016.

Brent Madison, G. (1981), *The Phenomenology of Merleau-Ponty. A Search for the Limits of Consciousness* (Athens, OH: Ohio University Press).

Brisley, L. (2012), 'The Will to Remember: Problematizing the Ethico-politics of Mourning and Melancholia', *International Journal of Civic, Political and Community Studies*, 10(2): 61–72.

Bruzzi, S. (2000), *New Documentary: A Critical Introduction* (London: Routledge).

Buali, Sh. (2012), 'A Militant Cinema. Mohanad Yaqubi in conversation with Sheyma Buali', *Ibraaz* (2 May 2012), available online at: http://www.ibraaz.org/interviews/16.

Butler, J. (1990), *Gender Trouble: Feminism and the Subversion of Identity* (London: Routledge).

Camus, A. ([1942] 1955), *The Myth of Sisyphus and Other Essays* (New York: Knopf Doubleday).

Carter, S. G. (2008), 'Constructing an Independent Moroccan Nation and National identity through Cinema and Institutions', *Journal of North African Studies*, 13(4): 531–59.

Carter, S. G. (2009), *What Moroccan Cinema? A Historical and Critical Study, 1956–2006* (Lanham, MD: Lexington Books).

Caruth C. (1995), *Trauma: Explorations in Memory* (Baltimore, MD: Johns Hopkins University Press).

Caruth C. (1996), *Unclaimed Experience: Trauma, Narrative and History* (Baltimore, MD: Johns Hopkins University Press).

Chaaban, J., Ghattas, H., Habib, R., Hanafi, S., Sahyoun, N., Salti, N., Seyfert, K. and Naamani, N. (2010), 'Socio-Economic Survey of Palestinian Refugees in Lebanon', report published by the American University of Beirut and the United Nations Relief and Works Agency for Palestine Refugees in the Near

East, available online at: http://www.unrwa.org/userfiles/2011012074253. pdf, last accessed January 2016.

Chapman, J. (2009), *Issues in Contemporary Documentary* (Cambridge: Polity Press).

Chen, N. N. (1992), '"Speaking Nearby": A Conversation with Trinh T. Minh-Ha', *Visual Anthropology Review*, 8(1): 82–91; reprinted in Minh-Ha, T. T. and Chen, N. (2000), 'Speaking Nearby', in Ann E. Kaplan (ed.), *Feminism and Film* (Oxford: Oxford University Press), pp. 317–35.

Cohen Hadria, M. (2005), 'Nothing New Under the Western Sun. Or the Rise of the Arab Experimental Documentary', *Third Text*, 19(1): 33–43.

Combs-Schilling, E. (1991), 'Review of *Morocco, Body and Soul*', *American Anthropologist*, 93(2): 517–18.

Cooke, M. (2007), *Dissident Syria: Making Oppositional Arts Official* (Durham, NC: Duke University Press).

Cordon, J. (2002), *Revolutionary Melodrama. Popular Film and Civic Identity in Nasser's Egypt* (Chicago, IL: ME Documentation Center).

Deffontaines, T. M. (1993), 'De la musique avant toute chose', *Ecrans d'Afrique*, 5/6: 3–4.

Deleuze, G. (1986), *Cinema 1: The Movement Image* (London: Athlone Press).

Dickinson, K. (2016), *Arab Cinema Travels. Transnational Syria, Palestine, Dubai and Beyond* (London: BFI & Palgrave).

Djebar, A. (1957), *La Soif: roman* (Paris: R. Julliard).

Djebar, A. (1985), *L'amour, la fantasia: roman* (Paris: Livre de Poche).

Doane, M. A. (2003), 'The Close-up: Scale and Detail in the Cinema', *Differences: A Journal of Feminist Cultural Studies*, 14: 89–111.

Donadey, A. (1996), 'Rekindling the Vividness of the Past: Assia Djebar's Films and Fiction', *World Literature Today*, 70: 885–92.

DoxBox, ArteEast and Network of Arab Arthouse Screens Press Release (2012), 'International Film Community Stands in Solidarity with Syria by Screening a Special *DOX BOX Global Day* Program', 2 March.

Foster, T. (1995), 'Circles of Oppression, Circles of Repression: Etel Adnan's *Sitt Marie Rose*', *PMLA Modern Language Association*, 110(1): 59–74.

Gabous, A. (1998), *Silence, Elles Tournent! Les femmes et le cinéma en Tunisie* (Tunis: Cérès Editions).

Génini, I. (n.d.), 'Interview' Marocorama, available online at: http://www.maro corama.com/index.php?page=presse&id=8&lang=fr.

Gertz, N. and Khleifi, G. (2006), 'From Bleeding Memories to Fertile memories: Palestinian Cinema in the 1970s', *Third Text*, 20(3/4): 465–74.

Gertz, N. and Khleifi, G. (2008), *Palestinian Cinema: Landscape, Trauma, and Memory* (Edinburgh: Edinburgh University Press).

Grossmann, R. (1984), *Phenomenology and Existentialism. An Introduction* (London: Routledge & Kegan Paul).

Guneratne, A. and Dissanayake, W. (eds) (2003), *Rethinking Third Cinema* (New York and London: Routledge).

Hafez, S. (2006), 'The Quest for/Obsession with the National in Arabic Cinema', in V. Vitali and P. Willemen (eds), *Theorising National Cinema* (London: BFI Publishing), pp. 226–55.

Hassan, F. (2001), 'Speaking for the Other Half', *Al Ahram*, 1 March 2001, available online at: http://weekly.ahram.org.eg/2001/523/sc3.htm, last accessed October 2008.

Hennebelle, G. (1976), 'Arab Cinema', *MERIP Reports*, 52: 4–12.

Higbee, W. (2013), *Post-Beur Cinema. North African Émigré and Maghrebi–French Filmmaking in France since 2000* (Edinburgh: Edinburgh University Press).

Hight, C. and Roscoe, J. (2001), *Faking It: Mock-documentary and the Subversion of Factuality* (Manchester: Manchester University Press).

Hillauer, R. (2005), *Encyclopedia of Arab Women Filmmakers* (Cairo: American University in Cairo Press).

Hitchcock, P. (1997), 'The Eye and the Other. The Gaze and the Look in Egyptian Feminist Fiction', in O. Nnaemeka (ed.), *The Politics of (M)Othering. Womanhood, Identity, and Resistance in African Literature* (London: Routledge), pp. 69–81.

Hongisto, I. (2015), *Soul of the Documentary. Framing, Expression, Ethics* (Amsterdam: Amsterdam University Press).

International Media Support (IMS) Denmark (2009), 'Paving the Way for New Film Talent in the Arab Region', 17 December, available online at: http://www.i-m-s.dk/article/paving-way-new-film-talent-arab-region, last accessed June 2011.

Jacir, A. (2007), 'Coming Home: Palestinian Cinema', *Electronic Intifada* (27 February), available online at: http://electronicintifada.net/content/coming-home-palestinian-cinema/6780.

Jezequel, Y. (2006), 'Au Coeur des Traditions musicales Marocaines', *Film Fest Amiens*, available online at: http://www.filmfestamiens.org/?-Maroc-Corps-et-ames-&lang=fr.

Junka, L. (2006), 'The Politics of Gaza Beach: At the Edges of Two Intifadas', *Third Text*, 20(3/4): 417–28.

Kapchan, D. A. (2002), 'Moroccan Female Performers Defining the Social Body', *Journal of American Folklore*, 107(423): 82–105.

Kapchan, D. A. (2008), 'The Promise of Sonic Translation: Performing the Festive Sacred in Morocco', *American Anthropologist*, 110(4): 467–83.

Kaplan, E. A. (1997a), *Looking for the Other. Feminism, Film, and the Imperial Gaze* (London: Routledge).

Kaplan, E. A. (1997b), '"Speaking Nearby": Trinh T. Minh-Ha's Reassemblage and Shoot for the Contents', *Looking for the Other. Feminism, Film, and the Imperial Gaze* (London: Routledge), pp. 195–217.

Kennedy, T. (2015), 'Michel Khleifi: Filmmaker of Memory', in Josef Gugler (ed.), *Ten Arab Filmmakers. Political Dissent and Social Critique* (Bloomington, IN: Indiana University Press), pp. 52–75.

Khanna, R. (2008), *Algeria Cuts. Women and Representation, 1830 to the Present* (Stanford, CA: Stanford University Press).

Khannous, T. (2001), 'The Subaltern Speaks: Assia Djebar's *La Nouba*', *Film Criticism*, 26(2): 41–61.

Khatib, L. (2008), *Lebanese Cinema. Imagining the Civil War and Beyond* (London: I. B. Tauris).

Khatib, L. (2013), *Image Politics in the Middle East. The Role of the Visual in Political Struggle* (London: I. B. Tauris).

Khélil, H. (2007), *Abécédaire du Cinéma Tunisien* (Tunis: Simpact).

Kozloff, S. (1988), *Invisible Storytellers. Voice-over Narration in American Fiction Film* (London: University of California Press).

Lahlali, El Mustafa (2013), *Contemporary Arab Broadcast Media* (Edinburgh: Edinburgh University Press).

Laine, T. (2007), *Shame and Desire. Emotion, Intersubjectivity, Cinema* (Brussels: Peter Lang).

Livingston, D. (2008), 'Lebanese Cinema', *Film Quarterly*, 62(2): 34–43.

Lury, K. (2010), *The Child in Film: Tears, Fears and Fairytales* (London: I. B. Tauris).

MacFarquhar, N. (2002), 'The Saturday Profile; Weaving Nile's Daily Life into Dream of Change', *New York Times*, 22 June.

Majaj, L. S. and Amal A. (eds) (2002), *Etel Adnan: Critical Essays on the Arab-American Writer and Artist* (Jefferson, NC: Mcfarland).

Marks, L. U. (2010), 'Experience – Information – Image: A Historiography of Unfolding in Arab Cinema', in D. Iordanova, D. Martin-Jones and B. Vidal (eds), *Cinema at the Periphery* (Detroit, MI: Wayne State University Press), pp. 232–52.

Marks, L. U. (2015), *Hanan al-Cinema: Affections for the Moving Image* (Boston, MA: MIT Press).

Martin, F. (2011), *Screens and Veils. Maghrebi Women's Cinema* (Bloomington, IN: Indiana University Press).

Martins, C. (2011), 'The Dangers of the Single Story: Child-soldiers in Literary Fiction and Film', *Childhood*, 18(4): 434–46.

Masri, M. (2005), 'An Interview with Mai Masri', Interview for Human Rights Watch, 2001, in R. Hillauer (ed.), *Encyclopedia of Arab Women Filmmakers* (Cairo: American University in Cairo Press), pp. 232–5.

Masri, M. (2008), 'Transcending Boundaries', *This Week in Palestine*, 117, available online at: http://www.thisweekinpalestine.com/details.php?id=23 51&ed=149&edid=149.

McDougal, J. (2006), *History and the Culture of Nationalism in Algeria* (Cambridge: Cambridge University Press).

Mohanty, Ch. T. (1984), 'Under Western Eyes: Feminist Scholarship and Colonial Discourses', *Boundary*, 2(12/13), 31: 333–58.

Mohanty, Ch. T. (2003), '"Under Western Eyes" Revisited: Feminist Solidarity through Anticapitalist Struggles', *Signs*, 28(2): 499–535.

Mortimer, M. (ed.) (2001), 'Reappropriating the Gaze in Assia Djebar's Fiction and Film', in *Maghrebian Mosaic. A Literature in Transition* (London: Lynne Rienner), pp. 212–28.

Mostafa, D. S. (2015), 'Jocelyne Saab. A Lifetime Journey in Search of Freedom and Beauty (Lebanon)', in J. Gugler (ed.), *Ten Arab Filmmakers. Political Dissent and Social Critique* (Bloomington, IN: Indiana University Press), pp. 35–50.

Mulvey, L. (1975), 'Visual Pleasure and Narrative Cinema', *Screen*, 16(3): 6–18.

Murphy, D. (2006), 'Africans Filming Africa: Questioning Theories of an Authentic African Cinema', in E. Ezra and T. Rowden (eds), *Transnational Cinema, The Film Reader* (London: Routledge), pp. 27–37.

Naficy, H. (2001), *An Accented Cinema: Exilic and Diasporic Filmmaking* (Princeton, NJ: Princeton University Press).

Naficy, H. (2006), 'Palestinian Exilic Cinema and Film Letters', in Hamid Dabashi (ed.), *Dreams of a Nation: On Palestinian Cinema* (London: Verso), pp. 90–104.

Naim, A. (n.d.), 'Assia Djebar: le cinéma, retour aux sources du langage', *BabelMed*, available online at: http://www.babelmed.net/letteratura/236-algeria/1511-assia-djebar-le-cin-ma-retour-aux-sources-du-langage.html, last accessed 20 June 2014.

Neidhardt, I. (2005), 'Palestinian Society as Reflected in its Cinema', in R. Hillauer (ed.), *Encyclopedia of Arab Women Filmmakers* (Cairo: American University in Cairo Press), pp. 206–8.

Nichols, B. (1991), *Representing Reality: Issues and Concepts in Documentary* (Bloomington, IN: Indiana University Press).

Padgaonkar, L. (2011), 'Director Profile: Mai Masri', *Wide Screen*, 3(1): 1–4.

Peteet, J. (1997), 'Icons and Militants: Mothering in the Danger Zone', *Signs*, 23(1): 103–29.

Pisters, P. (2007), 'Refusal of Reproduction: Paradoxes of Becoming-Woman in Transnational Moroccan Filmmaking', in K. Marciniak, A. Imre and A. O'Healy (eds.), *Transnational Feminism in Film and Media* (New York: Palgrave Macmillan), pp. 71–92.

Portail du Film Documentaire (n.d.), 'Retrouver Oulad Moumen. Un Film de Izza Génini', *Film-documentaire.fr*, available online at: http://www.film-documentaire.fr/Retrouver_Oulad_Moumen.html,film,1249, last accessed 26 April 2011.

Pullen, C. (2008), 'AIDS Orphans, Parents and Children in Documentary: Disclosure, Performance and Sacrifice', *Media, Culture and Society*, 30: 663–76.

Quilty, J. (2005), 'Film Review', *Daily Star*, Lebanon, 10 May 2001, in R. Hillauer (ed.), *Encyclopedia of Arab Women Filmmakers* (Cairo: American University in Cairo Press), pp. 234–5.

Rakha, Y. (2002), 'Our Revolution, Interview with Abdel-Rahman El Abnoudy', *Al-Ahram*, 595, 18–24 July, available online at: http://www.mafhoum.com/press3/nas105-15.htm, last accessed 4 July 2016.

Rascaroli, L. (2008), 'The Essay Film: Problems, Definitions, Textual Commitments', *Framework* 49(2): 24–47.

Rhodes, G. D. and Springer, J. P. (2006), *Docufictions: Essays on the Intersection of Documentary and Fictional Filmmaking* (Jefferson, NC: McFarland).

Ricoeur, P. (1967), *Husserl: An Analysis of his Phenomenology*, trans. E. G. Ballard and L. E. Embree (Evanston, IL: Northwestern University Press).

Ringrose, P. (2006), *Assia Djebar: In Dialogue with Feminisms* (Amsterdam: Rodopi).

Rositzka, E. (2016), '"Floating Signifiers": die Transformation des Kriegsfilm-Genres am Beispiel der Kartografie', *Mediaesthetics*, 1, available online at: http://www.mediaesthetics.org/index.php/mae/article/view/45/97, last accessed 10 July 2016.

Saba, A. (1998), 'Etel Adnan's "There": A Meditation on Conflict', *Al Jadid Magazine*, 4(23): 1–5, available online at: http://qcpages.qc.cuny.edu/cmal/faculty/alcalay/adnan.pdf, 31 July 2014.

Salti, R. (2006), *Insights into Syrian Cinema. Essays and Conversations with Contemporary Filmmakers* (New York: ArteEast).

Salti, R. (2010), 'This Woman's Work: Filming Defeat in the Arabic Ideom: Poetry, Cinema, and the Saving Grace of Hala Alabdallah', in F. Laviosa (ed.), *Visions of Struggle in Women's Filmmaking in the Mediterranean* (London: Palgrave Macmillan), pp. 167–82.

Samak, Q. (1977), 'The Politics of Egyptian Cinema', *MERIP Reports*, 56: 12–15.

Samara, R. (2010), 'La poésie de Daad Haddad', Mission Laique Francaise CHAM, available online at: http://www.mlfcham.com/index.php?option=com_content&view=article&id=156:la-poesie-de-daad-haddad&catid=100:daad-haddad&Itemid=238, last accessed 30 January 2016.

Scott, K. and Van de Peer, S. (2016), 'Sympathy for the Other: Female Solidarity and Postcolonial Subjectivity in Francophone Cinema', *Film-Philosophy*, 20: 168–94.

Shafik, V. (2005a), 'Film in Palestine: Palestine in Film', in R. Hillauer (ed.), *Encyclopedia of Arab Women Filmmakers* (Cairo: American University in Cairo Press), pp. 202–5.

Shafik, V. ([1988] 2005b), *Arab Cinema. History and Cultural Identity* (Cairo: American University in Cairo Press).

Shafik, V. (2006), *Popular Egyptian Cinema. Gender Class, and Nation* (Cairo: American University in Cairo Press).

Shohat, E. (2003), 'Post-Third-Worldist Culture: Gender, Nation and the Cinema', in A. Guneratne and W. Dissanayake (eds), *Rethinking Third Cinema* (New York and London: Routledge), pp. 51–78.

Shohat, E. and Stam, R. (2003), *Multiculturalism, Postcoloniality, and Transnational Media* (New Brunswick, NJ: Rutgers University Press).

Smith, D. J. (2009), 'Big-eyed, Sad-eyed, Wide-eyed Children: Constructing the Humanitarian Space in Social Justice Documentaries', *Studies in Documentary Film*, 3(2); 159–75.

Solanas, F. and Getino, O. (1969), 'Towards a Third Cinema,' available online at: http://revolutionenausdemoff.de, last accessed 20 July 2010.

Spivak, G. S. (1988), 'Can the Subaltern Speak?' in C. Nelson and L. Grossberg (eds), *Marxism and the Interpretation of Culture* (Urbana, IL: University of Illinois Press), pp. 271–313.

Tarr, C. (2005), *Reframing Difference: Beur and Banlieue Filmmaking in France* (Manchester: Manchester University Press).

Valassopoulos, A. (2014), 'The International Palestinian Resistance: Documentary and Revolt', *Journal of Postcolonial Writing*, 50(2): 148–62.

Van de Peer, S. (2009), Personal correspondence with Ateyyat El Abnoudy, throughout February.

Van de Peer, S. (2010a), Interview with Selma Baccar, Hammam-Lif, 1 March.

Van de Peer, S. (2010b), Interview with Jocelyne Saab, Beirut, 13 December.

Van de Peer, S. (2011a), Personal correspondence with Izza Génini, Paris, throughout February.

Van de Peer, S. (2011b), Interview with Reem Ali, Edinburgh, 18 May; trans. Yasmin Fedda.

Van de Peer, S. (2014a), 'Forgotten Women, Lost Histories: Selma Baccar's *Fatma 75* and Assia Djebar's *La Nouba Des femmes du Mont Chenoua*', in L. Bisschoff and D. Murphy (eds), *Africa's Lost Classics: New Histories of African Cinema* (Oxford: Legenda), pp. 64–71.

Van de Peer, S. (2014b), 'A Moroccan Homecoming: The Fabulation of Family and Home in Izza Génini's *Retrouver Oulad Moumen*', in R. Prime (ed.), *Cinematic Homecomings. Exile and Return in Transnational Cinema* (New York: Bloomsbury), pp. 269–86.

Van de Peer, S. (2015a), 'Morocco: Farida Benlyazid', in J. Nelmes and J. Selbo (eds.), *Women Screenwriters. An International Guide* (Basingstoke: Palgrave Macmillan), pp. 23–8.

Van de Peer, S. (2015b), Personal correspondence with Hala Alabdallah Yakoub, throughout December.

Vogl, M. B. (2003), *Picturing the Maghreb: Literature, Photography, (re) Presentation* (Boulder, CO: Rowman & Littlefield).

Waldman, D. and Walker, J. (1999), *Feminism and Documentary* (Minneapolis, MN: University of Minnesota Press).

Wedeen, L. ([1999] 2011), 'Tolerated Parodies of Politics in Syria', in J. Gugler (ed.), *Film in the Middle East and North Africa: Creative Dissidence* (Austin, TX: Texas University Press), pp. 104–12.

Westmoreland, M. (2009), 'Post-Orientalist Aesthetics: Experimental Film and Video in Lebanon', *Invisible Culture: An Electronic Journal of Visual Culture*, 13: 37–57.

Willemen, P. (1994), *Looks and Frictions* (London: British Film Institute).

Index